Emilio Castelar

Old Rome and New Italy

Emilio Castelar
Old Rome and New Italy
ISBN/EAN: 9783744782791

Printed in Europe, USA, Canada, Australia, Japan

Cover: Foto ©Andreas Hilbeck / pixelio.de

More available books at **www.hansebooks.com**

OLD ROME

AND

NEW ITALY.

OLD ROME
AND
NEW ITALY.

(RECUERDOS DE ITALIA.)

By EMILIO CASTELAR,

AUTHOR OF "THE REPUBLICAN MOVEMENT IN EUROPE,"

NOW PUBLISHING IN "HARPER'S MAGAZINE."

TRANSLATED BY

MRS. ARTHUR ARNOLD.

NEW YORK:

HARPER & BROTHERS, PUBLISHERS,

FRANKLIN SQUARE.

1875.

CONTENTS.

	PAGE
ARRIVAL IN ROME	9
THE GREAT RUIN	31
THE ROMAN CATACOMBS	52
THE SISTINE CHAPEL	70
THE CAMPO SANTO OF PISA	107
VENICE	132
ON THE LAGUNES	154
THE GOD OF THE VATICAN	170
THE GHETTO	246
THE GREAT CITY	265
PARTHENOPE	284

PREFACE.

TO THE READER.

THIS book is the record of the lively emotions awakened in my soul by the marvelous spectacles of Italy. It is not a book of travels. I have not designed to add one more to the excellent works we already possess in Castilian upon the artistic nation, for these are in the hands of all travelers. When a people, a monument, or a landscape made a profound impression on my mind, I took my pen and hastened to communicate that feeling to my readers with all fidelity. I have not, then, followed any order or itinerary in my book. I have placed my pictures where it seemed best, so that they do not bear any particular relation to each other; and I have sometimes returned to a town from which I seemed to have departed. Each picture may therefore form a separate work.

In these pages there is but little of the present life and manners of Italy. With that nation, the longer it lives the more it recollects. We must look at it historically and æsthetically. We must endeavor to connect its great monuments with the ages in which they were constructed, with the generations to which they owe their creation. In Italy, we must before every landscape or every ruin evoke the august shades which realize them, and gather the living ideas distilled from her fruitful bosom. Otherwise it is useless to travel there.

In her history there is an order which is not a natural order, but a human order, like the transition from the ancient world to the modern world—like the passing from the Middle Age to the Renaissance. By those buildings so famed for beauty, those statues so serene and lovely, have passed all the tempests of the human spirit. Knowledge has opened their wounds; and on seeing them, one feels in heart and brain the immense effort it has cost ages to create the modern spirit in which we breathe and live. For this reason a journey to Italy is a journey through all periods of history. And this is why an essay upon Italy, rather than a description, should be, in my judgment, a revival. I have intended to keep always in mind that above these great works of art, of archæology, history is visible. I am happy, quite happy, if I have succeeded in imparting to my readers the thoughts that, so to speak, are exhaled from the artistic works and the historical recollections of immortal Italy.

EMILIO CASTELAR.

MADRID.

OLD ROME AND NEW ITALY.

CHAPTER I.

ARRIVAL IN ROME.

At last we were at Civita Vecchia. As the boat rapidly neared the shore, our hearts bounded in our bosoms with enthusiasm. The buildings and all around spoke of antiquity. However little inclined to classical studies, one is tempted at such a moment to repeat the verses which Virgil puts into the mouths of the companions of Æneas. The emotions awakened by the first sight of Italy are enduring—not transient as the furrow of a vessel in the ocean. I sprung joyfully to land, and if our prosaic age did not quarrel with outward manifestation of high sentiments, I would have flung myself on my knees and kissed the earth. *Italiam, Italiam, primus conclamat Achates.* But in my excitement I forgot I was in Pontifical Italy. A custom-house officer stopped us, demanding the price of admission as at a theatre. A crowd of beggars, whose statuesque features bore the sad stamp of misery, with loud clamors divided our luggage among them as a rich booty. Then the police claimed our passports, now abolished in all civilized Europe; exacting another government duty, although they had been previously *viséd* and taxed by the Nuncio in Paris and at the Consulate in Marseilles.

Following our baggage, we entered a wretched store-house, dark as a dungeon of the Inquisition; an obscurity incomprehensible in this land of resplendent heavens and dazzling light, which gives to the eyes a feast of colors, and fills the mind with poetic rapture. For articles worn, or intended to be worn, custom-house dues were exacted. When these were paid, and we fancied we were free to move, all our effects were placed in a cart drawn by a number of ragged and shirtless lads, who cried, "To the custom-house!" A second time? These taxes and tariffs, this want of intercourse with the world—are these also of divine right? Is it essential to the exercise of the Pope's authority over consciences that he should incline to the economic errors of prohibition and the political errors of absolutism?

I compared this entrance into the Pontifical States with my arrival in the Swiss Cantons. Certainly, sentiments not less sublime are awakened at beholding those mountains crowned with eternal snows; those dark and shady groves beside which stretch meadows of tender green enameled with flowers; those azure lakes sleeping at the foot of gentle slopes, contrasting with hoary peaks half-veiled by clouds; those impetuous torrents of crystal waters; those villages peopled by a vigorous and hardy race, which realizes the greatest happiness known to human society—the union of liberty and democracy. Nothing disturbs the traveler in the contemplation of this grandeur. No policeman demands his name, no custom-house official searches his baggage. These mountains seem like impenetrable barriers, but liberty has thrown them open to the world, while on the Roman shore —those coasts which look so gentle and tranquil—absolutism has placed a cloud of spies and tax-gatherers, to inclose the country which nature has opened to all nations and to every breath of Heaven.

Nothing is more inconvenient than the registration of luggage; nothing more tormenting and ridiculous. On books, especially, custom-house officers fall with inquisitorial eagerness. And after having tossed about and examined every thing, they send the traveler's effects to the station, demanding another tax, which last forced contribution is equal to the first. Who can patiently endure such an administration? Is it possible that there exists in central Europe a beautiful and classic country, more remarkable for its glorious past than any other, under such injudicious and ruinous guardianship? Will not the Holy Spirit, which pours forth torrents of religious truth on the Church of St. Peter—will it not in mercy shed a few drops of political truth and economy, at once the happiness and riches of modern peoples? The soul shrinks from all that is administrative, to turn to the lovely and picturesque in this land of song and flowers. The heavens and the sea are of brilliant azure, the air mild and aromatic; the rocks which bind the coast are gilded and embrowned by the sun; on the trees the tender leaves come forth to meet the soft kisses of April; and among groups of merry and half-clothed children every now and then mingle the white tunics and gray serge robes of friars, looking like the living ruins of other ages, and moving like the *ignis fatuus* over the crumbling monuments of antiquity.

The hour of departure strikes. The whistle sounds. Civita Vecchia is the port of the Roman States; but there are no carts, nor barrels, nor burdens, nor laborers—nothing indicative of commercial existence except the custom-house officials placed there to obstruct it. I had often heard of the dreariness of the Roman Campagna, but I had not imagined its reality. Death seems to have swallowed even the ruins. Ravens and vultures have eaten even the bones of this huge corpse. There are eleven stations between the sea and the Eternal City, but no town near any of them. The officials call out the names, such as Rio Fiume or Magliana; sounds lost in distant echoes in the immensity of the desert. It is very strange to see a train in solitude, no one mounting or descending, no one looking on, no one loading or unloading. A circular hovel, surmounted by a wooden cross, is dignified by the name of "the station." They look like the tombs of savages. The train moves as slowly as a cart, so there is ample time to observe the immense horizon, the desolate plain, the vast marshes, some frightened horses and buffaloes, a few shepherds on worn-out ponies, or a cart with a poor fever-stricken family—the remains of a nomade race, dying in the desert where so many majestic remains of antiquity have fallen and are buried.

Economic errors are to be found in all ages and even amid much civilization. When Cincinnatus cultivated the Roman plains in the early days of the Republic, they might have been called the earthly Elysian Fields; a plantation of riches, an abode of happiness and abundance. Wine, corn, oil, milk, and honey were produced in such quantities by agricultural labor that Rome was sufficient for herself. But by degrees the great families took possession of the ground once owned and tilled by many. In order to avoid daily labor they converted agricultural land into pasturage. One slave was enough to guard the flock. Irrigation was suspended; the canals dried up, drainage was stopped. Water became stagnant in low places; those streams which had brought life in their flow, scattered death by their putrid emanations. Having conquered the known world, the Roman people were no longer employed with war and had forgotten the occupations of peace. The want of food and pleasure opened the way for despotism. From despotism came the moral death which is in tyranny, as material death is in the Pontine marshes. Well did Pliny say—*Latifundia Italiam perdidere.*

At last, at the fall of evening, when shadows hung over Rome, we arrived in the Eternal City; that city which gave us jurisprudence with her prætors, liberty with her tribunes, authority with her Cæsars, religion with her priests: that city on which the annals of the human race are written; the tomb of antiquity; the triumphal arch through which the modern ages have been ushered; the temple to which generations of Catholics have come for fifteen centuries, seeking spiritual light; the great school in which artists learn before thousands of statues and columns the secrets of the chisel; the battle-field on which lie buried the gods of ancient theologies, brought to the Pantheon on cars of triumph; the city the most august and most powerful that has ever existed on the earth; that which still directs the conscience of a part of the human family by the *prestige* of its history, by the mysteries which arise from its majestic ruins. I am penetrated with a deep sentiment of veneration toward this city, unique in the world. Babylon, Tyre, Jerusalem, Athens, Alexandria, have reigned in ancient story at different intervals and at certain periods, realizing each one its idea; then it has disappeared in the dust of its ruins, without other trace than the records of its existence, or the bones of its children in the earth. Paris, London, and New York will be great in history; but this Rome, which the ancients justly called Eternal, belongs to both hemispheres of times—the heathen and the Christian world.

With what emotions Rome inspires the traveler! He may be strictly Catholic; the impressions of his early education may remain unsullied, but at beholding these statues of antiquity, these fauns with their immortal smile, these goddesses in whose marble flesh appears to circulate the warmth of life and the blood of unfading youth; before that choir of Greek divinities in their dignified repose and Olympic serenity; in the wondrous harmony of outline and the splendid beauty of expression; the vitality which hangs on those lips almost vibrating with the hymn of classic poesy;—before those forms of stone, more animated and intelligent than their living guardians, he is overcome with sorrow for the death of art, and led to wish the temples of antiquity could rise from their ruins and continue their songs and sacrifices, the eloquent pages of Plato or the glowing words of Demosthenes, in the midst of that world of deities which pour upon the earth from cups of amber the nectar of eternal joy.

Goethe experienced this profound classical enthusiasm in the Museum of the Vatican: the abode of Catholic Pontiffs, by a miracle of art, has been converted into the Olympus of the heathen divinities!

Thus it happens in the Christian world. The great Basilicas, notwithstanding their colossal majesty, chill the warmth of our devotion. Those monuments of bronze and marble, sparkling with gold and jewels, bathed in light, and rich in mosaics and bass-reliefs, dazzle, but do not affect us. The coldness of marble touches the soul. But on entering, for example, the Catacombs of St. Clement; on seeing the damp earth which preserved for four centuries the seed of Christianity; on beholding by torchlight, in these subterraneous inscriptions traced by the hands of martyrs, the symbols of hope in the midst of the terrors of persecution, we hear in imagination the hymns of catechumens beneath the feasts of the Cæsars, ascending to the circus where ferocious beasts await their prey—and the sentiment of loving admiration inspired by all great sacrifices overcomes us by its sublime mystery, leading us to contemplate on our knees the secrets of eternity, and to desire the sleep of death in the sepulchre illuminated by the faith of the first Christians. How these emotions are stifled at sight of the Pontifical Court! I can not resist the temptation of repeating an anecdote from the most accomplished of Italian writers, Boccaccio:

"An old Florentine Christian took much pains to win souls to heaven, in order to secure his own eternal happiness; at length he met with one, either Jew or Mohammedan—I forget which—and endeavoring to open the eyes of his soul to divine light, succeeded so well that in a few days he was half converted. The idea of going to Rome then occurred to the infidel; a notion which much disconcerted the missionary, for he feared the licentiousness of that court would reduce his great work to ashes. What was his astonishment when the catechumen returned with feelings of gall toward his ancient faith and of honey toward the new, exclaiming, 'My father! I am quite converted; for if, notwithstanding the profligacy of the clergy, the Church exists, grows, and prospers, it is doubtless because, being the depositary of truth, it deserves the direct protection of Heaven!'"

I will not accuse the court which surrounds Pius IX. of licentiousness. I am not accustomed to speak without proof, and am always inclined to believe more good than evil of human nature. I believe Pius IX. to be venerable from his age and perfect morality. I suppose that the example of his unsullied character influences his whole court. But I say that neither he nor his followers comprehend the free, reasoning, and independent spirit of this age—perhaps too positive —which demands a pure and disinterested worship, in opposition to materialism; and which can never have that desire satisfied by the vain and pompous luxury with which the

Roman Court adorns religious ceremonies, changing them into the worship of sense. To which side do the errors of this generation incline? To that of industry and commerce. The marvels of modern progress have made us forget the sentiments hidden in the depths of the soul!

The exclusively luxurious tendency of its character may produce one of those idealistic reactions which mark the progress of the human race, as the sensuality of the Roman Empire operating on the conscience brought the too spiritual reaction of Christianity, and converted a world of epicureans into a world of monks. The ancient religion of the spirit may well experience a conscientious crisis in order to recover some part of the moral influence it has lost. But with this system of unrestrained luxury; of strangely dressed courtiers and pages clad in gold; of cardinals attired in purple and ermine; of bishops with Oriental mitres; of Swiss, who resemble harlequins; of noble body-guards, who throw black velvet mantles on their shoulders and wear silver swords by their sides; of servants clothed in all the hues of the rainbow; of lackeys, whose finery challenges the painted parrots of the tropics; of soldiers with uniforms like that of General Boom in the *Grand Duchess of Gerolstein*—with all this Eastern ostentation the Papal Court wanders from Christ and approaches Heliogabalus.

It is Palm Sunday. The great Basilica of St. Peter is going to bestow the benediction of Palms. Behind in the church the people are crushed together, as if they had not received with baptism the seal of Christian equality. From the grand altar to the great door are two lines of soldiers to prevent the multitude from pressing on the Pope. Although the assemblage is most numerous, it does not fill the immense space; for St. Peter's could contain sixty thousand souls. The words of military command resound loudly in the temple, where the voice of prayer should alone be audible. The butts of the fire-arms fall noisily on the marble pavement. Those present are strangers. The Roman citizen has almost disappeared in the inundation of foreigners called by the Pope to his succor. At the time fixed, the procession bringing Pius IX. appears. It is impossible for any one to give an idea of the different dresses worn by his retinue. To do so would necessitate a masquerading nomenclature like that of Bizancio. At length, after an army of courtiers, comes the Pope, seated on a gilded throne, and borne like the saints in our processions, wearing a robe of crimson velvet and a white mitre, his left hand holding the golden crosier, his right uplifted in benediction to those who implore it kneeling. St. Peter's appears a theatre. The stalls, raised on steps under the vast arches which support the wondrous dome of Michael Angelo, are occupied by ladies. The arrangement of these religious seats seems the same as that of the central area of the Grand Opera of Paris. Gentlemen whose costume is strictly *en règle* occupy the places below the stalls.

During the Mass, some talk, others walk about, and all occasionally use opera-glasses, sometimes turned on the ladies in the stalls, sometimes directed toward the cardinals. The noble guards—dressed like our cavaliers of the Court of Philip

IV., with trunk hose and silk stockings, short velvet jackets, the sleeves slashed and adorned with ellipses of satin; the mantle on the shoulder; the dagger with hilt of steel before; the black head-gear under the arm, and the white collar on the neck—join in the general conversation and mingle in the general promenade. The Swiss only are immovable. It is pitiful to reflect that they have been so weak-minded as to forsake the liberty of their native mountains to serve—poor mercenaries!—a foreign sovereign. Their costume was designed by Raphael, and in this the great painter did not prove himself a master of color—it is a mixture of strips of black, red, and yellow cloth; a helmet ornamented with a white feather covers the head, and each bears an elegant battle-axe. They look like lay figures dressed as harlequins.

After the conclusion of the function I went into the piazza or square of St. Peter. It was occupied by an immense multitude. Luxurious coaches traversed it in all directions, military bands performed warlike airs. The decoration of this piazza is admirable: in the centre the great obelisk, mute trophy of the victories of the Roman people in Egypt; at either side are fountains, which cast upward jets of sparkling water; to the right and left, intercolumniations open in colossal semicircles, half exposing the lovely southern vegetation of the adjoining gardens, and terminated by a magnificent diadem of statuary. On a height stands the Vatican, a palace which bears testimony to the genius of the first artists in the world; and below, at the end of an elegant flight of steps, the Church of St. Peter, crowned by the dome of Michael Angelo, who designed it grandly as an aerial temple ascending to the infinite, among the rosy clouds of that glorious heaven which extends over all, as a magic gauze of incomparable beauty, its mantle of golden light.

I must not forget to make an observation inspired by the festival. This city can not, notwithstanding so much splendor, perpetuate enchantment with the philtre of mysticism, nor ensnare in the nets of artifice. When Religion held in her hands arts, science, and politics, such a society was naturally governed by sacerdotal bodies. But from the time that all social employments became laic, a theocratic government became impossible. I noticed that the choirs of the Sistine Chapel have greatly degenerated. The sublime inspirations of Palestrina can scarcely find worthy interpreters. This falling off is explained by the difficulty which exists in our time of finding such singers as are required by the Papal Court. It is known that women are not allowed to sing in the choir of St. Peter, and for trebles they have recourse to boys from infancy reduced to the condition of those unfortunates who guard Eastern harems. Alexander Dumas says, in one of his books of travels, that he saw over the shop of a Roman barber the following announcement: "Here boys are perfected." I never saw any thing of this kind; but I know that the choirs decay, for there are now no families so despicable as thus to sacrifice their sons for money. And it is no longer possible that in order to support a religious and moral authority there should exist a city without a press, without a tribune, without the first rights constituting the personal protection of the people.

The internal tempest which rages in Rome is at once visible to the stranger. There are three thousand emigrants in a city of two hundred thousand inhabitants. Four hundred persons are now in prison for political offenses; and a priest of high position, an intimate friend of the Pope, and even an enthusiast for the temporal power, has assured me that Rome contains more than seventy thousand Garibaldians. Every thing indicates uneasiness. The city gates are defended by barricades. At nine o'clock in the evening all shrink behind their walls—and that in an age when other towns open their gates to welcome light and air, new ideas and new sciences—the products of every clime and the representatives of every race and nation.

At nightfall you meet guards at every corner, as in a besieged city. Passports are registered with astonishing minuteness. A State which scarce contains six hundred thousand souls keeps up a standing army of twenty thousand!

These twenty thousand men are of different nations and speak different languages. The greater number do not understand Italian. Thus the ties of blood and of language exist not among them, although they are bound together by the same religion and the same political sentiments. This is a serious inconvenience with regard to their manœuvres. French, as the language most generally understood, is used in the army; but it is unintelligible to the greater number of the private soldiers. In fact, to be able to live in Rome (not being born in the country) one must possess a mind of uncommon elevation—a soul capable of understanding her arts, her ruins, and her monuments. Those who are unable to hear the eloquent voices which awaken so many lofty ideas and inspirations, soon weary of this academical and monastic city. I do not speak idly; but having closely observed the Pontifical forces, I declare that I found an elegance, a refinement, and a distinction of manners one would seek vainly in any other European army. It is well known that if a great part of it is mercenary, or has been entrapped into the service, most of it is composed of high-spirited and romantic youths—with a chivalrous worship for old institutions, exalted in their opinions and tastes, some of them having lost their illusions, but all more or less eccentric and sentimental—seeking the exercise of arms and the turmoil of camps as food for that mysticism which formerly a more gentle and more religious generation sought in the silence of the cloister and the mortification of penance. These soldiers have come from the four points of the horizon; they belong to all Christian races, and speak all languages; so Rome maintains under the Popes the character of universality bestowed on her by the Cæsars. But this, which is a moral excellence, is a material disadvantage to the army. The notion of individuality, which the Germans have brought into modern history, is so deep-rooted that differences of race, of nationality, and of character continually show themselves in the ranks, and occasion innumerable conflicts. As the officers speak one language and the subordinates another, friendly relations scarcely exist among them, though these are even more necessary than discipline in times of danger. As the soldiers do not understand each other, there is no unity in their body; and from this the greatest difficulties arise, and the chiefs are obliged to struggle through them in directing the manœuvres. Catholic Rome chose Pagan Latin that all her children should have one spirit and one language. But the difference of pronunciation was so great that, though all spoke Latin, the monks of different nations did not understand each other, thus demonstrating the superiority of nature over law. Political Rome in our age has in her affliction selected the elegant and ductile language of Voltaire in addressing her soldiers—that language fatal to all idols and idolatries. The aristocracy of the Roman army understand it, but not the rank and file. And the troops are discontented, on account of the fatigue and difficulty of the manœuvres and the continual mounting guard to which they are compelled by the growing anxieties of the Papal Court.

Those nations which from their past history should send most soldiers, send fewest in proportion to their population. Spain destroyed herself to save Catholicism. Since the fifteenth century the bones of her children have whitened every battle-field where she found it necessary to defend her religion. She gave for it all the blood in her veins, and all the vitality of her spirit. But there are only thirty-eight Spanish soldiers in the Pontifical army. On the other hand, Holland, which protected the Reformation by its Princes of Orange, and introduced liberty of religious opinion into the modern world, has sent a great number of volunteers. This proves that while the freedom of worship has kept alive the Catholic faith in Protestant countries, intolerance has extinguished it in those places where it was most sincere and most exalted.

But leaving these reflections and returning to political questions, I can not understand what the Pope proposes to do with this numerous army, so disproportioned to his means, to his resources, and to his State. The shadow of the French Empire protects him. The day in which that shadow is withdrawn, no matter how valiant the Papal army, it will not be able to resist a hundred thousand Italian soldiers. While the French protection endures, the Pontifical army is useless; and without French protection the Pontifical army would be insufficient. It serves only to consume the succor which is sent to the Pontiff with full and lavish hands from all Catholic nations. But all this comes now from an exaltation of sentiment that can not continue. When Italy shall be convinced of her inability to struggle with Napoleon, or to promote the Franco-Prussian war with regard to the Roman question, the zeal of the faithful will diminish, the resources will fall away, and the army be speedily reduced. Then an insurrection will be not only possible, but easy; for the people still preserve the love of liberty.

It is wonderful what force and intelligence still remain in the physiognomy of these Romans, revealing all the indomitable pride of that ancient character which conquered the known world. The women are tall and majestic, with well-turned shoulders. Their complexion is pale brown, the lips full, the nose aquiline; black and brilliant eyes, made more beautiful by long lashes and artistic brows, a statuesque forehead, and head like the Madonnas of the divine Raphael; dark and curling hair falls in large masses on sculptured necks—they have the manner of Roman matrons such as commanded Coriolanus to die for his country, or Caius Gracchus to sacrifice himself for the people. The Roman youths inherit the beauty of their mothers, combined with manly vigor. The silence imposed by the Inquisition and the obedience exacted by despotism have not extinguished the spirit of this great people. The formula of ancient liberty yet trembles on their lips—*Civis Romanus sum!*

Side by side we see the Oriental luxury of the cardinals and the rags of a starving populace; here a gilded coach, and there a crowd of shoeless beggars; close to magnificent palaces of marble there are heaps of refuse, emitting horrible effluvia. And yet this city is the capital of Italy. At the fall of evening, in the sacred hour of poetic silence, under the pure heavens, glorified by the last rays of the setting sun, which give an air of mysticism to all around; from the height of the Pincio look on this city, with its eleven Egyptian obelisks, its three hundred cupolas, its groves of columns, its myriads of statues, and you see the seven hills from whence have sprung senators, consuls, and tribunes; the political and civil rights of antiquity, now the bases of our rights; contemplate the façade of St. Peter's, the Great Basilica surmounted by the dome foretold by Bramante and executed by Michael Angelo; the Titanic mausoleum of Adrian, over which are extended the wings of the brazen seraphim; there, to the left, the world of history, the walls on which are engraved a thousand victories, the Via Sacra where conquerors entered, the Forum, where the people gathered; those arches which twenty centuries have passed without destroying; those refreshing baths, copied so often by modern artists; the Coliseum, that mountain sculptured by Titanic chisels; the Quirinal, which contains the finest statues saved from the wreck of Greece; the Capitol, head and cerebrum of the world. At the sight of so many marvels, at the recollection of so much grandeur, at the contemplation of such monuments, framed in groves of cypress, like a funereal wreath placed by an invisible deity; at the soft music of bells which invite to vespers, like the voices of martyrs ascending from the Catacombs; the shadows of evening lingering sadly over the ruins, like the spirits of departed heroes—the heart, swelled by emotions, confesses that Rome is not only the capital of Italy, but the eternal centre of the world!

One must be Italian, must feel Southern blood in his veins, must have been educated in this glorious history under the painted wings of classic poetry, to comprehend all the influence which Rome exercises over the Italians. Those who desired to make Italy a monarchy, and afterward denied her the capital which is hers by nature, did but construct a headless body. It is easy to see that if Italy was a republican federation, the question of capital would be secondary. One can also understand that being a State adjoining other republican States, however analogous were the laws to those of Italy, it would preserve Rome, from respect to the Popes, to the nuns and the monastic character of the city; in the same way that

Freiburg has been kept, although it is between two Protestant and Liberal cantons like those of Vaud and Berne. But Italy having been constituted a monarchy from the natural aversion all European potentates have for republics, Rome is of Italy and Italy is of Rome, bound as the satellites to their planets and the planets to the sun. And in this city, now composed of churches and convents, where no trace of civil or political life is perceptible, where for all laic authority we see a few senators in painted coaches, followed by gaudily dressed lackeys (absurd parody on the ancient senators), this theocratic and monastic Rome, always kneeling on her marble ruins, must erect the tribune and the Forum, must allow liberty to the press, must call forth the ancient eloquence, encourage the discussion of all problems and the establishment of different schools; for the political spirit can not be driven from the sacred regions from whence it sprung.

In the mean time Rome is a city of the dead. I followed with a sort of archæological curiosity the ceremonies of the Holy Week. Some were Oriental from their ostentation, some Byzantine from their refinement, others trifling to puerility: all absolutely removed from this age, and from a religious stand-point inferior to the solemn majesty of Spanish worship. A Spaniard or an American accustomed to the severity of our towns in the Holy Week, to that severity for bidding shops to be open and carriages to appear in the streets, could hardly understand that on Thursday and Good Friday they work in this city as on other days; that all establishments are open, and more people throng the sausage-shops to admire hams decorated with laurels and flowers than the churches to visit the *Sagrarios*. He·could not comprehend that the twelve paupers served by the Pope in memory of the Last Supper of the Saviour laugh as if they were in a theatre, and snatch at the sweets and comfits as if they were at a merry-making or picnic. He would not believe that at five o'clock on Thursday evening a Penitentiary Cardinal enters the Great Basilica, and, sitting at the left of the tomb of St. Peter, pardons sins by waving about a wand, and touching with it the heads of the penitents, as if he were fishing in the air. I have seen very pious ladies laugh at all these absurdities.

But there is one grand and sublime ceremony, the Miserere of St. Peter. The music is exquisite, the effect surprising. Rome saw, in the sixteenth century, that Protestantism surpassed her in music, as she excelled Protestantism in the arts of painting, sculpture, and architecture. To prevent this inferiority, she naturally sought a master of song, and found the sublime Palestrina, the Michael Angelo of the lyre. The Pope forbade the reproduction of his Miserere, in order that it should be heard only in that church whose gigantic arches were completely in harmony with its sublimity. One day a noble youth heard entranced the Miserere. This youth, who may be called the Raphael of music, learned it by heart, and divulged it to the world. He was Mozart. The German genius came to steal the secrets of the Latin genius in the eternal war between both races. No pen can describe the solemnity of the Miserere! The night advances. The

Basilica is in darkness. Her altars are uncovered. Through the open arches there penetrates the uncertain light of dawn, which seems to deepen the shadows. The last taper of the *tenebrario* is hidden behind the altar. The cathedral resembles an immense mausoleum, with the faint gleaming of funereal torches in the distance. The music of the Miserere is not instrumental. It is a sublime choir admirably combined. Now it comes like the far-off roar of the tempest, as the vibration of the wind upon the ruins or among the cypresses of tombs; again like a lamentation from the depths of the earth, or a moaning of heaven's angels breaking into sobs and sorrowful weeping. The marble statues, gigantic and of dazzling whiteness, are not completely hidden by the darkness, but appear like the spirits of past ages coming out of the sepulchres and loosing their shrouds, to join the intonation of this canticle of despair. The whole church is agitated and vibrates as if words of horror were arising from the stones. This profound and sublime lament, this mourning of bitterness dying away into airy circles, penetrates the heart by the intensity of its sadness; it is the voice of Rome supplicating Heaven from her load of ashes, as if under her sackcloth she writhed in her death agony. To weep thus, to lament as the prophets of old by the banks of Euphrates, or among the scattered stones of the temple, to sigh in this sublime cadence, becomes a City whose eternal sorrow has not marred her eternal beauty. Thus she is enslaved. David alone can be her poet. Her canticle is majestic and unequaled. Rome, Rome! thou art grand, thou art immortal even in thy desperation and thy abandonment! The human heart shall be thy eternal altar, although the faith which has been thy prestige should perish, as the conquests that made thy greatness have departed! None can rob thee of thy God-given immortality, which thy Pontiffs have sustained and which thy artists will forever preserve!

Chapter II.

THE GREAT RUIN.

To see the Eternal City was long the dream of my existence, one of the most anxious desires of my heart. As a boy the Roman religion spoke to me of God, of immortality, of redemption; of all that enlarges the horizon of the soul even to the infinite. In youth the Latin language was my chief study—a study that to a plastic imagination showed in high relief the sweet verses of Virgil, the conciseness of Tacitus, and the grander periods of Titus Livius; those heroes of antiquity who lived for liberty and for their country.

On entering the portals of the University education, Roman literature and Roman law inspire the mind with an earnest desire to see those hills from whence so much light has shone upon human consciences; those sepulchres which inclose illustrious remains, which have nourished the plant of civilization upon our earth; the stones embrowned by sun and time, where consul and tribune have carved their names, apostles and martyrs their crosses—true mementoes, not of time, but rather of the universal effort to obtain and realize an ideal, that absorbs and torments man, but which also elevates and transfigures him; compelling him to be, as a warrior engaged in an incessant struggle, an agent and minister of endless progress.

Tired of politics in Madrid, of commerce in London, of gayety in Paris, and even of Nature in Geneva; wearied also with the positive tendencies of our age, visible at every step and at every moment, I took refuge in Rome, in order to spend some happy hours with history, art, and religion. But I was unable to disengage myself from a republican friend who, sure of the agreement of our sentiments and of my aversion for the holy office, unburdened his sinful conscience, and broke his enforced silence of twenty years passed under the Pontifical rod, by describing the abuses of Roman absolutism, of which I had heard much, and which I heartily detested; but the relation of which at that time did not harmonize with my desire to wander among the ruins, remote from all political labor, and to give free course to my dreams and reflections.

"To what a place you come in search of knowledge!" said he, cold by temperament, before the marvels I viewed with transport. "Here every body is interested about lottery tickets; no one for an idea of the human brain. The commemoration of the anniversary of Shakespeare has been prohibited in this city of the arts. Her censorship is so wise that when a certain writer wished to publish a book on the discoveries of Volta she let loose on him the thunders of the Index, thinking it treated of Voltairianism — a philosophy which leaves neither repose nor digestion to our cardinals. On the other hand, a cabalistic and astrological book, professing to divine the caprices of the lottery, has been printed and published under the Pontifical seal, as containing nothing contrary to religion, morals, or sovereign authority."

"I know all this," I said. "I have read it a hundred times in Dumesnil, Kauffmann, Othendal, and Edmond About."

"Then, knowing this, do you seek here new ideas? Rabelais knew this city—Rabelais. On arriving, in place of writing a dissertation on dogmas, he penned one on lettuces, the only good and fresh articles in this cursed dungeon. And priest though he was, a priest of the sixteenth century, more religious than our generation, he had a long correspondence with the pious Bishop of Maillerais on the children of the Pope; for the reverend prelate had especially charged him to ascertain whether the Cavaliere Pietro Luis Farnese was the lawful or illegitimate son of his Holiness. Believe me, Rabelais knew Rome."

Talking thus we turned into a cross street and soon found ourselves in a small square. A balcony of the principal house in this place was adorned with rich hangings of crimson damask. Fixed upon the balcony there shone a crystal globe with gilded ornaments, at one side of which was a golden handle. Before the house an immense multitude, ragged and poverty-stricken, were pressed together. There was a singular expression in all the eyes turned upon the balcony; in the hands were papers, images of saints, and scapularies; a sepulchral silence prevailed—a silence incomprehensible among the loquacious people of the South, and a solemnity suitable for a religious ceremony. My suspicions were confirmed when an acolyte came out on the balcony, and behind him some ecclesiastics of rubicund visage and obese proportions. After the ecclesiastics there followed a Prince of the Holy Roman Church, attired in rustling violet silk and a tunic of white lace. He wore a small calotte or cap, also violet, with a rich tassel, the color of the pomegranate blossom. The silence was broken by the joyful shouts of the multitude. Some of the peasants, who still preserve the antique statuesque beauty in the open forehead, the aquiline nose, and full lips, fell on their knees and folded their hands ecstatically, offering up prayers that sounded like conjurations. Others drew forth pictures of their holy protectors, mostly grimy, and kissed them in transport. Others jumped in the air, extending their arms, and pronouncing incoherent phrases. It was Saturday, the day for sorcery. Twelve o'clock approached, the bells began to sound the hour, and the crowd became still more anxiously excited. The cardinal lifted the golden handle and gave several turns to the globe of crystal. The acolyte put in his hand and drew forth a number. It was the official and Pontifical lottery! The Garibaldian was right. Is this a place for the intellect?

Let us plunge into antiquity as a diver in the sea. Our life is so short, our being so little, that to arrive at an idea of the infinite, to which we are attached by invisible ties—to comprehend the immortality of which we dream—we must set behind the limited visible horizon and the unlimited rational horizon, behind every thought of life, interminable perspectives, distant and immense, presentments which overcome us with beauty, glowing colors on magic palettes, the inspirations of celestial poetry, the ideas we have evoked from the dust of ages and the abyss of history!

Is it true that we have before us a trembling light, pale and almost imperceptible? It is like that of the glow-worm—like that which we call an idea? Is it true that with this light we can kindle the material world, dissipate it, and offer it to the spirit as the smoke of a sacrifice? Doubtless. Nature appears to our eyes a thousand times, like a multiform image of conscience. The light is no more than the golden veil behind which is concealed the Infinite Mind, which grouped in scales of musical harmony suns and their satellites. The universe, that universe which overcomes us by its vastness, is the poem of our sentiments, the mysterious apocalypse written with words of stars, with lines of constellations in this immeasurable ether, of whose real existence we are certain, in that immensity without borders or foundations which we call space! As at the feet of men the Pagan gods have fallen, like to the imperishable gods created and destroyed by the imagination, whose bones lie in heaps in the great necropolis of the Roman Campagna, so may worlds be ruined and retain among their cold ashes the warmth and vitality of our spirits!

While protesting with vain reflections against human littleness, I arrived alone face to face with the Roman Coliseum. The first impression it produced was one of astonishment. If I had not been born on the sea-shore, and accustomed from childhood to its expanse, I should have been overcome by emotion. Seeing the Coliseum for the first time in manhood, my changing and lively fancy carried me back to my Professorial chair, where we read the epigrams of Martial, and there rose to my lips the verses which we meet with in the learned guide-book published by Roman archæologists :

> "*Barbara Piramidum sileant miracula Memphis*
> . . . . .
> *Omnis Cæsareo cedat labor Amphitheatro.*"

These were the gardens of Nero! Here he walked, clothed in purple, shod with azure buskins; his temples crowned with laurels; his eyes fixed on the heavens; in his hands a cithern; on his tongue ancient Greek verses, and in his heart evil passions—like a demon who tries to be a god, and, possessing for a moment the divinity of art, turns and falls into the abyss. He was consul, tribune, dictator, Cæsar, sovereign pontiff—all blessed him—all adored him; but, alas! he was despised by his own conscience. Posterity has not been so lenient toward him as toward the other emperors, for Nero was always a tyrant without remorse.

There have been so many with dead consciences! There have been so many that murder, burn, destroy whole cities, and believe these actions are meritorious in God's eyes! To-day there is a Cæsar of the North of Europe, who, in order to grasp the sceptre of Germany, has laid hold of unhappy France, and at the echo of his cannon—amid fire, ruin, desolation, and the groans of the dying—has invoked the name of God as the accomplice of his crimes! Nero murdered his mother; but he felt on the sea-shore the grief of Orestes, and heard the murmurs of the Eumenides. Nero oppressed humanity; but in his last hour he proclaimed aloud that he ought to have been an artist, but not Cæsar. The Pagan religion did more to preserve the conscience and its jurisdiction over life than pretended Christianity.

I have been false to Nero, since his name is united to that of the Coliseum. In this place was the reservoir of the Roman gardens, and before that a colossal statue of the divine emperor with the attributes of Apollo, the god of light and harmony, holding the lyre to whose melody the Muses danced, and on his temples laid the green laurel of Daphne. The family of Vespasian, in hatred of the son of Agrippina, had destroyed his golden house full of immortal works, tearing down the Colossus and building the Amphitheatre in its place; but they could destroy neither the name nor the record of the Apollo statue of Nero; and this name, degenerated and corrupt—Coliseum—leaves to-day this colossal monument!

Indeed, it looks less the work of men than of nature. These gigantic proportions, these immense masses, seem not to have been created by human strength, but by the power of the Great Architect, of the Great Artist who has raised the eternal pyramids of the Alps, and has built up the wondrous cone of Vesuvius by the creating fire whose reverberations resound with the manufacture of crystals and granite. It is only when we observe the harmony of its arches, the sequence of its columns, the rhythm of that architecture which ascends to heaven as a canticle, that we find those enormous blocks have been distributed by human thought, and that the Amphitheatre has been sealed with the stamp of its laws.

Now the Coliseum is for the most part in ruins. When it was all perfect, two flights of steps supported it as huge pedestals. Four stories are placed above. Eighty open arches, forming eighty entrances, surround the first story. At the sides of the arches are raised half-columns attached to the wall, and belonging to the severe Doric order. Upon this first story there extends a cornice, and over the cornice other eighty arches, by the sides of which are placed half-columns of the lighter and more graceful Ionic architecture. Another cornice, the same as the preceding, completes the second story, and serves as a base for the third, also cut in arches, and ornamented with columns, but of the rich and florid Corinthian order. The monument is completed by an airy portico, resembling a chiseled crown-light, ornamented by pilasters, and having openings through which the heavenly azure of the sky seems to look more brilliant. This vast building is fifty-two metres high. To define it in a few words, I would call it a circular mountain, raised, sculptured, and chiseled by the labor of man. The side toward the north-east is in the best preservation. On its walls the succession of arches can be best studied, the harmonious staircase formed by the columns, the order and the grace of its cornices, the severe majesty of the first story, and the lightness of the upper part, which crowns all, and gives to such an enormous mass the finish and beauty of a jewel.

In these monuments we see the conceptions and character of Roman architecture; Grecian grace and beauty is replaced by colossal grandeur. The Coliseum is a monument worthy of a sovereign people, of a conquering people, of a Titanic people—of a people which counted legions of slaves and armies of workmen, on whose shoulders alone were borne to giddy heights these immense blocks of stone. Those who constructed the Coliseum had seen the East and its huge buildings, on which they desired to lay the Orders of Grecian architecture as a garland. Roman architecture has not the beauty of the Corinthian, which took for its model the lovely form of a Grecian woman—of that goddess the mother of all the arts. The Roman buildings are less beautiful but more majestic than the Greek, and there floats over them the invisible conception of a universal, assimilating spirit, which has united Grecian harmony and Asiatic magnitude, abounding on the earth and in history, without touching an ideal that soars to be lost among the heavens in rosy clouds and mysteries, half light, half shadow. Later Roman monuments, constructed on as vast a scale, we shall see tending to useful ends—practical, immediate, like all improvements. The god Eros, the Greek god of love, has been replaced in Rome by the god of all uncleanness—the god of that substance which covers and fertilizes the fields, as Hellenic metaphysics have been replaced by right and morality, with principles and sciences relating more immediately to life and society.

The Coliseum has all the characteristics of Roman architecture. It can be better learned in this great example, left miraculously by past ages, than in the pages of Vitruvius, probably altered and interpolated by the learned of the Renaissance period. Look at this mortar, that seems hardened as granite is hardened by the irregular internal movements of the planet! Look at the cellars and vaults—contrivances unknown among the Greeks—admirably constructed in this land of strength and empire! Behold the arches which the Hellenic world never erected, and that look like the triumphal gates by which history entered with a new life and a new spirit! See how the Roman has placed a plinth to support the Doric pillar which the Greek rooted in the bosom of the earth as the trunk of a tree! Contemplate those three Orders, always separated in Greek architecture, and united here in an ascending scale: first, the most simple and severe, the Doric, at the base; then the lightest and most elegant, the Ionic, in the centre; and lastly, the most florid and ornate, the Corinthian, crowning the whole as the diadem and capital of the monument! The spirit of a constructive people is visible in the whole building. The Roman has united the three Orders in his erections, as he has united the Greek gods in the Pantheon, and his style is the great epilogue of antique genius. Rome took from Greece her metaphysics and her religion, from the Sabines their women, from Spain her swords, from the East her arches, and from Etruria her bows. Thus it may be said that Greece is the flower, and Rome the fruit, of ancient history. Monuments like the Coliseum are, in fact, but the mighty bones of the immense organism which composes the Eternal City.

And to think that this edifice, which has conquered twenty ages, with all their destruction, was built in less than three years! It was erected, as we have heard, by some emperors of the Flavian family, under whose domination Tacitus cursed despotism and mourned the republic. Titus, whom universal adulation named the delight of the human race, burned Jerusalem; on her calcined stones he immolated a million and a half of Jews, and destined the rest to die in the gladiatorial shows of Syrian cities, to be trophies of the triumphal entry of the conqueror by the Via Sacra, to raise on shoulders livid from the lash the masses of this amphitheatre, and to be devoured by hungry beasts in the circus!

Titus—after having loved Berenice as Antony loved Cleopatra, after having heard his own victims call him Messiah, after having been called a god by those Egyptians whose fields gods visited, after having consecrated under the shadow of the pyramids nine bullocks to the god Apis, after having organized an escort of Oriental Satraps, and enjoyed through an entire day the cruel honors of triumph beneath the arches of the Eternal City—demolished the golden house of Nero, exchanged the statue of the sun for that of Cæsar adored by the populace; he dried up the lake which extended between the Mount Cælium and the Esquiline Mount, tore down the groves, cut up the pasturage on classic shores, and raised the greatest amphitheatre the world has yet beheld, solemnizing its inauguration by a hundred days of feasting, in which there were combats of stags, elephants, tigers, lions, and of men—terrible struggles, which sprinkled with hot blood the face of Cæsar and those of his people. Nine thousand animals perished during those sanguinary orgies upon the arena. History, which has preserved their number, does not mention that of the human sacrifices; doubtless because slaves were more worthless than wild beasts to the Cæsars.

Titus sought something to assuage his insatiable thirst of ambition, and sought it vainly. After having the world under his hand, there was no more for him to obtain; he had upon his shoulders the mantle of the Cæsars; all submitted like sheep to his authority; the world was subdued and silent. But, unable to attain his wishes and satisfy his ambition, the heart of Titus was broken. He had nothing to desire, or had but desires that were vague and infinite, which dissipated themselves in fantastic dreams, exhausting with them his existence. Certain it is that, despising the throne, a profound sadness took possession of him: his frame was attenuated by a kind of internal consumption; his respiration was heavy with sighs and his heart with sorrow; his eyes were filled with tears and his life with illusions; his sleep became oppressive; his past was remorseful, his future terrifying; till one day, wandering in the poisonous Roman Campagna in search of a spot where to sleep away his disgust, he expired, looking up to heaven with eyes inflamed by the fever of infinite and unsatisfied desires. While I thought of the life and death of Titus, I wondered at the boundless ambition of a Cæsar to rule the heavens as he possessed the earth, without any other advantage than to keep beneath his foot the seething mass of his crimes, and to heap upon his head the maledictions of humanity.

Indulging these thoughts and recollections, I went over the whole monument. I observed and studied it as the naturalist might study a mountain. I went through all the passages, so spacious that a hundred thousand spectators could enter and depart with rapidity, and without incommoding each other. I mounted to the highest steps, from whence can be seen the Roman Campagna: before me were the distant lagunes; to the right the Arches of Titus and of Constantine, the Pyramid of Caius Cestus, and the Basilica of St. Paul; on the left the Catacombs of St. Sebastian, the Via Appia with its double row of tombs; behind, the Palatine, the Forum, the Via Sacra, the Arch of Septimus Severus, the Capitol. In whatever place, ideas are preserved like a rich treasure; those scenes are suggestive of recollections; they are the true West of the ancient régime, the true East of modern progress.

I was so much absorbed that evening came upon me imperceptibly. The city bells announced the hour for vespers; the owls and other birds of the night began their first cries; I heard the hoarse and monotonous croak of the toad and frog in the distant lagunes, and the chant of a procession entering the neighboring church; spiritual voices mingled with those of nature, which made my meditations still more profound and silent, as if the soul escaped from the body to attach itself, after the manner of parasitic plants, to the dust of imperishable ruins.

The full moon rose in the serene and tranquil horizon, and lent with her melancholy rays fresh poetic touches to the arches, to the columns, to the vaults, to the scattered stones, to the desolation of the place; to the cross reared in its centre, as an eternal vengeance taken by the gladiators, obliging the most abject of the Roman people to bless and adore the once infamous gibbet of slaves, now transformed into the standard of modern civilization!

At the splendor of the rising moon, at the echo of the bells which sounded among the uncertain shadows, I seemed to see, awaking from their dust, the souls of departed generations, coming with silent flight to revisit those spots consecrated by their souvenirs and beloved even in the tomb. I wished to stay the spirits, and tell them, alas! all that passes in our world. I would have said: "If you be souls of tribunes, of senators, of Cæsars, know all that you loved has perished, and that already ages have worn even the steps of your altars by their kisses; all those gods you believe immortal have passed away, and the ideas by which they were animated, whirled like withered leaves in the abyss of history, have been loosened from the human spirit by continual renovation of ideas. No more do the Nereids move gracefully in the foam of the sea; no more do nymphs of marble whiteness sigh in the murmuring rivulet! The god Pan has dropped his pipe, once filled with the melody of the groves. To the intoxication of the Bacchantes have succeeded maceration, penance, and an indifference to the charms of nature. A Nazarene, a son of Israel, of the slaves, of that race which raised with a chain on their foot and a lash on their shoulder the mighty Coliseum, has conquered and buried the gods who inspired Horace and Virgil, who sustained Scipio in the plains of Carthage and Marius in the putrid fields— the gods who brought forth art and directed victory! In vain did Tacitus look contemptuously on the followers of this obscure youth, a poor carpenter of Judea! in vain Apuleius ridiculed them in his apologies and fables! Not even the immortal scorn of Lucian could dissipate the breath that exhaled from those lips, the truth and justice which poured from that infinite mind! The gods died, and upon their corpses dead Rome has fallen! The Forum is now a field where cows graze peacefully. The Coliseum is a pile of ruins, where Romans preserve and worship the gibbet of ancient slavery. The Via Sacra is no more. Upon the Capitol are performed the religious ceremonies of the Nazarene. Those you thought disturbers of the public peace have the altars and monuments once sacred to the gods of Cato and Camillus. Barbarous hordes from the North stifled the oracles, interrupted the sacred rites, delivering (as if it were a spoil) the human conscience to crowds of cenobites, who issued from the sewers and Catacombs. And when the new creed had taken possession of souls, when it had substituted its altars for those of Pagans—as if the human mind was condemned to weave and unweave continually the same web of ideas—new champions, new tribunes, new apostles, new martyrs arose to overthrow the faith of their ancestors. And the human conscience passed through new phases, and the human heart experienced new tortures, and new extremes of sorrow troubled the bleeding earth.

As my lips murmur these vague and incoherent imaginings, my ears seem to hear sounds of wailing. Is it the moaning of the wind among pines and cypresses? Is it the last sigh of the meadows sinking in the arms of night, or the echo of a great city, of its orisons and lamentations, like the expression of overwhelming and deep emotion?

"Sunt lacrymæ rerum!"

In imagination I beheld a festival in the amphitheatre. This enormous pile was not now a skeleton. Here stood a statue, there a trophy; opposite, a monolith brought from Asia or Egypt. The people entered, after having washed and perfumed themselves in the public baths, mounting to the top to disperse over the places previously assigned to them. At one side was the gate of life, through which passed the combatants; at the other the gate of death, through which were dragged the corpses. The shouts of the multitude, the sharp sound of the trumpets, mingle with the howling and roaring of wild animals. While the senators and the emperor arrive, attendants of inferior municipal rank scatter parched peas among the people, which they carry in wicker baskets like those of our traders at fairs. The ground is brilliant with gold powder, with carmine and minium to hide the blood, while the light is tempered by great awnings of Oriental purple, which tinges the spectators with its glowing reflection.

The senators occupy the lowest steps. Behind them are placed the cavaliers. Above are those fathers of families who have given a certain number of children to the empire. Beyond these are the people. And on the top, crowning the whole, are the Roman matrons, clothed in light gauzes and loaded with costly jewels, perfuming the air with aromatics carried in golden apples, and kindling all hearts by their soft words and tender glances.

While the spectators look to the emperor to give the signal for the commencement of the festival, conversation is carried on in a loud murmur. Look at that glutton—he is so rich that he knows not half of his possessions! Lolia Paulina is wearing emeralds worth sixty million sexterces — a small sum compared with the enormous robberies of her grandfather in the oppressed provinces. He who accompanies Cæsar stole at a supper of Claudius a golden cup. These reckless madcaps salute the orator Regulus, for they fear the venom distilled from his viperous tongue. He is honored, while generals who have conquered barbarian hordes, and died in defense of Rome, have been ten years unburied. The doctor Eudemus arrives, and his pupils in corruption and debauchery are not behind. That child of eight years is already depraved. That lady, who belongs to one of the most noble Roman families, has quitted the list of matrons and become degraded.

Cæsar is received by the people with loud acclamations; he is always welcome at festivals and especially at massacres. The priests and vestals offer sacrifices to the protecting gods of Rome. Blood flows; the entrails of the victims are quickly consumed in the sacred fire; the music sounds, the multitude vociferates, and at an Imperial signal come forth the gladiators, who salute the crowd with a smile on their lips, as if a delicious feast awaited them instead of a cruel and relentless death.

These unfortunates are divided in several categories. Some guide cars, painted green; others shelter themselves behind round bucklers of iron, on the outside of which sharp knives are fixed. They throw their tridents in the air, and catch them again with much dexterity. Their costume is a red tunic, azure buskins, a gilded helmet surmounted by a shining fish. The equestrians conduct their horses with great agility in the circus. The light is reflected on the steel breastplates, collars, and bracelets. Their robes are many-colored, and bring to mind Oriental dresses. Last come the duelists — a body all handsome, all unclothed, all imitating in their artistic attitudes the positions of classic sculptures. They are saluted frantically by the people, for they are the strongest, the most exposed, and the most valiant.

They were born in the mountains, in the desert, among the caresses of nature, breathing the pure air of the fields and of sacred liberty. War and war only has torn them from their country. Rome has fed them for the sake of their blood—blood to be offered in sacrifice to the majesty of the Roman people. Some of them now about to wound and murder each other have contracted close friendships. Perhaps some are brothers by nature, brothers by sentiment, obliged thus to endanger and immolate themselves, when, united by the same sentiments, they wish to bury their swords in the heart of Cæsar, and to avenge their race and country.

Already they lie in ambush, they search, they threaten, they entice and persist in this boisterous and bloody strife. If any one, moved by terror for himself or compassion for his opponent, draws back or seems to shrink, the master of the circus tortures him with a red-hot iron button applied on his naked shoulder. The crimson blood flows and smokes in the circus. One man has slipped and fallen. The people shout, believing him dead, and hiss when he rises. He loses heart after vain and desperate efforts to keep on foot. This one falls, pierced by a single wound given through his buckler. That one writhes in insupportable anguish, which looks like an epileptic spasm. Two are mortally wounded, but in falling fling away their swords, and embrace each other as a support and help in the death agony. Mutilated limbs, torn intestines, groans of anguish, the death-rattle of the expiring, faces contracted and fixed, last sighs mingled with lamentations, cries of rage and desperation;—all this is a grand spectacle for the Roman people, who shout, clap their hands, become intoxicated, infuriated; following the combat with nervous anxiety, straining their eyes from the sockets to see more of the slaughter, opening their lungs and nostrils to inhale the bloody vapors.

Anger seems to float as the master passion over all this feast of blood. Antique sculpture, generally of an Olympian severity, has left us the lively image of this anger in the statue of the dying gladiator. Over his dilated eyes hang his dark and knitted eyebrows. His robust frame is subject to a wonderful tension. His head is advanced, and makes an inclination over his breast in order to aim his thrust aright. His body is in the act of rushing forward to the combat, supported only on the right foot. His left arm threatens, at the

C

moment that his right wrist, strongly contracted, prepares to give a mortal blow. The statue is the image of hatred. And hatred has engendered in Rome a thick cloud of anger, of curses that found a terrible satisfaction in the Apocalyptic night of eternal vengeance, in the night of the victories of Alaric, of the orgies of barbarians, the sons of slaves and gladiators!

Who, who can turn aside Rome's punishment? All her power, all her majesty, all her greatness have been destroyed for an idea. There in the Catacombs hide obscure sectarians who oppose spiritual light to ancient sensuality—to the Pagan and Imperial religion, dogmas which Rome can not admit without perishing. These sectarians fly the light of day, and bury themselves fearfully in the Catacombs. There they paint the Good Shepherd who guides them to eternity, the Dove which announced the termination of the great deluge of tears in which our life is overwhelmed. There they intone hymns to an obscure tribune, poor and feeble; who did not die as a conqueror, but humbly and ignominiously on a cross. From thence have come forth those confessors of the new faith, to seal it with their blood on the arena of the circus. The old man, the youth, the tender maiden, have heard without trembling the cries of the Asiatic tiger, the roar of the lion of Africa. Hungry beasts of prey have come from the dens still visible in the foundations of the circus, and fixed their teeth and claws in the defenseless bodies of the martyrs. While panthers, hyenas, tigers, and lions divide the palpitating remains; while they drink the blood of these Christians with insatiable fury, the Romans give thanks to Cæsar, believing that a superstition has been destroyed with the lives of the unbelievers, and that with the blood the beasts have devoured a heresy!

And now emperors have died, and prætors are dispersed, and the stones of the Coliseum have fallen, and a new idea has replaced the ancient belief, and converted them from being persecuted to persecutors; has attempted in its turn to destroy new sects, to stifle new opinions—not being able to arrive—neither with its excommunications, nor its inquisition, nor its tortures—at the immortal idea of the human spirit, that shines eternally among gods and ruins, among those who die and those who suffer, among creeds and dogmas, perpetual as the sun in the choirs of the universe.

Chapter III.

THE ROMAN CATACOMBS.

IF the Roman city above ground is curious and wonderful, that which is hidden beneath is still more astonishing. Above, the wind shakes the ivy and the vine upon the walls, and all around reveals the faith of other ages. Below, in the solemnity of darkness, where the coldness and humidity of night are eternal; in those caves and grottoes formed in the depths of the earth, those silent vaults, whose obscurity is sometimes lighted by false fires, the product of decaying bones heaped there for ages, there is now no living soul. But in other times —times sacred and solemn—those Catacombs contained the germ of that faith which gave vitality to the human conscience and enlightenment to the world.

I turned with religious reverence toward those places hallowed by the veneration of so many ages, my mind overcome with tenderness and emotion; indeed, the Roman Campagna invites to meditation on the instability of human greatness and the worthlessness of the greatest earthly majesty.

There remains only a recollection of that population which once filled the world. Of those institutions which supported the weight of so many ages, we see but the traces. Broken walls, a few arches, some columns, half-legible inscriptions, ruined sepulchres, mutilated statues—things looking like the débris of a great shipwreck, the spoil of a terrible tempest. I understood there, among so much destruction, the mystic strength by which some souls are sustained, the contempt for an unstable world, where all is so soon and surely lost, wasted, and consumed; I understood their aspiration for the rest of the grave—their noble impatience for the possession of the infinite in another world less uncertain and more durable.

I, who have the ideas of my time, who believe in the everlasting character of the Universe, who look on death not as annihilation, but as renovation—I feel disposed to melancholy reflection, and fancy I hear the trumpet of the Last Judgment sounding over the trembling spheres, and the lamentations of the prophets over the ruined cities.

I saw in the mountains of the Apennines remains of antiquity: crumbling tombs strewed around; broken arches of gigantic aqueducts, towers ruined as if they had been struck and shattered by a thunderbolt. In all these fragments of half-pulverized buildings I seem to see some of the grand Apocalyptic visions; the remains of planets scattered by the swords of destroying angels in the solitude and immensity of space. The face of the beloved Apostle, idealized by the sculptor's hand in modern ages, eternally youthful as the gods of the heathen, eloquent as a Grecian orator speaking the language of Plato—he who put the Word nurtured in the shade of the Piræus in harmony with the fundamental doctrines of Christianity—this face that the Renaissance has realized in its pictures and statues I saw at Patmos—among the Greek islands whose lovely shores smile like sirens. At the sight of the blue Mediterranean and its classic shores, its coral-strewed waters, whose murmur is like an ancient canticle, I saw this ideal face, mystic as a prayer, sweet as hope; I saw it as I read in the Revelation the punishment of the dishonored Babylon, while good and bad angels fought rudely in the air, and the rocks struck the planets, and the dead, bursting the grave-clothes and the sepulchres, obtained their bodies, and went up to the Last Judgment to hear in that supreme moment their sentence from the Eternal Judge of all the Earth.

We went to the Catacombs through heaps of ruins. The desolation of the landscape added to the sadness of our souls. Exiles, and wandering far from our country, our hearts seemed blighted as the immense tract of volcanic soil through which we passed. All spoke of death and decay. We could have fancied ourselves in some infernal sphere, if Nature, with the fresh dews of morning, the green grass between the stones, and the early spring flowers—the butterflies hovering above, the tender leaves shooting from the buds, the birds' nests already formed in the young foliage—all the sweet beauties of April—had not shown us the loveliness of life and the ever-new delight of Nature's festivals.

Oh Nature! immovable in the midst of movement, unique amid variety, surrounded with ether which penetrates every pore, forming the spirit and its atmosphere, with the continual succession of organic beings which change and are transformed. Oh Nature! durable and unchangeable; subject to death and to eternity; to the limited and the infinite; diffused over the immensity of space and compressed into organic beings: from the stars which irradiate the heavens, to the flowers which perfume the air with their aroma; from the impalpable gases that evaporate, to the great mountain chains with their glaciers, where the snow whitens the volcanoes struggling with internal fires; from the almost imperceptible nebulæ, to the great worlds which travel through space; from the grain of sand drifted by the wave, to the farthest stars of the Milky Way, whose light reaches us in twenty thousand centuries—poor outcasts clinging to this little planet. In that vast circle, whose centre—according to modern science—is found every where, and whose circumference is nowhere, there happens not the annihilation of a single molecule; nothingness exists not; it is the shadow of our thoughts, the apprehension of our folly, the phantasm of our feelings, an idea without reality, which the confined limits of our reason and the incurable imperfection of our language has obliged us to place in the eternal ocean of life. It is true that stars have been extinguished in our solar system, as fauna and flora have disappeared from our world; but the warmth of universal life is enduring, and the growth and progress of the most perfect organism is unceasing.

Let us then enter these subterranean caverns with our thoughts absorbed by the infinite, and our hearts resting on the hope of immortality.

The Catacomb most generally visited is that of San Sebastiano, and the one most deserving of deep study is the Catacomb of San Calixto. About four miles eastward of Rome, between the Via Appia and the Via Ardeatina, under heaps of all sorts of débris and rubbish, close to cypress groves, which deepen the sad solemnity of the landscape, lies hidden the largest and most remarkable of Christian cemeteries. It was a refuge for the persecuted, a dwelling-place for martyrs, a rest for the dead, a temple for the living, the assembly of those bold innovators who brought a new light into the world and a new sentiment into life. I advise my readers not to visit these sanctuaries without taking with them the books and maps of the celebrated Catholic archæologist, Bossi. As the explorer of American woods—that land of the future—advances armed with his short hatchet in these untrodden paths, cuts down the trees, drives away the reptiles, roots up the brushwood, and creates by his labor a habitation for his family, so the archæological explorer of a subterranean world plunges into shadow, into the asylum of birds of the night, into crumbling dungeons, between labyrinths of grottoes, liable to be crushed by fragments from the fragile walls, to be lost forever in some corner of those cities of the dead, in that tomb of palpable darkness, mingling his bones with those traces he wished to snatch from the silence of sad and ungrateful forgetfulness.

How many times the light and spongy soil rained sand on the forehead of such a one! How often a shower of stones and bricks fell at his feet, covering him with thick clouds of dust, and oppressing his overcharged and exhausted respiration! How often he lost his way in that immense labyrinth—

could not find the North in that ocean of darkness, and fancied he had also lost the outlet, and had found a certain death of slow starvation! By the uncertain light of a dying lamp, the bold miner in human affairs, the diver into the abyss of time, reads the inscriptions traced fifteen centuries ago by one of those sectarians who collected human remains in the great circus, and placed them in the earth with prayers whose echoes are still heard, and tears whose exhalations remain in that blessed atmosphere.

The first thing which astonishes one on descending into the tombs is the gigantic labor of those who excavated them, without having either the mechanical or chemical means of our civilization. Though it is said these subterranean cities were opened for quarries, their especial peculiarities, their galleries placed one over the other—there are even as many as five stories of tombs—their disposition, that preserves a certain regularity, reveals a perfectly conceived and matured plan to which the construction of these passages has been submitted, probably by the early propagators of the new creed, who left there the germs of those doctrines which were to feed the souls of future generations. Even the nature of the soil has been studied with scientific attention. They have carefully avoided the argillaceous clay and chalk, the overflow of water, and all places that easily retain moisture; they have dug the tombs and temples in soft granular stone—volcanic, but hard and consistent, less accessible to damp forged by the creating fire, and suited to all kinds of durable building. For it was essential to preserve these asylums not only from the fury of men, but from the calamities incidental to nature.

To this end the early Christians sought the protection of the laws. And the Roman law protected, before all, and above every thing in the world, the places sacred to sepulture. The soil which was the property of the dead was undisturbed by the living. If land was sold, bequeathed, or given away, neither sale, testament, nor donation was valid to alienate the sepulchre, which was always excepted—always held in the possession of the families who placed there the ashes of their kindred. Thus the Christians could open graves in the depths of the earth, raise lofty monuments, and, under the title of adjacent ground, annex much land to the sepulchre—like the sepulchre, sacred. The Christians, profiting by the protection of the law for their cemeteries, took land, opened subterranean galleries, and there deposited the treasured remains of those of their sect and of their family. A series of Roman arches constitute the true nucleus of the Catacombs. Thus by a superstitious respect of Pagans for the rights of property, the Christians obtained a home for their worship and a resting-place for their dead. The same emperors who persecuted the Christians as believers respected them as proprietors. Collective property, such as was the property of the early Christians, had a legal existence in the code of laws and in the sanction of the tribunal. If there were confiscations, as in the reigns of Valerian and Diocletian, they were passing, exceptional, and interrupted; soon effaced by a restitution which proved the lasting nature of the right, as the restitution of Galieno and of Magencius. Yet, notwithstanding, the empire pursued illicit societies, and declared as such those religious communities which sacrificed to their dogmas the integrity of their lives. And Rome, which acknowledged the epilogue and synthesis of the ancient world, which admitted into her temples all the divinities worshiped among Asiatic peoples—Rome rejected the God of the Israelites and the God of the Christians; doubtless the other gods were, like her own, gods of nature, while the God of the Jew and the Christian was the God of the spirit, come to displace the material and powerful goddess of the earth—the goddess Rome. Notwithstanding this hatred, confirmed by so many persecutions, Rome respected all benevolent associations having for their object the interment or the praying for the dead; not questioning as to their religious belief when that tended to recognize immortality. Protected by this respect of the Roman people for the dead, the early Christians prepared their temples and cemeteries.

And the burial-places of the primitive Christians were necessarily very extensive. The Romans burned their dead, and collected their ashes in vases of marble or porphyry; while the Christians, who believed not only in the immortality of the soul, but also in the resurrection of the body, buried their dead entire in the sepulchres. Thus the cities of the dead soon assumed proportions as colossal as the cities of the living; and under triumphal arches, under the magnificent circus, under the temples containing the gods they believed eternal, under palaces where emperors reigned who thought themselves omnipotent,—beneath all these there extended cities of tombs toward the four points of the horizon—cities with their streets, their crossways, their squares; cities of the dead, who, notwithstanding, quickened a new spirit destined to destroy ancient Rome and to build upon her ruins another civilization!

Let us note the difference between the Catacombs of the first century and those of later times—the third century, for example. The former were more beautiful and more highly ornamental. Marble was frequently used in the first century; brilliant stuccoes, lively colors, artistic relievos, frescoes worthy of a place beside those of Pompeii; classical inscriptions with high-sounding and noble names of aristocratic families, monumental sarcophagi, all constructed and beautified by those artists—a little Pagan, it is true—who embodied by their pencils and their artistic chiseling the essence of classic inspiration, whether they represented the transition of one course of ideas to another, or of one epoch to another in history. Such is life! The most transcendent revolutions separate themselves timidly from their origin, and still cling to the old institutions they seek to destroy. The Church, although born under the malediction of the Synagogue, collects and consecrates its books, uses and extends its language. Christianity, although increasing under Pagan persecution, copied its symbols and sanctified its arts. Philosophy separates itself from theological science, but preserves many of its maxims, and binds rationalistic formulas to the phrases of the ancient schools. The mystical painters of the

Middle Ages had their example in the painters of the Catacombs. Here is the true genealogy of Cimabue and of Fra Angelico. Here the dove which accompanied Venus in the ancient picture, serves now, with the olive-branch in her beak, to announce the promise of the resurrection. Perhaps it is not as well designed or chiseled as the beauteous dove of Greece, which built her nest among myrtles and lentiscus, and which accompanied with her melodious warble the hymn of Hellenic temples; yet Christianity has conveyed beneath her white wings the sublime enlightenment of a new spirituality. Thus it is with the human soul. It believes in the sentiment that has transformed it, which it thinks has grown by sudden and miraculous revelations, when really it has been transformed, when it has grown by internal effort, persevering and constant, which has slowly elaborated the new ideas, food of so many generations, attributed in the excitement of the heart and imagination to the miracles of the prophets, of angels, and teachers; just as the artist or poet attributes to the smile of the chaste muse floating in space, or concealed among the rosy clouds of heaven, the inspirations which arise in his own soul!

The Catacombs of Apostolic times are more ornate than those of later ages, when Christianity was considerably extended. I can only attribute this fact to the same reason as that given by the Comte de Richmont, in his erudite work on Primitive Christian Archæology, and not to any connection with the classes which belonged to the new religion. History contradicts this latter view. The power of the Christian association worked the wonders of the first Catacombs. The artists, who belonged always to the past by the poetry of their recollections, or to the future by the poetry of their hopes, were touched to the heart by the new faith, and expressed their sentiments in the solitude of the Catacombs. The insignificance of the persecuted sect sometimes served them as a shield against their persecutors. The first Cæsars feared the Stoics, whose humanitarian principles contrasted too strongly with the fundamental idea of the Romans—the idea of the incontestable superiority of the great city. But they did not fear the Christians, who seemed confounded with those Jews whom they brought away captive after the taking of Jerusalem; a people whom they saw with contempt in the exhibitions of the circus, in combat, in agony, in tortures and death, serving by their sufferings to amuse the populace.

When Christianity increased in the third century; when the number of its churches terrified those who beheld ruin and desolation in the abandonment of the Pagan temples; when the tendency of the times was to separate from the ancient faith, and the disposition of the people was also to abandon the ancient Empire; when, among so many moral and material ruins, came, like a flock of hungry vultures to an unburied corpse, the irruption of barbarians, who scared them by their shouts, the clanging of their arms, and the ferocity of their instincts; the last Romans attributed these misfortunes to the first Christians, who being persecuted resorted, for better security rather than as a new idea, to subterranean shelter—took refuge for a time only in the easily wrought Catacombs, not thinking of pictures or relievos, for they were not religious temples, but hiding-places for fugitives.

We passed from the Catacombs of San Sebastiano to those of San Calixto. Through the former we were rapidly conducted by a monk, who guided us, candle in hand, through the caverns, muttering prayers as he went along. In the latter we had a layman for a guide—much more intelligent, and much less hasty—who seemed better taught by his own experience and less given to recitations. The darkness was profound and the silence unbroken. We descended from the busy scenes and storms of life to the deep shadows and the repose of death. The farther we advanced the more we were interested. If our guiding light had been extinguished, how could we have quitted the abyss! And what repose, what stillness in that region of the dead! The fugitives once hidden there conquered the world. The doctrines there planted have for ages covered with their shadows altars and temples, feeding them with their vitality, and sustaining the human heart with the Christian's hope.

Who that had seen the two as they once were—Christianity and Paganism—would not have said that the caverns were destined to disappear: and the greater—that structure raised in the air and light as the abode of pleasure and of vice—destined by its false brilliancy, by its apparent power, by its pretended strength, by the courtiers who encircled it, to endure for ages! Yet the Cæsars have departed, the senate crowned with laurels is no more. There were the soldiers with their burnished armor; the priests who were oracles of the past and prophets of the future; the proud and wealthy nobles, the slaves of the circus, the gladiators, the triumphal arches, the colossal monuments; the obelisks, witnesses of so many ages, and the spoil of so many battles; while beneath all these lived an obscure and feeble sect, proclaiming a high-toned morality in the midst of the general depravity, and having for their only power—prayer! for their only victory —martyrdom! Above, the temples were magnificent; surrounded with gardens and meadows, where innumerable birds sung in aviaries; marble vestibules adorned with wondrous statues, where the cunning of the sculptor gave to the inert stone all the warmth and vitality of the soul; museums for the preservation of the swords of the early heroes, and of the trophies they took in field and city; while below, in the darkness—close to those wonders of history, close to those miracles of art—lay the sombre temple of Christian worship, entered like the dens of wild animals, and peopled by some humble figures symbolical of sorrow, pursued by despotic cruelty, and often tortured in drunken orgies!

Who could have predicted the triumph of these humble sectarians? One is astonished and terrified to see how they were ridiculed by the most admired writers of antiquity. Lucian has left among his immortal works the burlesque sketch of a Christian martyr named Peregrino. This unfortunate, according to him, fancied he was immortal, and having to live eternally, he despised earthly torments and desired death. As the crucified Founder of Christianity told his disciples that all men were brethren, they held their goods in common, and, victims of their own ignorance and folly, they fell into the hands of the most covetous or skillful. They crowned all these absurdities by dying in the flames!

After this bitter manner the reformers of the world were judged by a writer of ability, a philosopher of elevated ideas, a satirist of the highest order, and one too who felt the indifference to death common at that period, who might have known that the philosophers of Greek science and the gods of Pagan worship rather deserved his contempt, and who should have felt in his inmost soul the necessity of a reformation.

Then these fanatics in creed, superstitious by temperament, secluded in darkness, believers in the crucified Jesus, these insane preachers, these passionate sectarians—the feeble, the poor, the ignorant—were, after all, those summoned to awaken and to call down the living flame of the spirit on the intoxicated and corrupt world, which poisoned with its orgies and its vices not only the human conscience, but even material nature.

What strength had they? Arms? Their word. What riches? Their faith. What power? That of resignation and suffering. Had they legions? The legions of martyrs. Had they property? That of the tomb. What they really possessed was a force which is unconquerable, a weapon that is never blunted, riches that can not be lost, possessions that can not be exhausted. The mysterious light without shadow, and which grows not dim; the living fire, which quickens and is not quenched; the immortal soul of nature, the acting spring of society, the air in which the soul is free; an unfailing faith bestowed on them by Heaven with the gift of miracles. The conquered were conquerors; the proscribed became powerful; the dead were givers of life; the weak, with hands pierced by the nails of the cross, vanquished the savage fierceness of barbarians.

Such reflections must of necessity force themselves on those who wander through this immense labyrinth of subterranean passages. They are the furrows in which were planted the first germs of the Christian religion. There they were long guarded from persecution, as the seed corn under the frost-bound earth in winter. From thence they sprung into life. The martyrs of a progressive idea fall, but rise again. The work they build is not interrupted, although it seems to our poor vision incapable of kindling the moral world, as flame can kindle the material world. We who respect all that has contributed to the education of humanity, children of this preeminently synthetical age, behold and admire the place where was contrived the great moral revolution against the excesses of ancient sensualism. The epigraphic signs, the half-effaced figures, the hieroglyphic sculpture on sepulchral stones, the holy images of those times, transport us to the ages of Christian persecution. We seem to hear the religious psalmody half repressed by terror; to behold the arrival of those who brought the remains of the martyrs collected from the refuse of the circus, to deposit them in urns, and raise at their tomb the altar whereon burned the mystic lamp. We see painted in fresco and sculptured on stone the miraculous fish which represented the Saviour; anchors, symbols of hope; the crook and bag of the Good Shepherd; the lamb resigned to the holocaust; the ship of the Church defying all tempests; the mystic vine whose roots and branches overspread the world; the divine woman upon the waters of the sea, with her child in her arms and the star on her forehead; the supper in which the eucharistical bread was divided among the primitive Christians—a frugal supper and one nourishing to the soul, a lively protest against the orgies of the empire; the resurrection of Lazarus, coming forth from the sepulchre rejuvenescent and beautified by the divine Word which fell on his mouldering flesh, and awakened it to a new life, as the evangelical doctrine kindled anew the old world.

I can not enter into the artistic controversies which have so much excited those learned in Christian archæology. I can not say, with M. Paul Rochette, if these paintings were the inspirations of ancient art, or if they sprung spontaneously from the new faith, according to the Cavaliere Bossi and his French commentator, whom I have previously quoted. To me it has happened as to him — I did not see heaven, which Ozanan saw in the eyes of the worshipers. I did not perceive the spiritual expression of the paintings of the Middle Ages in the frescoes of the Catacombs. I saw that the faces had something of the immovable impassibility of ancient paintings. But it is observed that art is not in classic serenity, in that peculiarity of outline and perspective which gives it an Olympic character. Some drops of melted lead have warmed that flesh. Some lightning flashes have kindled those eyes. The forms are contracted by grief, and the lips sigh with sorrowful desire. These are the mysterious beginnings from whence issued in after ages the Angels of Fiesole, the Martyrs of Fra Bartolomeo, the Conceptions of Murillo, the Virgins of Raphael. And the artist who studies these symbolical figures sees in them the first glory of the genealogy of modern art—of that pictorial art that we have added to the antique.

Christians or philosophers devoted to the past or to the future, men of faith or of science, when you penetrate into that abyss, when you wander through that darkness, when you study those half-blotted frescoes, or touch those sacred relievos, you feel through your veins an emotion of terror always produced by the sight of sublimity.

I confess that all the religious sentiments and recollections of my childhood took possession of me, as if the first faith was still living. I remembered the humble church of my native village with its religious festivals; the Virgin Mother among clouds of incense, and the melody of the organ; the processions which came forth to bless the fields in the May mornings, when the poppy unfolded her petals among the corn, and the thorn-tree glowed with rosy blossoms; the chant of the Litany repeated by many voices; the sound of the bell floating in air and inviting to vespers, while the last splendors of day died over the mountains, and the first stars of the evening arose in the immensity of heaven.

But when these emotions left space for reflection, I saw the power of a new belief which appeared at the expiration of the ancient worship. Such sentiments are experienced in going through those subterranean caverns, where people seem to wander like moving corpses in immense pantheons. The obscurity and silence, if too much prolonged, fatigue, chill, and petrify. One wants the warm air and the light—above all, the light. And when we leave the Catacombs and breathe the atmosphere of the Roman Campagna, and see the sun flashing on the snows of the Apennines, and inhale the aroma of the dewy grass and the opening flowers, and listen to the chirp of the young birds which welcomes the maternal caress, while the swallow ascends in the pure sky, and the nightingale warbles in the groves—our hearts bless the beneficence of Nature, which offers an eternal theatre to all tragedies and infinite pages to the epochs of history.

Chapter IV.

THE SISTINE CHAPEL.

Rome is a city of perpetual sadness. Her cypress groves murmur an elegy. Her fountains weep the death of her god. The moon shining on her marbles evokes pale and mournful shadows. Upon all sides there are heaps of ruins with their crowns of green nettles. There are traces of where a Titanic army has been in the dust of Rome beside her funereal urns. The gigantic stones, the Cyclopean walls, the colossal columns, are the bones of this race conquered by the bolts of heaven, annihilated by the vengeance of God. A volcano which for long ages has lain cold is less majestic in the sterile solitude of its crater than this dead Rome. Yet fossil bones incrusted in the mountains since the Deluge teach less than these bricks scattered in fragments, these stones with half-effaced inscriptions.

All is desolate. The sepulchres are empty. Death has not forgiven the dead ashes. Nature, in her insatiable voracity, has metamorphosed the bones fallen on her bosom. The dust of Cæsar, of Scylla, of Cincinnatus, of Camillus, is perhaps whirling in the air, perhaps mingling with the frail and beautiful wings of a butterfly, or woven into the fibres of the grass which the wild goat divides with his sharp teeth. And notwithstanding—when they were grouped together in the frame, when the warm blood animated and gave them vigor and vitality—these atoms supported the weight of the heavens, ruled the world at their pleasure, and governed with a brittle sword the humanity which has long since mouldered away!

And what remains of all this? Some handfuls of dust, heaped on other dust, among which have been lost Cæsars and tribunes, conquerors and vanquished, Romans and barbarians, masters and slaves, without weighing more in the balance of the universe and in the gravitation of the globe than other ashes.

After a long time spent among ruins, one becomes accustomed to the inhabitants common to such places. You are not startled by the bird of night which hides in the crevice of a sepulchre; nor at the bat issuing from a catacomb; nor at the owl or the cuckoo sitting in the nocturnal solitude on the stones of the Coliseum. You like to meet the dwellers on the height. It is useless to search for them in a degenerate and submissive race. The worthy inhabitants of Rome are the men carved by the chisel in immortal marble. They are the figures designed and perfected by genius. And among these figures—those which yet retain the sacred fire on the forehead; those which preserve the nervous contraction of awakened thought; those which breathe a tempest from their colossal lungs; those which look like gods, with a resemblance to things earthly—are the statues of Michael Angelo.

After the Genius of the Capitol had fallen in the dust a thousand years, lulled by the miseries of the Middle Ages, it shook off its heavy sleep and arose, flinging aside the mountains of ruins heaped upon its shoulders, and went to search for that Titan of art, Michael Angelo—solitary, unapproachable, and sublime—to communicate to him the secrets of the chisel, and to invite him to dig under the walls of Catholic Rome for the remnants of Roman antiquity. They were powerful, robust, herculean, these Roman heroes: those strong lungs were needed to inhale a human spirit with their breath; those nervous arms to direct the war-horse—to pass as conquerors from Tigris to the shores of Betis. On those broad shoulders the earth reposed as on other Caryatides; in that forced and almost impossible position they attacked Jerusalem and Alexandria; their hands seem to brandish the lance with which they opened the veins of cities and ingrafted their people upon the native race, and the gigantic and slightly curved shoulders are those which drew the enormous burden of the conquered gods.

These feelings were awakened by the sight of the Sistine Chapel, which I visited on my return from the Via Appia and the Via dei Sepolcri. In that temple of art, smoke-stained by tapers and incense, you see only colossal figures, and can neither comprehend the ideas nor personages represented. Strongly moved by my long walk between two or three leagues of tombs, I fancied I saw in the Alcides of the vault and in the various groups of the Last Judgment the spirits hidden in the ruins; those souls which float above the stones over broken arches; those souls wandering near the Forum, retenanting colossal and violent human bodies, as if shaken by the hurricane of the Last Day—all in due proportion and harmony with their historic greatness. The figures of Michael Angelo are antique heroes that have risen from the sepulchre!

The Sistine Chapel takes its name from Sixtus IV. His pontificate was stormy and agitated. Machiavel learned some of his political intrigues from the conduct of Sixtus. He was the first who showed how immense was the political power of the Popedom, and, while exciting wars against the Italian magnates, was praised as the author of the *Principe*. In his time and at his instigation Julio de Medici was assassinated in Santa Maria dei Fiori, at Florence, when he was worshiping God at high mass. In revenge the Medici hung from a window the bishop appointed by the Pope for Pisa. The riches of Sixtus IV. were enormous, because they proceeded from the sale of benefices. Pietro Riaria was a Cardinal at the age of twenty-six, Patriarch of Constantinople, and Archbishop of Florence, and died satiated with gold, blood, and pleasure, like Balthazar or Sardanapalus. Contending parties fought at the gate of the Vatican, and stained with blood the steps of the altar of St. Peter's. But the Roman court increased its possessions, and raised churches with its riches. At this time licenses to pillage were granted to bandits for money, and a Lord Chamberlain said to Innocent VIII., who had bought the pontifical throne by simony, and who sold safe-conducts to robbers—"Your Holiness does well, for God wills not the death of a sinner, but rather that he should *pay* and live."

But if the Sistine Chapel owes its name to Sixtus IV., it is indebted for the marvelous decoration of the vault to Giulio II. This was the classic period of Italian horrors. If, as says Alfieri, man is born more robust in the Italian peninsula than in the rest of the world, his strength may be known by his crimes, for never did any country show greater. Pisa succumbed among her marshes, after a resistance that had something of the furious madness of suicide. A Duke of Genoa, raised from the plebeian class to the supreme dignity, was assassinated and quartered; his members, divided among the enemy, were fixed as trophies upon the walls. Three thousand citizens were decapitated on the Prato, and the sanctity of the convents was outraged. The Venetian nobles were roasted to death in a cavern in Verona, the woods having been set on fire for that purpose. Nor did infants at the breast escape the slaughter. In those fearful times even the women turned cruel. A countrywoman of Tuscany cut off the head of a Spanish soldier who had robbed her house, and ran to present the bleeding trophy to her husband, believing her honor to be thus satisfied. The Swiss ravaged Milan; the Germans Venetia; the French Ravenna; the Spaniards the rest of Italy.

Gaston de Foix used to show his shirt red with Italian blood. Bayard exercised the terrible cruelties of the feudal ages. A way of springing mines was invented by Pedro Navarro. Then the great captain gained his victories at the cost of terrible struggles. Italy was a field of slaughter. Lines of unburied corpses covered it from the defiles of the Abruzzos to those of the Alps.

But in the midst of all these horrors the genius which governs and the voice that commands are those of Giulio II. Austere in his habits, an Italian in his inmost heart, formed by battles into the bronze of heroism; clever and dexterous enough to be able to subtract or add to his calculations, like arithmetical figures, kings, emperors, and peoples; gentle in his spiritual authority, because it served to maintain his political power; implacable in his punishments as a priest of the Old Testament; quick to make hostile incursions and to besiege cities even amid the rigors of winter; holding in one hand the spiritual thunderbolt ready to launch on the enemies of the Church, and in the other a match to fire cannons and drive the barbarians from Italy.

There is certainly a resemblance between the temperament of Pope Giulio II. and that of the artist Michael Angelo. The one attempted to form by his wars a race of heroes who should be able to defend his country; the other to draw from the bosom of the earth a race of Titans who should excite others to glory. He proposed to Giulio II. to erect his tomb after this fashion: A mountain of bronze and marble, broad at the base, and with an elevated pedestal; a staircase and richly sculptured cornices; several genii in those violent and virile but harmonious attitudes of which he alone knew the secret, supporting the cornices on their heads, and having the nations in chains under their feet. The Arts and the Virtues were represented by beautiful women, weeping and wringing their hands in sorrow. Over the four corners of the first cornice were active and contemplative life—Saint Paul, whose word is a sword, and that Moses who almost appals us, and whose face flashes with the lightnings of Sinai. Below are trophies, tributes of nature and recollections of history. Cybele, the earth, holding a winding-sheet with the attitude of a *Madre Dolorosa* who embraces the crucified Lord lying on her loving bosom, and looking to Urania, the heavens, who smilingly links the soul of the Pope, like another star, to the choir of his blessed souls!

Michael Angelo went to search out the best marbles of the mountains, and returned well supplied with huge blocks suited to his purpose. Then he took his hammer and chisel, and commenced to break and plane the pure material, seeking—with breathless eagerness and extreme effort, among a shower of stones which started upward at his blows—the image already formed in his own imagination. But when he was engaged in his herculean labor, envy sought to destroy him. Bramante, a genius of that unnatural age, desired his ruin. The one chiefly an architect, the other mainly a sculptor, each should have endeavored to perfect himself—not to injure the other.

The grandiose statues of Michael Angelo appear to the greatest advantage under the bold arches of Bramante. There —between those broad lines, under those prodigious curves, placed in one of those courts, or near one of the great temples where the perspective is incomplete—the statues of Michael Angelo display their tragic attitudes, their gigantic members, which seem animated by a ray from the Divinity, and struggling to mount from earth to heaven. Bramante and

Michael Angelo detested but completed each other. Thus it is often in human nature. Those two men knew not that they were laborers in the same work. And history is silent on such points till death has passed over her heroes. Armies have fought till they have been almost annihilated on the field of battle; men have hated and injured one another by their calumnies; the learned and powerful persecute and seek to blot their fellows from the earth, as if there was not air and space for all; they know not, blinded by their passions and warped by the prejudices of envy, that the future will blend them in the same glory, that to posterity they will represent but one sentiment; friends and enemies will alike leave traces of their footsteps among the arts, and all distinct personality is but a laborer employed to erect this immense series of triumphal arches called ages; and all individual intelligence is a facet of the prism called human genius, which disperses in a thousand varieties the divine light in which the universe is floating. Society is like nature. Evil is in the circumstantial, in the fortuitous, in the limited; but it disappears in the combined, in the universal, in the eternal. Thus it appears that in certain ages all individuals seem perverse, all people blind, all actions sinful. Here we perceive a monster, there a slaughter, yonder a superstition; and afterward, when the genius of the age succeeds in separating itself from old prejudices, new opinions arise like beneficent clouds of consoling dew, refreshing the atmosphere and sustaining the world with new life and energy.

And the same holds good with regard to the universe.

Lightning, poison, pestilence, and catastrophes are accidents which never perturb the serenity of the great whole; the eternal light of Cosmos changes not for any inequalities on the bosom of nature. The viper stings a man, but it can not poison all humanity. Death cuts off the individual, but it does not destroy the species. I have ever revolted against the cruel belief in the eternity of evil. And I have always combated another idea not less terrible—that of complete death and the total annihilation of consciousness. We shall resolve these antinomies hereafter. All contradictions will be reconciled by death. Bramante and Michael Angelo, enemies during life, are reconciled in immortality.

Let us follow the history of the Sistine Chapel. Bramante urged upon Giulio II. the desirability of intrusting Michael Angelo with the frescoes of the vault. But the great sculptor did not yet feel himself sufficiently acquainted with fresco painting, and he frankly said so to his Holiness. The latter would not allow any contradiction, refused to tolerate disobedience, or to listen to the best of all reasons—the impossibility of performing the desired task.

This affair was a great trouble to Michael Angelo, because, close to the Sistine Chapel, Raphael was painting the Chambers of the Vatican with his usual calmness and self-possession in difficulties. The first sculptor of his age ran the risk of being the second painter. This thought wounded his vanity, but did not dishearten him. Finding that resistance to the Pope would be his ruin, he sent for the best Florentine fresco painters, learned from them the principles of their art, and dismissed them. Then he shut himself up alone in the chapel, contemplating that immense vault, lofty, dark, and empty, like chaotic space before the creation. He commenced to people it. On attentively observing the figures, a strange reflection makes them seem as if they had been painted by lightning. They look as if they had issued from the flashes of a tempest, and been produced from the fury of a giant. Lips have been sketched to breathe a lamentation of Jeremiah, a stanza of Dante, a malediction of the Prometheus of Æschylus.

The soul of Raphael produced his figures without effort—as it is said the Virgin was delivered without pain. Each of them seems to have been born like Cytherea from the foam of the ocean, in a pearly shell, with a smile upon the lips, the rays of Aurora on the head, and heaven in the eyes. They have been raised by a gentle wave and left on the rude shores of reality. The figures of Michael Angelo struggle, turn, suffer—are mounted on the blast of the hurricane; they have for light a conflagration; they express all the intensity and power of sorrow—they are the giant offspring of the extreme despair of genius in delirium, desirous of marking reality with the stamp of infinity. They all seem to carry in the flesh the burning iron of the artist's idea, and cry hopelessly, like the shipwrecked for the land, from the world that is visible and finite to that which is unseen and everlasting.

It is necessary to comprehend all the troubles which tore the heart of Michael Angelo while pursuing his work. Raphael is always sustained by his *innamorata* who loved him, by his disciples who obeyed him—surrounded by a choir of angels; but the great sculptor was alone, separated from the world, reduced to a perpetual companionship with his own ideas, without love and without friendship, isolated as a mountain with the tempest beating on its summit. After having studied the first rudiments of the art, he essayed the commencement of his wonderful composition. His colors mingle, the paintings fall asunder. He flies to Giulio II. to beg he would free him from his promise. The Pope insisted on its performance. San Gallo, a painter, suggested to him an easy way of avoiding the difficulty. Up to this time the scaffold constructed by Bramante was suspended to the roof by cords. At each extremity of his work, which was like a bundle of rags, the scaffold was unsteady. In place of this, Michael Angelo, by the advice of San Gallo, made another, which was quite fixed and secure. Then he sketched the heavens which were to contain his figures. But when he had so much space he was overcome by despair, from the fear of being unable to fill it. He locked the chapel door, and rushed out to wander alone, like a madman, in the Roman Campagna. The broken arches and aqueducts, resembling giant skeletons; the ruined masses where the shepherd rested, and up whose rugged sides goats clambered; the Apennines with their snowy summits, and slopes dotted with monuments; the cypress groves, pine-trees, and willows, which give the country the aspect of the largest cemetery ever seen by man; the lagunes, covered with rushes, and crossed by wild buffaloes and by melancholy looking boats, occupied by beings who seemed like the dead revisiting the earth; sepulchres gilded by the sun's rays, like fragments of shattered planets fallen amid the desolation; fantastic clouds like evaporations from ashes; volcanoes in the brightness of the desert, more replete with interest than peopled cities — such a spectacle must strengthen and invigorate the mind, and enable it to produce something superior to human power, something sublime.

But it was essential that he should abandon himself to solitude and his inspiration. Time is the great helper of the artist. Against his inspiration, against his solitude, against his time, the impatience of the Pope was exerted. He was aged, and he ardently desired to see the work completed before his death. Three great works Michael Angelo had been compelled to perform or invent for Giulio II.—his sepulchre, his statue, and the vault of the Sistine Chapel. The tomb was stopped on account of its difficulty and costliness. The bronze statue, erected in a square at Bologna, was melted down and converted by the Bolognese into a piece of artillery. They called it Giuliana, and discharged it against the Papal party. These having failed, the Sistine Chapel was all that remained to him for glory. Leaning on his crosier, the Pope would enter to interrupt, torment, or hasten the artist. Michael Angelo at one time let fall a board at his feet. "Do you know that I should have been killed had it struck my head?" cried the Pontiff. "Your Holiness will avoid all accidents by not coming here to distract me," expostulated the painter. Giulio II. took the hint and departed. But a few days after, when the artist was still more absorbed in his wonderful creation, the Pope re-appeared. "When will you finish it?" he asked. "When I am able," replied Michael Angelo, covering his figures with a thick black veil, which shrouded the whole of the vault.

On another occasion, so great was the impatience of the Pontiff to see the progress of the work, that he went into the chapel, and, in spite of Michael Angelo, mounted, with great difficulty, the steps of the scaffold. The painter contrived to get between the Pope and the painting. Some authors say that the latter then designedly let fall his crosier on the ribs of the artist. (It is certain that he once caned his valet for saying that Michael Angelo was half mad, like all painters.) He immediately descended from the scaffold, flung away his pencils, rushed to his house, mounted his horse, and fled from Rome. But deeply enamored with his work, which now began to start out of chaos, he soon returned to finish it. The Pope would certainly have had him taken on the road, or would have declared war against any city which harbored him without his sovereign consent, as, at another time, he was on the point of making war upon Florence, in which town the artist had taken refuge on flying from the Pontifical displeasure. At last it appeared—that work, not for an age, but for humanity. The Renaissance had found its representative. It was the age of the great growth of man. The mariner's compass grew in the ocean; painting grew on the land; the discovery of America grew in our planet; philosophy grew in the human mind; the classic arts re-appeared and grew in history; the telescope grew in the heavens; and all grew in the love of God.

Would you like to see how the world has grown? Do you desire to measure her stature? Then compare the measured and rigid figures—narrow-chested, meagre, and lustreless—left by Fra Angelico in Florence as the testament of the Middle Age, with those bold, athletic, gigantic, and herculean figures left by Michael Angelo in the Sistine Chapel—the glory of the Renaissance.

Imagine a vast plane ceiling, lighted by twelve windows, and divided from the side walls by a cornice. Time, the smoke of the incense, and the waxen tapers have toned it to a duskiness which increases its mystery. They do not seem pictures; from the powerful incarnation, from the prominence of the design, from the relief of the figures, they appear sculptures. It is the apotheosis of the renewed human body. On the frieze of the cornice and over the windows, stretched out, on foot, and in improbable attitudes and positions, are vigorous undraped athletics, with nerves vibrating as the strings of a harp, and with fibres hardened by gymnastic exercises; beautiful youths who have fought for Rome on battle-fields, or who, turning to the classic shores of Greece, have guided the car with its four coursers in the Olympic games. The genius of Michael Angelo called again upon earth the heroes of past ages; converted stones into men; and, audaciously scaling the summit of Catholic Rome, as if it was the ancient Olympus, celebrated with rapture a new existence and a new era—the resurrection of gods, philosophers, poets, of the arts—and of his country!

Here classical reminiscences are concluded. The remainder of the roof has neither precedent nor sequence. It remains there, fixed on the human mind, like the first verses of the Bible, or as the isolated peaks of Mount Sinai, of Calvary, or the Capitol, in the plains of history. There are sibyls and prophets. The former come from Delphi, Cumæ, Erythræa, Libya; after having collected among the oaks of Dodona, on the shores of the Ægean and Tyrrhene seas, from the grottoes of Posilippo, or the gulfs of Corinth and of Baiæ, the prophecies, the hopes, the promises of redemption which poets have expressed in their verses and philosophers in their discourses. The prophets come from the desert, from Mount Carmel, from the caves of Jerusalem, from the primitive groves of Lebanon; after having collected the consolatory hopes of the priesthood, they unite with the sibyls in the Sistine Chapel as two Titanic choirs, whose combined strength supports the roof from which issue these marvelous paintings, unique from their size, from the scriptural allegories and tragedies they so admirably depict.

Chaos submerged in shadows; the first light dawning over the waters; Adam sleeping profoundly; Eve newly created, awakening in the ecstasy of love and enchantment with the life she beholds blooming around—the life she breathes and absorbs with delight; the first sin committed in the world, depriving the first human pair of Paradise, and the first sorrow which burdened the heart, robbing it of peace and innocence; the Deluge whirling its green waters of bitterness crossed by the lightning, and swelled by the hurricane up to the heights where the last men climb to save themselves in the extremity of desolation and despair; the sacrifice of Noah on the mountain as a sign of the perpetuity of nature and of the salvation of the species;—all grouped, all united—giants, sibyls, prophets, storms, hurricanes, floods—around that majestic and sublime figure of the Eternal Father, who animates and invigorates all these creatures by His creating breath, governing them by His powerful and protecting hand, and irradiating their minds by a ray from His own omniscience!

After examining the combination, let us go into particulars. How wonderful is each of these figures! One can not comprehend how the poor genius of man has performed so much. I have seen artists, in mute contemplation before these frescoes, let fall their arms in astonishment, and shake their heads in desperation, as if saying, "Never can we copy this!" The three fates whom Goethe saw in a cavern holding the thread of life are less sublime than these sibyls. The giants of the Bible and of classic poetry are inferior to these prophets. Isaiah is reading the book of human destiny. His cerebrum is like the curve of a celestial sphere, an urn of ideas, as the tops of high mountains are the crystal sources from which descend great rivers. The angel calls him, and without dropping his book, he slowly raises his head toward heaven, as if suspended between two infinities. Jeremiah wears the sackcloth of the penitent, which suits the prophet wandering near Jerusalem. His lips vibrate like a conqueror's trumpet. His beard falls in wavy masses upon his breast. His head is inclined like the crown of a cedar struck by the lightning. His melancholy eyes overflow with tears. His hands are vigorous, but swelled by bearing the tottering stones of the sanctuary.

He is thinking of the complaint and the elegies of the Children of Israel, captives by the waters of Babylon, and the pitiful lamentation of the Queen of Nations, solitary and desolate as a widow.

Ezekiel is transported; his spirit possesses him. He speaks with his visions as if occupied with a divine delirium. Invisible monsters hover around and shake their wings in his hearing, producing apparently a violent tempest like the roaring and surging of the ocean. The sea-breeze fills his mantle as if it were a sail. Daniel is himself; absolutely absorbed in writing, relating to the world the history of the chastisement of tyrants, and the hopes and happiness of the good; the punishment of Nebuchadnezzar — changed from a god into a beast; the crime and punishment of Belshazzar, surprised by death in the midst of the orgy where he feasted his concubines, giving them wine in the cups stolen from the sacred temple; the condemnation of the courtiers of Darius, devoured in the pit by hungry lions. After this a space of seventy periods of years passes; at the end of which, according to the prediction of the angel Gabriel, will appear a humble youth, clothed in white linen, who shall awaken with his sword the dead sleeping in the dust of ages, and make the firmament glorious with a new splendor. Jonah is terrified, as, rising from the bosom of the sea to go into the desert, he watches the fate of the great city of Nineveh. Zachariah is the most aged of the group. He staggers, as if the ground was rent under his feet by the trembling of the earthquake announced in his last prophecy.

What is most admirable about those colossal figures—and this we can never weary of admiring—is, that not only are they decorations of a hall, the adornments of a chapel, but men—men who have suffered our sorrows and experienced our disappointments; whom the thorns of the earth have pierced; whose foreheads are furrowed by the wrinkles of doubt, and whose hearts are transfixed by the chill of disenchantment; men who have seen battles and beheld the slaughter of their fellows; who have looked on tragedies where generations are consumed, and who see falling on their brows the damp of death, while seeking to prepare by their efforts a new society; whose eyes are worn and almost blind from looking continually at the movable and changing glass of time, and at humanity exhausted by the slow fire of ideas; men whose powerful and concentrated nerves support the weight of their great souls; and upon the souls the still greater burden of aspirations which admit not of realization; of impossible dreams and of painful struggles without victory; with no satisfaction on the earth, but with boundless desires for the infinite.

I should like to define these figures. For all that in them approaches humanity in respect to form and organization, they are really superhuman. All those gigantic and extraordinary beings which the various cosmogonies assume to have sprung from the first fruitfulness of the newly created planet, teeming with life and expansion—all of them are believed to have been of gigantic stature. But for all that they possess of spirit or durability, all are alike human, all the offspring of those two elements of our existence which have produced so much grandeur — aspiration for the infinite and sorrow for reality, against which the soul is in perpetual warfare, against which it ever dashes despairingly, longing vainly to diffuse itself in the invisible, in immensity, in the mysterious, and returns baffled to fall upon its narrow bed of clay with sighs and trembling.

The humanitarian, conciliatory, and universal spirit of the sixteenth century is seen in these sibyls of Paganism, who are raised to the level of the prophets, placed side by side with them, repeating the same sentiments, declaring the same truths, like two separate choirs, whose voices and canticles blend in harmony and are confounded in the heavens. The same union takes place in the laboratory of the atmosphere, where the vapors exhaled from distant seas are mingled, just as the electric fluid leaps from mountain to mountain!

How remote and barbarous seem those iconoclasts who destroyed the beautiful statues of the gods, believing them to be representations of the Devil! How distant we feel from that narrow spirit which condemned ancient history, thinking it worn-out and useless! The sibyls are the oracles of Paganism. When night has flung her shadowy mantle over the earth, and the Pleiades issue from the sea; when the waves, beautified by phosphoric splendors, die on the sandy shore; under the branches of mystery, on the stones embrowned by ages, clothed with a white tunic, floating as a cloud and crowned with vervain; the kindling altar in front, the idol raised on her shoulder; the people motionless around, the citharas of the maidens sounding in her ears, her eyes fixed on heaven and her hand on her heart; all the nerves agitated, and the soul delirious with emotion—the sibyl tells her oracular secrets in mystic verses, collected from leaves and confided to the mercy of the wind; she there discovers the shadow of the future, and forcibly wrenches the embryo of the hereafter from the womb of future ages yet sleeping in the abyss of eternity!

St. Augustine read the mysterious books of these women. In his enthusiasm he acted like Michael Angelo—he placed them in the city of God. They predicted the coming of the Saviour. "*Pertinent ad civitatem dei,*" he exclaimed. It was these same sibyls who, before Cæsar, according to a pious legend, descended from the marble altar, because the hope of nations had been born, and the prophecies of ages had been accomplished. Virgil deserved that St. Geronimo, after having saluted the birthplace of Christ in Bethlehem, should pay similar honor to his sepulchre at Posilippo. He deserved more; he deserved that St. Augustine should count him among the highest witnesses in favor of Christianity, among those men of learning who drove away his doubts and fortified his faith. "I would not so easily believe all this, if it had not been long foretold by a noble poet in the Roman language." He also deserved that the great poet of the Middle Ages should invoke him, exclaiming,

"*Per te pœta fui, per te Christiano.*"

And all because Virgil repeated the oracle of the Sibyl of

Cumæ; the advent of a mystic child, before whose presence the order of the ages would be changed, and nature would lose her evils, the lion his ferocity, the serpent his venom, the fields their thorns, labor its weariness; and without the necessity of eating bread in the sweat of his brow, man would be satisfied with the produce of the fields, the vine by a natural process bringing forth grapes, the corn its ears, the trees their fruits, the hills be crowned with flowers, the fleeces of the sheep dyed with the colors of the rainbow, the sting taken from the bee, whose honey would be left upon the lips; and the universe, as a tree waved by the celestial zephyr, should intone a sublime canticle which would make men forgetful of the music of the flute of Pan and the melodies of Orpheus, being the incommunicable hymn of the new age of justice!

It is true that history, in its modern universality, has destroyed and overcome many hatreds. The Romans and the barbarians, that fought furiously as irreconcilable enemies up to the latter part of the ancient period, were brothers, children of the same race. And those prophets of Jerusalem, those insatiable readers of the future, those invincible enemies of tyrants; those mysterious sibyls, wandering over the sands of Libya, by the ruins of Persia, by the sea of Ionia, by the grottoes of Cumæ, appearing in the extremity of the Grecian Archipelago and at the Cape of Messina, like disembodied spirits to tell of ideas without substance; those philosophers who have passed the Piræus from the great Greece, and from the Piræus have traveled to Alexandria, sowing between the East and the West a track of ideas which have been the nursery-books of the world; and the sublime and obscure missionaries, not understood by Imperial Rome, who went from the Catacombs to the Circus, leaving with the blood of their veins the immortal stream which watered the faith; all enemies for ages, all mutually unknown, all separated by chasms, prejudices, and hatreds, all are united in the Infinite that has formed our spirit and kindled our religious conscience!

How sublime are the sibyls of the Sistine Chapel! How our eyes and our thoughts turn from one to the other without being able to fix themselves. These figures appear to be the mothers of ideas, the embodiment of eternal beings. Any one would say they hold in their fingers the thread of universal life, and that they weave the web of nature. They are the Persian, the Erythræan, the Delphian, the Libyan, the Cumæan. If you search for their genealogies, you must find Dante, Plato, Isaiah, and Æschylus; they are of the same race. If you seek for their resemblances in the modern world, you will have them in some of Shakespeare's personages, in some thoughts of Calderon, in some scenes of Corneille. There, in some respects, you will find their counterparts.

Read and study many treatises on the sublime, and then draw near to understand this grand conception. It is difficult to explain a certain cold shuddering that is only experienced twice or thrice in a lifetime; it is hard to comprehend an idea of which there are only half a dozen examples in history. But raise your eyes to the roof of the Sistine Chapel: there is the sublime, there the disproportion between our feeble being and the wonderful power of an impression which overcomes us, that crushes and annihilates us under its immeasurable grandeur! This is the sublime: an enjoyment in a punishment.

Sibyl of Persia! bowed by the weight of ages, thou rememberest how the infant world confided to thee her secrets and confessed her sorrows, and how before death, oppressed by years and labor, thou didst desire to write a cyclical poem on the leaves of thy brazen book! Thou of Libya! who comes upon us, rushing as if the scorching sand of the desert burned thy feet—to bring to man some great idea, gathered in space, where all ideas are transformed like mysterious larvæ. Erythræ! thou wert youthful as Greece, beautiful as one of the sirens of thy Archipelago, a songstress sweet as the earth of the poets, undulating and graceful as the seas which bring forth divinities, the friend of light, and trimming the lamp by thy side round whose brilliancy the human conscience shall hover as a butterfly! Maiden of Cumæ! virgin, like Iphigenia, immolated for kings, thou didst receive the kiss of Apollo upon thy lips, the shadow of the laurel on thy brow, the immortality of genius in thy bosom; thou wert formed to intone a song of harmony which should vibrate through countless ages! Thou, Sibyl of Delphi, leavest thy cavern, and there where the mountains are chiseled as if by the hand of a sculptor, where the air is filled with aroma, where the Tyrrhene Sea is most lovely, near the Gulf of Baiæ, looking like a Grecian goddess, and intoxicated as a Bacchante reclining on her couch of vine leaves, breathest the soft melody of hope!

Are ye of flesh? Are ye women? Have ye felt love, sorrow, and disappointment? Or are ye but the archetypes of things, the symbols of art, the shades of the muses invoked by all the poets, and that none have beheld but in unrealized and impossible visions the various forms of the eternal Eve—named alternately Sappho, Beatrice, Laura, Victoria Colonna, Héloïse—and who stand by the cradle and the tomb of all ages, smiling to us hopefully, awakening in us new aspirations, or flying to our arms as an illusion soon vanishing in the infinite.

This roof of the Sistine Chapel will always excite poetical imaginations. One of the most learned men in Europe has said that he spent thirty years in studying it. When Michael Angelo finished the painting he could not cast down his eyes for a moment without their being obscured—he had been so long in the habit of raising his head and looking upward. He met the object of his sight in the heavens. There, even to the heavens, he directed his gaze, his mind filled with boundless aspirations and with infinite sorrow. And this man, with so lively a sensibility, with so harsh and bitter a temper, with thoughts so extraordinary and tempestuous, lived in the period of the most violent changes, of the strongest contrasts, as the human spirit passes from sad discouragements to exuberant existence, from dark eclipses to sudden illuminations, from repentance to the orgy, from sensuality to faith, inclining, like a drunken man, sometimes to one side, sometimes to the other.

Let us imagine a body suddenly translated from the torrid

zone to the pole, from earth to heaven, from the peak of a mountain to an abyss, from the stormy sea to a downy couch, and perhaps we shall be able to form some conception of the changes to which the soul of Michael Angelo was exposed by the contradictions of his time. The Luzbel of the Bible, passing from angelical to diabolical nature, and the Luzbel of Origen, turning from the things of earth to those of heaven, may give some distant idea of the sudden transformations which that age experienced, and through which that man passed, who was steeped in the life of his century.

This division of ages is by no means arbitrary. History is like an almanac of the spirit; in a hundred years ideas radically alter, their essence changes, and the aspect of society varies considerably. In a hundred years the atoms of a people are renewed with the renovation of generations. Each age is a great personality engraved by anterior ages. The sword is often a chisel which obeys a conscience, and an unknown or misunderstood spirit. All ages have a philosophy peculiar to themselves. But the age that Michael Angelo filled with his large existence is the most contradictory of all ages. If at each alternate minute it grew light and dark, perhaps we should have in nature a resemblance of the time of Michael Angelo; that is to say, of that period in which the Middle Ages were concluded and the Modern Age began.

Constantinople fell; but the wounded Venice increased, and in all her power navigated a vessel closely covered at the sides by painted canvas, to obstruct the sight of the enemy, which flung a cable into the Adriatic to keep Europe and the

East united. The gods of the ancients were reborn, revealing in their frames of marble all the secrets of the sculptor's art, and the works of artists were burned in bonfires, stirred by a population of monks in the Piazza de Firenze. The Perugino Convent still preserved the penitents and the mortifications of the cloister, and the Farnese Hercules was erected on Roman soil to show all the force and power of antiquity. Ariosto wrote his sensual work—in which the heroes dance as in a brilliant carnival, and dream in delicate language the Platonics of Florence, with mysterious sentiments, with heaven concealed behind the sepulchre, and God hidden from the world. Savonarola, that political François d'Assis, invokes saints and angels, recommends fasting and penance, renews the imitation of Jesus Christ; summons Machiavel the Demon, calls up traitors, advises imposition, crime, and assassination, and restores the likeness of the Cæsars. The Florentine people selected for their chief the Crucified, while the Romans chose Cæsar Borgia, handsome, but vicious and infamous, a traitor, and stained with the blood of his brother and brother-in-law, which splashed his forehead, and that of the Pope, degraded by orgies like those of Nero, reproducing the erotic delirium of Heliogabàlus in conjunction with the slaughterings and poisonings of Tiberius.

These all pass and depart like shadows, and the French come from the North and support the Guelphs, and the Spaniards from the South to support the Ghibelines. The political power of the Popes and the political power of the

Emperors seem over and past, but the Pontificate appears renewed with increased vigor by Giulio II., and imperial power becomes more brilliant under Charles V. The spiritual authority of the Middle Ages re-asserts and restores itself through the medium of its arts and artists, who support the Vatican, converted by Leo X. into Olympus, when suddenly, at the voice of Luther, the blood in the veins of Rome is frozen. On all sides the plebeians arise to save or to renovate republics, and on all sides monarchies are restored. The arts, by which Michael Angelo wished to unite liberty, are the fatal circle, the brilliant talisman with which tyrants lull and tranquilize the people. Patriots seek a Brutus and scarcely find a Lorencino!

On this account Michael Angelo did not desire to finish his bust of the defender of the Roman Republic in unworthy Florence, given up to the Medicis. In that age cities surrendered themselves, falling in the dust, with their own sword in their bosoms, before the conqueror. The disgrace of Chæronea was repeated a hundred times, and a hundred Athens, steeped in gore, died on Italian ground. Ancona gave up her fortresses, to free them from the threatened invasion of the Turks, and they fell under the dominion of monks. The Popes converted all into Ghibelines, contradicting their previous history. Spain, which had sent Jews and Moors to serve in Rome, pillaged the city herself. The numerous revolutions which occurred in Italy from the tenth to the sixteenth century, and the fourteen millions of men fallen on her fields of battle, produced confusion and chaos. Can you not—when thinking over all this—can you not comprehend why the Moses of Michael Angelo looks on his time with so much disdain? Do you not understand why the colossal Jeremiah in the Sistine Chapel mourns with such a heart-rending lamentation?

But the greatest of all catastrophes drew nigh when Michael Angelo had finished the vault of the chapel — I mean the sacking of Rome by the Spaniards and Germans under the command of the High-Constable Bourbon. The Spaniards, deprived of their pay, suffered greatly from famine. Religious fury took possession of the Germans, enemies of the Pope. The Spanish general brought with him a chain, and intended to cut off the head of the Catholic high-priest the day he should enter into the city, which he called sacrilegious Babylon. The High-Constable wished to teach a terrible lesson to Clement VII., the enemy of his new master Charles V.

Rome had been restored by eighty years of artistic labor—reclothed with marble, painted by Raphael and his disciples, covered with statues which seemed to arise by enchantment from the ruins, enriched by Leo X. with all the ornaments of the Renaissance, filled with treasures by the people, who crowded as pilgrims to kiss his brazen slipper, to worship in his religious sepulchres, in his admirable temples; full of palaces erected by a wealthy and powerful aristocracy, she had reconquered her ancient fame, and shone in all her spiritual splendor, with as much glory as she had formerly done among the spoils of the world. Her great riches excited the cupidity of the Spaniards and the Germans, all of them warriors by profession, and consequently all of them addicted to pillage, then considered the proper harvest of the sword. Thus it was in vain to make a truce. Those twenty-five thousand men, Italian adventurers, Spaniards, by profession soldiers, German Protestants, drew onward, marching toward Rome, with the voracious hunger of the legions of Attila, of those birds of prey darting from the pole on the corpse of ancient Rome.

It was a morning in the month of May, 1527. The High-Constable demanded a passage for Naples; the Pope refused. The assault followed the refusal. The Spaniards wavered, but their generalissimo, the High-Constable, placed with his own hands the ladder against the wall of the Holy City. An archer took aim and killed him. In his death agony he covered himself with a Spanish mantle, in order that he should not be recognized, and so cause panic among his soldiers. The Spaniards entered by the walls near St. Peter's, the Germans by the gate of Santo Spirito, the Italians by the gate of San Pancrazio, like three torrents which rush together and mingle their waters in the same bed. The Pope had barely time to pass from the Vatican to San Angelo, under a shower of bullets, and Pablo Jovio flung over him a violet-colored robe, in order that the white Pontifical garments should not serve as a mark for the enemy's musketry. It seemed—so great was the turmoil—as if Genseric and Alaric—as if the Goths and Vandals had arisen to trouble the city. Here they fought hand to hand, there the houses were in flames, in every part slaughter and pillage! Some cut the fingers from the bodies of the vanquished to tear off their rings ; many who were consecrated to the service of the Lord were outraged on the altars. Many of the Roman women were cut to pieces to satisfy the blood-thirsty passions of the invaders. Young maidens threw themselves into the arms of their fathers and brothers, tearfully imploring death rather than dishonor. The night increased the horrors of the bloody saturnalia. By the light of torches the plunderers hacked down the pictures ; filled sacks with the ornaments, profaned the sanctuaries in searching for precious stones ; celebrated their victory by drinking wine out of the sacred chalices; beat and spit upon the cardinals; surmounted their military casques with mitres ; clothed the *cantinières* with the robes of the Virgin ; pronounced ridiculous and profane sermons, standing defiantly on heaps of dead and wounded, many of whom still breathed ; made fantastic processions ; decapitated many ; cut the ears from asses and placed them on the tortured faces of the clergy, throwing smoking intestines and bleeding hearts at the feet of the images. Terrible carnival! whose horrors were increased by the noise and rattle of muskets, the fall of ruins, the crackling of the flaming houses, the blasphemies and loud laughter of the drunken and voluptuous, the maledictions of the conquerors, the supplications of the conquered, the terrified rushing of the fugitives, the death-rattle of the dying, and the silence of the dead left naked on the smoking and ensanguined stones, as if that dreadful night were the last night of unhappy Rome—as if those were the fatal hours for the work of the exterminating angels of the world!

The desolation of that city was unequaled. Shut up in prison, the Pope, Clement VII., ate the flesh of horses and asses. The dead, avenging their immolation, engendered a pestilence. Before Rome had quite recovered from these fearful calamities, which occupied almost all the second half of the century, Michael Angelo entered her gates to conclude his labors, to enrich with another masterpiece the Sistine Chapel, to leave on the central wall the "Universal Judgment." The great tragedy just mentioned gave him inspiration; the death of his country's liberty, the new ruin of Rome, the triumph of reform over a part of the human race, the victory of time over his own life, of old age on his powers, of sorrow on his soul. While sketching his gigantic work, a thousand times he believed himself dying. At last, falling from the scaffold, he opened a wound in his leg, and, shutting himself up in his house, resolved to leave it no more till carried to the tomb. One of his friends, a physician, went to see him, called him by name, and, receiving no answer, broke his way into the house like a robber, and eventually succeeded in tearing him from his melancholy.

The fate of Italy is one of the wounds which remain in the heart, and consequently one of the inspirations of its conscience. The study of Dante, soothing and apocalyptic, animates and sustains it. Taking an outline with a very wide margin, Michael Angelo filled it in with designs from poetic visions, and from exquisite and life-like sculptures. For three centuries the great poem of Dante explained and beautified the Universal Judgment of Michael Angelo, as the poem of Homer gave vitality to the tragedies of Æschylus. The human frame and its organism, heretofore little studied by him, and almost unknown, is the principal element of his plastic conceptions. In the Universe he saw but man alone. His anthropology is less soft and harmonious than that of Greece —it is gigantic. His men are immense, like his ideas. From this arises a certain contempt which he occasionally shows for beauty in immortal serenity, and a certain unrestrained liberty with regard to the sublime. When young, he changed his living models for corpses. For twelve years he lived studying and almost analyzing the dead. One time he became infected with the virus of putrefaction, and was at the point of death from an effort to extract the sublime from a skeleton laid aside as useless by the world.

His profound study of the anatomy of the human form is visible in this picture, in this poem. All griefs have shaken those bodies whose nerves are contracted in violent agitation. All the figures are undraped. Michael Angelo dared much in the Sistine Chapel when he commenced the reaction against Renaissance—when hypocrisy went so far as to take the winding-sheet of the Middle Ages wherewith to shroud nature anew. It is difficult now to imagine the scandal which this audacity on the part of the artist produced in that age, already separated from the semi-Pagan days of Leo X. Aretino, who delighted in depicting all kinds of unveiled impurity, was much offended with the chaste nudity of true art. Biagio, Master of the Ceremonies to Paul III., implored the painter, on the part of the Pontiff, to drape his figures and not expose the human form so completely. "Tell the Pope," replied Michael Angelo, "that with regard to the pictures, they may be corrected in a few minutes, but his Holiness will find it difficult to improve the world." As a punishment to Biagio, he painted him with the ears of an ass in the depths of hell. The Master of the Ceremonies ran to complain to Paul III. of the affront put on his respectable person. "He has put me in the picture," he said, weeping like a child, and tremulous as an old man; "I beg your Holiness will take me out of that." "But where has he placed thee?" demanded the Pontiff. "In hell, your Holiness, in hell," replied Biagio, sobbing. "If thou hadst been in purgatory," said the Pope, "I would have removed thee, but I have no authority whatever in hell."

It is impossible to detail all that has been said about this wonderful fresco. The Academical School, which predominated during the past century, and so much resembled the hybrid and wearisome narrowness of many literary critics, terrified at all greatness, which overwhelmed its own irremediable littleness, has treated it as an ill-designed daub. There is one writer who describes this great work as a collection of frogs. Three hundred undraped figures—some of them half clothed at a later period by Volterra, who earned for himself by this artistic profanation the name of *Braghetone*—three hundred nude figures grouped together in a mural picture with fifty feet of height and forty of breadth. One readily understands that it cost much time and labor. One is disposed to examine it with the same attention with which one listens to an air of Beethoven. Those who are naturally irreverent and unimpressed in presence of art will after some time feel and admire its beauties, and become absorbed in the profound contemplation of that marvelous masterpiece of genius. The artist should not attempt to imitate it, because there are certain personalities in history, there are certain styles in art and literature, whose individuality is so powerful, whose stature is so elevated, whose centre of gravity is so removed from the sphere of general gravitation, that to follow them would cause a vertigo, and the bold mortal attempting to imitate them would but expose himself to a perilous fall. Go into St. Peter's after having gazed at the figures of Michael Angelo, and you will observe in the colossal statuary—violent, exaggerated, and in bad taste—you will see the utter ruin mediocre artists have made in trying to copy the unique and almost superhuman genius of Michael Angelo, who must remain the wonder of ages—like Dante, like Shakespeare, like Calderon—alone in his inaccessible solitude.

Nature is but little represented in the picture; Michael Angelo has only depicted air and light. The planets are not seen revolving majestically through space, nor the sun dyed in gold and crimson, nor the mountains rent in pieces, nor the raging sea tossed in foaming waves by a terrible tempest; nothing of this—in the blue air, in the air alone, passes the awful scene occupied solely by human bodies and celestial clouds, and over both the anger of the Eternal. All appears horrible, all frightful, in that picture, as if no one could be saved, so forcibly does terror dominate all other sentiments.

In the first compartment there is the boat of Charon on a leaden river, and at the left we see the lurid and sinister light of Purgatory. Above are the dead, awakening at the sound of the trumpet, raising the marble of their sepulchres, rending their grave-clothes, shaking the dust from their almost naked skeletons and the sleep from the nearly empty sockets of their mortal eyes. Among the dead there arise many who have scarcely recovered the power of motion; they struggle violently to help themselves; agitated by uncertainty, listening to the irrevocable sentence, bearing on their shoulders the weight — more or less heavy — of their worldly works. Among those who move rapidly, there are some who despair, others who pray, more who hope, and many who help and support each other. To the right of Christ is a bright group of women already saved; who all intone a hymn, and among them one is sublime—a mother who has just heard the judgment on her daughter, whom she folds in her arms with a rapturous embrace, assuring herself of the happiness she can scarce believe. Near the women is a group of angels, who appear by their melancholy to receive in their faces a shower of tears, borne to them by the wind. Below the angels are the blessed, many of whom recognize each other, after many ages, and embrace on the heights of the Eternal City. In the centre, Jesus in anger curses, condemns, punishes, without heeding the prayers of his mother, separating himself from the lost ones, without even looking toward them lest he should alleviate with his glance their eternal torments. Adam, in majestic old age, is by his side, resuming his humanity, as

Christ returns to the heavens. But where the genius of Michael Angelo is shown in all its grandeur is in that immense torrent of the condemned, who fall overcome by the terrible sentence, some inert as withered leaves, others contracting their bodies in agony, as if they could rebel against their eternal doom, already biting their hands and tearing their hair, already awe-stricken by the sight of the flames before them, and delirious from terror; all in the most cruel physical and moral torture; Titans, full of life, of flesh and blood, offering an abundant food for torment; Titans, who roar, curse, and revile; who spit horrors from their mouths, and struggle furiously with the serpents twined around their bodies, and look in the air for a cloud to cover them, and fall with a fearful shuddering, as if at the first contact of their flesh with the molten lead in the eternal fire!

Attention can not be for long concentrated on the sublime. On feeling a profound emotion, the nerves are shaken and the brain is furrowed as if by an electric shock. I felt my temples palpitate, as if the swelling veins were about to burst from the torrent of gigantic thoughts excited by that Chapel, which comprehends all of human life from the Creation to the Universal Judgment. I wanted air, and went out to breathe it in the Roman Campagna, around whose ruins the lovely season of April had flung her green and joyous mantle. But on turning, I beheld, in the azure of the heavens, the outline of a stupendous work, over which floats the soul of Michael Angelo, who designed the dome of St. Peter's, and which appeared gilded and glorified by the last rays of the setting sun; a temple slowly stretching itself to the infinite, as if to say to Jehovah that the eternity promised to Rome by the gods of Antiquity was realized in the Ancient Age by its tribunes and its heroes, strengthened in the Middle Age by its Popes and learned doctors, and saved in the Modern Age by the genius which raised that Cupola as the summit of history, as the crown of the spirit, as the tiara of the world!

Chapter V.

THE CAMPO SANTO OF PISA.

I NEVER believed there could be in the world a town so dead as Toledo. But then I had never seen Pisa. The difference between these two beautiful places is, notwithstanding, very great. In Toledo, adjoining edifices which have been wonderfully preserved, such as the Cathedral, there are buildings almost in ruins, as the church of San Juan de los Reyes and the palace of Charles V. The ruin and the desolation justify the solitude.

But in Pisa all the monuments are standing, all are most carefully preserved, all are white and renovated by modern restoration—some painted in lively colors. Yet still the solitude is indescribable. You would say that those palaces expect their inhabitants, and are prepared to receive them, but no inhabitants come to take possession. In the month of May, on the day of my arrival, I happened to stand on the central bridge of the Lung' Arno at two o'clock in the afternoon, and I can assure the reader that, being alone, completely alone, I was almost tempted to fancy the large town had been destined solely for my particular person. It is precisely the place for an egotist. It was most melancholy to see those two broad rows of fine buildings, really elegant houses; those numerous bridges, those magnificent road-ways, that exquisite cleanliness; the river below, the smiling heavens above; at one extremity the arched trees waving gracefully with the breath of the fresh sea-breeze, and no one, absolutely nobody but myself, at that hour and in that delicious place, to contemplate and enjoy so much beauty.

I felt inclined to shout aloud, feeling sure that the echo would be my only response. A stranger once made a bet that he would go round the walls of Pisa on horseback without meeting a living soul, and he won his wager. The English and the Russians whose lungs have become diseased by the severity of northern climates, in order to prolong their days for a short time, take refuge in Pisa, where they are sheltered by the mountains from the keen winds of the North, and secured by the solitude from all great emotions. Thus you see from time to time very pretty young girls, with that flush on the cheek and that brilliancy in the eyes which are indicative of consumption, accompanied by some of their family, looking sad and gloomy, as if they had already mourned and wept the inevitable stroke of separation. These circumstances contribute to the general depression of the town, called, with good reason—" dead Pisa."

But, notwithstanding the present dejection, there was a time in which her liberties astonished Italy, and her commerce was a marvel of the world; a time in which the sea brought even to her gates the tributes of Corsica and Sardinia; a time in which her ships transported the Crusaders to Asia, and brought from Asia gold, purple, and ivory; a time in which her warriors aided the German Emperors against the Roman Pontiffs, and the chiefs of Barcelona against the Moors of Majorca; a time in which pirates dreaded her power, and the Saracens trembled on the coast of Africa at the gleaming of her lances; and in which the columns brought to Pisa from distant expeditions formed a trophy of the first victory of the arts. Then the last masters of mosaic from Constantinople filled with brilliant stones the arches of her monuments; then the first painters who divined the secret of design animated with mystic figures her walls and cloisters; then the Jews heaped her with riches, protecting themselves under the shadow of her toleration; then Nicolas and John of Pisa, who must be numbered among the men of genius of the Middle Ages, chiseled and polished her marble, and produced those white figures which appear the early visions of a new age of inspirations—awakening the mind to the splendor of new ideas almost before they appeared, like those birds which announce the coming day in the hours of darkness.

The liberties of Pisa brought forth her commerce; commerce produced riches; riches the arts and sciences. The machinery of Buschetto in the eleventh century raised enormous weights, whose gravity would conquer much modern mechanism. The light vessels, with their graceful triangular sails, brought in the tenth century pieces of rustling silks, which, from their brilliance, their quality, and color, might be called radiant apparitions of Ancient India in the midst of the darkness of the Middle Ages. Serpents of bronze from

Egypt twined around columns of granite, and winged horses from Greece and Byzantine cupolas beautified and embellished the city. Thousands of workmen thronged the quays when her laws were based on the principles of liberty. But the Republic expired, and Pisa is a corpse! Perhaps it is on this account that her chief monument is a cemetery. In the zenith of her glory and splendor Pisa predicted her sad destiny, and erected the building most suitable for her future history—she erected the Campo Santo.

With my soul saddened by the melancholy of the town, in the midst of that oppressive solitude, where the soft murmur of the sea-breeze is alone audible, I turned to visit the magnificent monument which was to cause me so much emotion and to give me so much instruction. The place in which the Campo Santo is situated is the most deserted part of the town. In vain the high mountains of Pisa lift their azure peaks in the ether of a splendid horizon; in vain the luxurious vegetation of spring—flowers, butterflies, and birds' nests cover with their profusion even the bare stones of the round towers in the walls; in vain the magnificent baptistery (close to the Campo Santo, and which appears the high dome of a subterranean temple) shows its chiseled buttresses; in vain the white leaning tower, looking like a gigantic column beside her sharp-sounding bells, and the cathedral, adorned with costly jewels, sends forth her harmonious litany; in vain all attempts to awaken a new life; the nettles which spring up over this immense desert and all around recall and inspire the sad ideas of death and decay.

The Campo Santo is a vast and severe structure, with high walls and narrow entrances : a marble tomb for the whole city. The Pharaohs of Egypt, the Cæsars of Rome, the Oriental Satraps have raised pyramids, fortresses, and mounds to serve as burial-places, and to conceal the worms which shall gnaw their bodies and their purple; but none of these superb monuments where despots perpetuate eternally in death the isolated pride of their lives—none of them can bear comparison as to grace and beauty with this cemetery of citizens, who there mingle and confound their bones, and whose cold ashes, purified by the sharp scythe of death, irradiate the same warmth, the same enthusiasm, that in life animated their free bosoms.

The exterior is extremely simple. It appears like an immense mausoleum hewn out of one solid stone. The perspectives of death give extraordinary solemnity to every object in life. Always when man wishes to figure death he also expresses immortality. In vain he paints its last agony as the sorrow of sorrows; in vain its ultimate asylum as the shadow of shadows; there, in the hollow of the empty grave, in the depths of the unfathomable abyss, there always extends the mysterious light of a new existence. We all know that man, that epitome of creation; that mineral subject to the laws of gravity and to the limits of extension; that vegetable which can not exist without air and light and water; that animal who is born and nourished like other mammalia; that microcosm whose spherical head copies the circle of the heavens, and whose sparkling eyes reflect the lustre of the stars; that angel who exalts himself through time and space, and essays to contemplate and understand in their purity the archetypes of nature, of which things are but shadows; the great musician of the worlds, the high-priest and the poet among all beings; he who can deduce universal laws from particular actions, and extract from the rough matter the impalpable essence of the spirit; he who observes and admires the music of the spheres; he whose aspiring thoughts seek to unfold the secrets of nature—he can not bury himself entirely under a few shovelfuls of clay without burying with him at the same time all creation!

And, notwithstanding, no monument can express nothingness so well as this parallelogram—irregular, solemn, and death-like. We all require an obscure dwelling under our feet, which awaits the moment of our death like the desert the rain-drops. We all have a sepulchre. The nakedness of the exterior of the Campo Santo of Pisa, the monotony, the uniformity, are the nakedness, the monotony, the uniformity of death. As the gate opens, you fancy it is the gate of eternity. The cold of those vaults petrifies your bones; the silence of those graves deprives you of utterance. I felt completely isolated, like a dead man forgotten in his coffin.

I, wandering without home, without country, asked myself if that journey was not the symbol of my last voyage, if that passing visit to the cemetery was not the anticipated picture of the day in which men should come to fetch my body and throw it into a pit, that its putrid miasma should not infect the air they breathe. The guardian of the dead, who was standing near the gate, invited me to enter. The most melancholy ideas struggled in my brain, and fell like corrosive drops upon my heart. The sound of a pickaxe digging the hollow graves, and the jingling of the keys carried by the guardian, fell painfully on my ear. But, nevertheless, I entered, thinking that death is, after all, as natural as life, that the tomb is the cradle of Eternity. And the great gate closed behind me!

If, as I believe, and as I hope, after passing from life to death, we go from this to another and to a happier world, I greatly doubt if the short journey could offer as much variety and interest as the interior of the Campo Santo of Pisa. I beheld with ecstasy the lofty arches covered with precious woods; the broad walls adorned with every possible combination of color; the oval windows of immense height, with their light columns and their elegant ornamental roses; the cypresses and the ivy; the honeysuckle pushing its fragrant blossoms into the central court, its leaves rustling softly in the breeze; the rude monuments of monastic times shadowed by the cross, joined to the beautiful tombs of classic ages, adorned with nymphs and fauns; the bacchanalian vase of Paros marble, with its sculptured figures of the priests and of the god of wine, by the side of the *Madre Dolorosa* with her son in her arms, overcome by the contemplation of death and her tears of agony; the trophies of the Crusades close to the native offerings of the Romans; the friezes of the great Grecian temples mingled with the architraves of the altars of the tenth century; a bust of Brutus, and the Roman Tribunes under the white wings of the marble angels wrought by Christian sculptors; the recumbent statues upon the pavement looking as if sunk in the eternal sleep, those which are erect on their pedestals stretching forth their arms as if to enter conquerors into immortality; the saints and virgins, the patriarchs, the doctors, the seraphim, the cherubim, the choirs of the blessed, the demons, gnomes, and monsters floating on the many-colored atmosphere of the gigantic frescoes which cover all the walls; an indescribable chaos in those four Gothic galleries—a chaos over which the sound of the bell comes like the trumpet of the angel, and the noise of the pickaxe like the response of the dead opening their tombs at the great summons; a chaos where all ages, all civilizations, all arts crowd together in confusion over the fragments of a world in ruins—a picture of the Valley of Jehoshaphat at the supreme hour of the Universal Judgment!

And, notwithstanding, when you have once recovered from your first sensation of astonishment, you find nothing more regular than that chaos. Four walls, four galleries, four series of oriel windows; a court-yard in the centre; at the entrance by the principal door a chapel; and in the middle of the little gallery to the right a church; in the cultivated part of the court is a wonderfully luxuriant vegetation of leaves and flowers; at the extremities there are four tall, dark-green cypresses—melancholy trees, nourished like the plants by food from the dead.

There are few Gothic buildings in Italy—very few. This architecture of the Middle Ages has not been able to eradicate the enduring Paganism with which the country of the arts is impregnated. It appears that when the architects proposed to erect the Catholic structure, which they intended to finish for One and the only God, the goddesses sighed from the bottom of their streams or the hollow of their trees, to entreat them to continue the antique columns crowned with garlands, immortal as themselves. The Gothic architecture is the architecture of the thought and judgment, not that of the imagination; it is rather the native spirit than the plastic genius. Consequently it can not be the architecture of Italy. The Campo Santo of Pisa is Gothic. But with what motherly devotion she has gathered all the arts to her bosom! It imported but little to the Italians that a sepulchre should represent the heathen fables opposed by Christianity. Whatever they found most beautiful they placed in their cemetery, and they filled it with the bones of Christians. The mother of the Countess Matilda—of that lady who was Catholic *par excellence*, of that firm friend of the Popes, of that most orthodox heroine—rests in her sarcophagus, on which there is a sculpture of Phædra. Diana kissing the forehead of Endymion sleeping is one of the marbles of the Campo Santo. Pagan busts are placed close to the images of the saints. The lamps lighted by religion illumine the face of Brutus. Near the mausoleum, where the cavalier of the Middle Ages folds his hands and bends his knees in prayer, we find Augustus, and Agrippa, the founder of that Pantheon where for the last time the gods of antiquity took refuge. A bacchante sleeps the sleep of intoxication, with the empty cup by her side, under a fresco which represents the macerations of a cenobite, joined to the tomb from which is suspended the crown of white roses consecrated to innocence, and over which are expanded the wings—as if covering a nest—of the Guardian Angel. The Good Shepherd, buried in the catacombs of the martyrs, and sculptured on a sarcophagus which the early Christians watered with their tears, leads his sheep to the Church; a few paces off there is a bass-relief, whose tritons formed part of the court of Neptune in the depths of ocean, before nature had been robbed of her divinities. Meleager follows the chase beside the altar where Henry VII. worships. On a capital dedicated to Mary the Virgin, full of mysticism, and almost at her feet, are Etruscan figures in all the reality of life. The sculptor, Della Robia, has there a Madonna in terra cotta, similar to the Byzantine Virgins; and on a marble column from Egypt, close by, is a head of Achilles. Andrew of Pisa has chiseled the Prophets and Evangelists with all the rigidity of Catholicism in the midst of bacchantes, represented on other bass-reliefs with the Grecian voluptuousness. Here is an Emperor of Germany, seated in his sacred chair; there an Arabian winged horse; yonder, Venus with all the graces of love in the dominions of the dead. How these men knew by artistic and supernatural intuition that all generations and all ages are reconciled in the abode of death! These sculptors knew that combatants who fall in the light of the sun, hating and cursing each other under opposing standards on the battle-field, are united there in the region of shadows. These men understood that human wretchedness may drive them from life, but nothing can deprive them of death. Although you destroy and seek to annihilate your enemy, though you burn his body and give his ashes to the wind, his atoms are there, in the laboratory of universal life, in the immense bosom of nature; and after a time your children will absorb them and bear them in their hearts. The hatred of men is so great that it desires not the peace of the dead. And yet, while contemplating the Campo Santo of Pisa, I thought, before the dead of all generations and those monuments of all epochs, that as we have in our bodies the particles of all pre-existing life, and in our consciences the ideas of all generations, so we have in our lives a part of all ages, and that nothing is more stupid and inhuman than to separate ourselves from other human creatures by our creeds, when children of all times, individuals of all humanity, by those altars which seem to us most full of superstition, those dedicated to household gods, by the Egyptian Pyramids, by the Sphinxes of Babylon, there has passed the spirit of humanity—has passed before arriving at its present plenitude, as great rivers pass by beds of ice, of stone, and mud, before pouring themselves into the immensity of ocean.

This is the true Campo Santo of a people, the true Pantheon of the Middle Ages. In those days people were more preoccupied about death than life. The cemetery was the Eternal City; hell and purgatory the epopee; the jubilee the great association of races, and the crusade the great war. The Middle Ages gravitated around a sepulchre. The strongest and richest among the people shaped his boat, wove his sail, and went by the Eastern Sea to Constantinople and to

Syria, to go from thence to Jerusalem; and after a thousand difficulties, after perilous encounters, burdened by the weight of the enormous armor of that period, and the cross on their bosoms, to seek amid the thickest of the desert, under the brilliant heavens, on burning hills, in the violence of the wind that seemed like a voracious fire, the sepulchre of Christ; to die beside his sacred body, and to be covered with that earth sanctified by the tears of his followers and by the blood of Calvary. The citizens who remained on the shores of Italy desired also to participate in this benefit, to sleep in the bosom of the promised land, and to mingle their ashes with those of the prophets. And the republican equality would not admit of privileges in death. The great commerce of the city accomplished the wishes of the inhabitants. The squadrons arrived even at the gate, loaded with holy earth from Jerusalem. In this earth was buried the bones of the people. It was of a devouring quality. In twenty-four hours it consumed the remains confided to it, as if it was an earth of fire. The greater part of the salts which performed this prodigy have evaporated after so many ages; but still, according to the learned Valery, it consumes a dead body in forty-eight hours.

I looked on it with enthusiasm. A coverlid of green velvet, on which a rain of roses seemed to have fallen, ornamented it; the wild rose extended its thorny branches around, and clouds of white and pure butterflies—like the souls of children, in my imagination—enjoying that aroma and drinking the sweet juice of those plants which extended themselves in festoons and garlands of life over the habitation of the dead. Earth, most holy earth of Jerusalem, trampled by my feet, thou hast germinated the idea of God, and has long guarded it in thy bosom, in order that the Modern Age may repose in thy depths; thou hast collected the bones of those prophets who kindled the faith in the human conscience; from thy clay has been moulded the immortal cradle of our civilization, and that divine Martyr who sacrificed himself in thy mountains to save the world from slavery and the infamous yoke of destiny has made thee as fruitful and as sacred as the seeds of martyrdom! Land of Jerusalem! philosopher or Christian, Jew or Catholic, man of the past or man of the future, whoever presses thee must be stirred with profound emotion, because thou art part of ourselves, and enterest, immortal earth, into the composition of our life!

But let us leave the court, and look again upon the gallery, contemplating, not the tombs, but the paintings. The Italians are essentially artists, and can not understand that an art can exist alone and isolated. They employ both sculpture and painting for their monuments; they inscribe them with verses and inscriptions, that they may contain sentiments, and afterward with music that they may have voices. Let us not forget that the Campo Santo of Pisa was erected in the thirteenth century. To understand it well, it is necessary to comprehend the age of its birth, because architecture never loses — least of all in religious monuments — its symbolical character.

The thirteenth century began with being the age of Catholicism, and ended with being the age of heresy. The human spirit was exalted with faith in the commencement of the century, and inflamed with passion at its conclusion. It began with Innocent III., who saw the human conscience submissive beneath his feet, Europe on her knees before his altars; and ended with Boniface VIII., who felt the blow of the laity on his cheek, and died with rage at his own impotence. It opened with Ferdinand III., of Castile, who merited to be reckoned among the number of the saints, and closed with Alphonso X., who deserved to be counted among the number of philosophers. Pedro II., of Arragon, was born under the protection of the Church, grew up in her bosom, lived to give battle to the infidels, and died fighting for heretics. And these rapid changes are the general law of the century. James I., of Arragon, in the first half of the century, bought and obtained by entreaty lands for the Church, and Pedro II. forced tribute from the Pope. The saints who directed the Crusades and its armies worked miracles before the walls of Verona against the Pontifical troops. The war for the sepulchre of Christ was suspended. Moorish science dominated over theological knowledge. Doubt became mixed with reason, irony entered into literature, the sentiment of nature into art. Human intelligence had passed from the period of faith to the period of reason.

Do you now comprehend why the cemetery of Pisa has been so tolerant? In looking at its galleries and paintings, you behold two hemispheres of time. The arches are animated with one idea, the walls by another. There is the

Gothic, and here the distant announcement of the Renaissance. One could not write the history of the arts without saluting as one of their birthplaces this Campo Santo. You can not enter into it without evoking the ages in which it was constructed. And you can not call up these ages without bringing to memory the name of Nicolas of Pisa. Born in the lap of mysticism, he died in the bosom of a new age. Between his cradle and his tomb there are two worlds. The human spirit changed its character while this man lived, who reckoned seventy-one years. But he felt the change; he announced the death of mysticism. His fathers, his masters, made him kneel, fold his hands before Byzantine statues, bow beneath the terrors of the representation of the Universal Judgment; and later he went and prostrated himself before Grecian figures radiant with beauty, elated with that essentially human civilization suckled at the fruitful breast of liberty. Nicolas was born in the seventh year of the thirteenth century, and died in the seventy-eighth. If I had to express this age in one single symbol, I would select one of his figures, and demonstrate from it that the mystic thought is still visible in his brow, but that the Greek form is seen in its body, as a young plant shooting in the earth, bathed in new-fallen dew.

John of Pisa, the architect of the Campo Santo, also a sculptor, looked with the same eyes as Nicolas of Pisa. Compare the works of these two men of genius with the gigantic mosaics and the extraordinary pictures that are but a few paces removed in the centre of the Cathedral—works brought from Constantinople, or wrought by Byzantine artists. The virgins, the saints, the Byzantine angels have an expression of sublime terror, but also of coldness, the rigidity of death; the virgins, the saints, the statues of Nicolas and of John of Pisa already aspire to the serenity and the perfection of the Greek. It is the world of nature that opens to the breath of the new spirit. It is human beauty, which leaves the shroud of monastic loveliness in the obscurity of the cloister. These stones are trophies of the battles of the spirit; or, to define it better, they are trophies of its victories.

While Nicolas and John were modeling the stones to build cemeteries or to form statues, a little shepherd, keeper of a small flock, sketched on the clay, in the dust, or the sand strange figures. This Tuscan shepherd was the father of painting: he was Giotto. His fame filled the fourteenth century. This extraordinary man was, with respect to painting, what Nicolas of Pisa was with regard to sculpture. In his genius there was already the marks of the genius of Raphael. There are the arms of his saints still rigid, the outlines of the body sharp and angular, the feet deformed, as if they could not stand quite steadily; but the heads are full of benevolence, the faces full of grace, of that grace which ever comes to Byzantine artists in their extremity—that grace, daughter of the serenity of the spirit and twin-sister of hope. We see there that if the bodies sketched by Giotto belong to the earth of his time, the heads approach the heaven of the new age. Those faces were caressed by the breeze of the morning, bathed by the light of Aurora. The artist was submerged in the bosom of nature, meeting in her the immortal inspiration. His pencil is a new efflorescence of the human spirit. Look at his Job on the wall at the left! It is blotted, like the recollection of those days; it is undone, like the faith which animated him; he is seen through a cloud, distant, far distant; the wall is injured by the damp and the sea-breeze, which strips it in pieces from the wall; disfigured, stained by late restorations, you see Job in the same manner that you behold fantastic figures in the clouds, variegated by the sun of the west; nevertheless you see him as a penitent who complains of God without daring to curse Him, surrounded by infidel friends, between the devil, hideous and terrific, and the sweet and beautiful angel on the right, floating in a luminous horizon. I know not why, but that damaged fresco appeared to me as a symbol which Giotto had traced without wishing or thinking of doing it, or perhaps it was done by some contemporary of his own accord in the critical and extraordinary epoch of that century, between the demon of Feudalism, then struggling to exist, and the angel of the Renaissance, which was then issuing from its larvæ.

I can scarcely explain why this cemetery appears to me to be altogether a cemetery of the Middle Ages. A disciple of Fra Angelico, of that mystic in whose retina was painted angels and cherubim, from whose hands no Christ and no Virgin ever came without prayers and tears—a disciple of that sublime monk who painted on his knees, and who has left a gracious remembrance in the immense fresco he produced on almost all the western gallery of the Campo Santo

—has painted a figure which could only have been designed in times of greater sensuality than the present, and which is illustrative of extreme curiosity. Noah is uncovered and drunk upon the ground. A young woman covers her face with her hands, but watches him through her half-open fingers. Fra Angelico would have cursed his pupil Gozzoli.

But this is the new age, the period of the Renaissance of nature, till then despised; the age of the awakening of the sentiments until then blinded; the age in which the faun tramples the fields again, and crowns his horns anew with garlands of ivy; the age in which the nymphs give themselves up on couches of roses to all the joys of life; the age in which the rivulets intone a hymn of new eclogues; and between the delirious rapture of existence and the awakening of all the antique divinities a new Prometheus comes forth, without chains, who with his hand dashes the sea aside and discovers a new world; with his foot propels the earth, obliging it to revolve in infinite space; collects the stars with his telescope, as the hunter takes the birds in his net, and, weighing them in his hand, forces them to murmur in his ears the secrets of the skies.

Yes, that cemetery is the testament of the Middle Ages. I fancy I see in those walls the departure and the last adieus of those times which preceded our age, as chaos precedes the light. The Middle Age, in the mortal agony of its literature, reproduced the dance of death. This curious poem could not be wanting in the Campo Santo of Pisa, and in the immortal heaven of its paintings of the fourteenth and fifteenth centuries. Orcagna, the great Orcagna, painted it there. Look at it, and remember all the other monuments you have ever chanced to see, and there you will perceive the entire genealogy of art. The mausoleum in which the Princess Beatrice reposes is, so to speak, the cradle of the new thought. There Nicolas of Pisa studied. In the works of Nicolas of Pisa, his son, John of Pisa, the architect and sculptor of the cemetery, studied; in the works of John, Andrew of Pisa studied; and in the works of Andrew, Orcagna. After Orcagna came Guiberti, who sculptured the gates of the baptistery of Florence, the triumphant gates of the Renaissance, named by Michael Angelo the gates of Paradise. And before these gates the great artist waited to study design. And this grand and glorious creation of art has this noble genealogy: the mosaics of Venice, the mosaics of Pisa, Cimabue, Nicolas of Pisa, Giotto, John of Pisa, Orcagna, Guiberti, Masaccio, Leonardo di Vinci, Michael Angelo, Raphael. Immortal spirit of man! Never wast thou so great as after having newly encountered the human form, the plastic beauty, at the cost of extraordinary efforts, after eight centuries of maceration, of fasting, and of penance. The fresco of Orcagna is the fresco of the dead. The design is nevertheless incorrect, the bodies of the figure still disproportioned, the perspective is still absent, but the faces have a sublime expression, and a soul which irradiates the thought, which is kindled by the eyes and illumines the forehead. At the left, a cavalcade of ladies and cavaliers in gala costumes stop before the bodies: three swine-herds—one recently dead and swollen, the second decomposed and eaten by worms, the third a fleshless skeleton. A cold shudder comes over one at seeing those three spoils of death in the midst of the crowd of cavaliers richly attired in velvet and ermine; the ladies with their luxurious adornments; the dogs and the falcons for the chase, all the signs of a life devoted to the combat or to pleasure. In the centre, the aged, the infirm, the dying call upon death in verses which the painter has copied to add to the effect of his performance. "O death, medicine for all trouble!" But death will not hear them; he withdraws from those who desire him to strike at those who want him not and forget him; to enter with his cutting scythe into some pleasant grove, in whose shade repose two lovers, contemplating each other with delight, and listening to the song of the troubadour, who sings the happiness of sentiment, surrounded by love and flowers. Yonder, on a high mountain, the penitents pray for all; but below there is a great confusion—kings, nobles, pages, bishops expire; and these souls are collected by the angels, and by demons with wings of bats and with horrible faces. Here the monastic ages finish. The souls mostly gathered by the demons are the souls of monks. And joined to this fresco, as if looking at it, we find the Final Judgment and Hell.

Long after having visited the Sistine Chapel, one is moved by the anger of Jesus, the tender pity of Mary the intercessor, the despair of the reprobates, the ecstasy of the blessed. Solomon, coming out of his grave and shaking off the earthly dust from his eyelids, looks uncertain as to his lot, whether he is destined for celestial heights or the infernal abyss; the avenging genius who draws by his hair into eternal darkness a monk who had sought to conceal himself among the blessed, and the angel of mercy who leads toward the abode of the saved a young worldling, already lost among the condemned; the woman who wrings her hands with desperation at the entrance of the unfathomable eternity; the old man who casts himself at the feet of Jesus to relate his good works and to ask the divine clemency; the guardian angel in the centre of the picture, melancholy, overcome by infinite sorrow, looking with his large and profound eyes full of contending emotions as the souls drop like a cataract of gall into the abyss, in the seas of molten lead—the souls he had vainly protected against the wickedness of the world beneath his sheltering wings, and which he vainly wished to save from the justice of the divine anger with his prayers in the supreme hour of judgment; terrible images of horror and desolation, which appear in grim reality on those tombs in that asylum of the departed, represented by some cold, rigid, and fleshless figures in the last day of the universe.

In the paintings of all these great pictures, you discover, however, that mystic times have passed, and that the period of the Renaissance has not yet arrived. In none of them—in not one of the immense number of personages depicted on these walls do you find either the idealism of Fra Angelico or the naturalism of Buonarotti. Human history is a struggle between thought and reality. In these pictures we find that the idea evaporates, but that nature has not yet arrived. The mystic spirit is quenched, but as yet there has not been substituted that adoration of the human organism which made such great painters and such great sculptors—the artists of the Renaissance. Michael Angelo threw himself on a dead body with the appetite of the hyena; he examined and studied so closely that he had each one of its bones engraven in his memory. His favorite study was that of the nude, as if he wished to bring man back to the primeval innocence of Eden. But anatomy was prohibited in the Middle Age. Those unhappy artists of the fourteenth and fifteenth centuries were not able to study the structure of the human body. Their forms were confined within their clothing, as if in a bag or in a winding-sheet. Man still holds too much before his eyes his ever-present transgression, and is ashamed of his own body, of the eternal shadow of sin. But though he finds himself thus degraded, he discovers that it enables him to embrace a new idea. The figures of the Campo Santo of Pisa are figures of the clouds, uncertain and unknown beings, which arise in the limits of two epochs. After all, if we look at the human history, we find it thus with all men—all are condemned to stifle half the ideas they have learned, and half the dear aspirations of existence; all are dragged onward by the interminable current of circumstances, without knowing whither; all are forced to the labor of renovation, without knowing wherefore; more or less all cast off the habiliments of the soul—the innocence of childhood, the passion of youth, the faith of the cradle—in the cross-ways of the journey; all at one time or other fall, subdued by fatigue and exhaustion, on a heap of dry illusions, which successors scatter with their feet, or cast into a pit, and all continue repeating ceaselessly the same herculean labors, and representing the same tragedy without completing it.

Do you believe that death is the end of our being? I have never thought so. If it be, then the universe has been created solely for destruction; and God is a child who has formed the worlds like a castle of cards, for the pleasure of overturning them. The vegetable consumes the earth, the ox and the sheep graze upon the vegetable, we eat the ox and the sheep, invisible agents which we call death or nothingness consume us; in the scale of existence some creatures serve only to destroy other creatures, and the universe is like an enormous polypus with a capacious stomach, or, if you desire a more classic image, a catafalque upon which burns a funeral torch, and is erected like the eternal statue—fatality. Some are patient because they have been born lymphatic; many are heroes because they have much blood; others are thinkers because they are bilious; more are poets because their nerves are excitable; but all die of their own characteristics, and all live while their stomachs endure, while their hearts, their brains, their spines are sound. What we call virtues or vices are tendencies of organism; what we name faith is but a few drops of blood less in the veins, or some irritation in the liver, or some atoms of phosphorus in the bones; and what we term immortality is but an illusion; death alone is real and certain, and human history is a procession of shadows passing like bats between day and night, all to drop one behind the other into that obscure, empty, and unfathomable abyss which is called Nothing—the unique atmosphere of the universe.

Oh! no, no, I can not believe it! human wickedness can never so much affect me as to obscure divine truths in my soul. As I can distinguish good from evil, so I can separate death from immortality. I believe in the Almighty, and in a vision, the Almighty in another and a better world. I leave below my body, as armor which fatigues me by its weight, to continue my infinite ascension to the heaven of heavens, bathed in light eternal. It is true that death exists, but true also that there is a soul; against reality, which would shroud me with its leaden mantle, I have the glow and fire of thought; and against fatalism, that would confine me by its chains, I have the force and power of liberty. History is a resurrection. Barbarians buried the ancient Grecian statues, but they live again in this cemetery, producing immortal generations of artists with kisses from their cold lips of marble. Italy was as dead as Juliet; each generation flung a handful of earth upon her corpse, and placed a flower in her mortuary crown; yet Italy is alive again! To-day tyrants sing the *Dies Iræ* on those fields where the members of unhappy Poland were divided. Yet soon humanity approaches, collects the bones picked clean by the vultures of the Neva, and Poland is reborn, standing like a statue of faith, with the cross in her arms, on her ancient altars! I have always been impressed with the thought of immortality in cemeteries. But I felt it more than commonly in the Campo Santo of Pisa, filled with so much life, peopled by so many beings that give inspiration, and consequently immortality, as the trunks of trees distill honey when bees have inhabited them.

Insensibly the night fell over me. The grave-digger finished his work, the noise of his shovel ceased, and the guardian came to beg I would retire. But I prayed him to leave me there another hour, in the bosom of night and of the shadows. I wished to submerge myself in the melancholy of nothingness, to anticipate my being in that place of silence and eternal repose by a long contemplation of the earth of the departed where so many generations sleep forgotten. There I remained leaning against a tomb, resting my forehead upon the marble, my eyes fixed on the picture of death and on the monsters of the Universal Judgment, illuminated by the last splendors of the expiring day, awaiting the greater sadness which the darkness of night would bring upon me. But no; the fresh breeze of the sea came to awaken me from my melancholy dreams; the sweet flowers of May raised their blossoms, before drooping from the heat; a penetrating and intoxicating aroma, full of life and fragrance, diffused itself in the air; the winged glow-worms began to hover between the shades of the cloister and the lines of tombs, like wandering stars; while the full moon rose above the horizon, floating majestically in ether, with her pale, pure rays lighting up the faces of the funereal statues; and a nightingale, hidden in the thick branches of the highest cypress, chanted his song of love, as a serenade to the dead and a supplication to the heavens.

Chapter VI.

VENICE.

The night advanced upon us as we crossed the campagna of Padua, directing our way toward Venice. The sky was cloudy, and at intervals between the showers there were moments of great clearness and beauty, in which the first stars of evening floated in the limpid atmosphere. But on the border of the horizon, toward the northern extremity, on the side of the mountains, the clouds emitted flashes of lightning; while on the other extreme, toward the south, from the side of the sea, fringes of purple, formed by the vapors of the lake, mingling with the last glimmer of daylight, gave a copper-colored tint to the scene and a fantastic appearance to nature; it was impossible to doubt that the region which we were about to visit would satisfy all our desires and reward our longing, as these natural beauties were revealed between the sublime mysteries of the fading light. Notwithstanding the beauty around, my impatience was excessive. I observed that vegetation became extinct, that we passed dried-up canals full of mud, on whose borders some marine plants grew sadly. But, though I continually put my head from the window, hoping to see the final point of our journey, I saw neither the celebrated lagune nor the beloved city; it seemed as if it fled from my impatience and escaped from my desire. I had such an idea of the fragility of this beautiful Venice, continually combating the winds and the waters, that I feared she would disappear before I was permitted to behold her, and bury herself in the sea-shell in which she was born, as a living miracle of human history.

 I shall always remember the day in which for the first time I saw the Alhambra. I ran to seek it without a guide and without any companion, desiring a solitary interview, like all the assignations of love, with the Maga of the East lost in our mountains. I went through a door which I do not remember, for I scarcely noticed it. I saw at the left a magnificent fountain of the Renaissance, which in no way responded to my desires or conceptions. I lost myself in the superb alamedas—promenades planted with rows of trees at either side, freshened by the pure breeze of the morning, and illuminated by the splendid sun of Granada, whose rays, pouring through the thick foliage, formed upon the ground flickering arabesques of light and shadow. I stood before that magnificent judiciary gate, upon the slope of a hill, in the architecture of which the Arabesque, without losing its graceful elegance, has taken all the solemnity of the Gothic. I entered, expecting to find the palace beyond the gate. It was not there; I only beheld a hall, used as an armory, and an altar of the Middle Ages, before which a lamp was burning. Round about there was a long row of small round towers; in the centre of the grand square a most beautiful palace of the sixteenth century, but in direct opposition to my preconceived impressions; and in the distance, upon an elevation covered with laurels, its light galleries resembling minarets, stood the Oriental Generalife. I looked for the Alhambra, the palace, the magical grotto of stalactites, beautiful with brilliant Asiatic colors, where were extinguished, at the close of the fifteenth century, those who came like lions to conquest at the beginning of the eighth century. But not one of the numerous doors at which I knocked was the entrance to the Alhambra. I feared that a genius, a witch among those left in the groves by the magic of the Middle Ages—certainly unlike the lovely goddesses with which classic antiquity peopled them—had stolen the Alhambra that night, the grand building continually threatened with decay, in order to mock at my impatience. We are born and we live so unhappily that the accomplishment of a desire appears to us a falsehood, the realization of hope a deception, as if our sad experience had taught us the bitter lesson that in the world nothing is true but sorrow.

So, in that moment I doubted the proximity of Venice, or feared that for me Venice had disappeared. At last we arrived at the entrance of the great Venetian lagune. The air brought to our ears the sweet voices of the bells announcing the Angelus, and reminded us of the sublime emotion of Byron, when one evening he fancied he heard the combination of these same echoes from the borders of the horizon gliding over the waters, as the stars of heaven to the Mother of Christ, with the moon at her feet, and with the mysterious white dove waving its wings on her forehead, in that sublime hour of love and adoration. It was true that I went to see Venice. How many times in the long hours of the winter evenings, my mother, who was remarkable for her love of letters, related to me mysterious Venetian stories of events much discussed at the beginning of the century: the decapitation of Marino Faliero, the banishment of the young Foscari, the matchless heroism of Dandolo, the ungovernable passion of Othello, the splendor of the banquets immortalized by Paul Veronese, the espousals of the Doges with the waters of the Adriatic in the gondola covered with brocade and moved by golden oars; the infinite sorrow of the last of Venetian Magistrates when he fell lifeless at signing the judicial record which delivered up his country to Austria for a criminal error of Napoleon; all these simple narrations, half historical, half legendary, in which there was always an outline of a traitor or a dungeon to excite the interest of tragic terror; some sittings of the Council of Ten to sustain the dramatic power, and some moral teaching to fortify in my mind the two great ideas, whose worship I shall never renounce—liberty and my country.

Recovering from one of those natural transitions to other recollections, I saw in my mind historic Venice—those noble children of ancient civilization, priests of her last household gods—funeral cortége of her last days—who conquered fatality, saving themselves in the uninhabitable lagunes from the irruptions of Attila and his ferocious Huns, to preserve in a mysterious and unique city, anchored like a beautiful ship in a Grecian port, her classic liberties; which induced them to struggle with the waves when society was uselessly hiding itself in cloisters; to extend their labor and commerce as a safeguard, when in the terrors and uncertainties of the tenth century the strongest arms fell with dismay, regarding the end of the world as a necessity, and the Universal Judgment as a punishment; and, in fine, to unite and treasure up riches in her moles, in her canals, in her palaces chiseled by marvelous sculpture; in her public monuments, singularly beautiful and majestic, decorated by a continual festival of shades and colors; in her bronze and marble trophies, the remains of three civilizations lost in an infinite series of shipwrecks; Venice being thus Asiatic and Greek, Roman and Byzantine, never German—the synthesis of three great ages in history, the precious stone in the nuptial ring of the Eastern union, of the world of mysteries, with Europe, the world of the new life, of the new civilization.

And as it is impossible to renounce the nation as the race to which we belong, I, a Spaniard, felt at that moment crowding upon my memory the historic recollections of the service rendered to civilization by Venice and Spain, united in the memorable maritime crusade. One day the Crescent shone over Constantinople. The Byzantines and Greeks fell one after the other under the Turkish cimeters, turned ominously toward Venice. The isles were taken captive, their sons were made rowers in Turkish galleys; the Mediterranean, the sea of civilization, became a lake of Oriental palaces. But the vessels of the Spanish cities—of Barcelona, of Valencia, of Cadiz—joined themselves to the ships of Genoa and of Venice, and moved onward to oppose the Turk; which resulted in that remarkable victory of Lepanto, in which the waves were crimson with human blood and boiled under the fire of the cannons; in which fatalism was driven backward in its devouring career before the power of Western civilization.

But, above all, I went to see the town for which we felt so much sorrow and sadness during her long captivity in this century. How many times I had beheld her in dreams, surrounded by her islets, like Niobe among her wounded children, cursing men who would not succor her, and despairing of the justice of God who tolerated her oppression! How often had I fancied I heard in the mysterious echoes with which her shores repeat the murmurs of the Mediterranean a long lament for Venice! How often had I believed I should see her one day in her despair fling herself, like Ophelia, into her lagunes, and disappear under the waters with her double crown of marble and of sea-weed upon her brow, and her melancholy death-song upon her lips! Venice was for us a City-Christ, suspended with infamous punishment by the four great nails of the Quadrilateral. Venice bereft of some of her pearly crowns, her robes of velvet, her gilded barges; those lions of bronze with their eyes of diamonds, those crocodiles of emeralds and rubies, those costly jewels with which the privileged genius of her painters adorned her, and only showed her ruined fragments of marble, stained by the rain of her tears, as a mendicant shows his bones covered with rude skin through his tatters! The history of this martyrdom, the lament of her past servitude, the numberless elegies wept by so many poets, by so many illustrious orators in the dungeons of Venice — all these recollections struggling in my mind augmented the emotion produced in my soul at the sight of those mysterious shores made illustrious by genius and heroism.

While still excited by these thoughts, the train entered the lagune of San Marco. The heavens, as I have said, were on one side clear and bright, on the other dark and cloudy, with occasional flashes of lightning, at intervals obscured by clouds or brilliant with stars, altogether of so singular an aspect that I did not weary of looking at it, demanding its light to drink in that spectacle, the object of so many desires, the subject of so many dreams. The immense lagune, which still preserved in its tranquil surface something of the brightness of the day, shone in all the expanse of the vast horizon like an extended looking-glass crossed by bands, sometimes of opal where it reflected the stars, sometimes of amethyst where it mirrored the clouds, kindled into a blaze every now and then by vivid flashes of lightning. The smoke of the locomotive, the breeze from the lagunes, the clouds over our heads, the waters beneath our feet, and the broad range of vision, made us imagine we were far from the earth, or cruising in some distant, extraordinary, and unknown region. Between the uncertain sights, the fitful shadows, outlined fantastically as if in a half-darkened mirror, we discovered the buildings of Venice, here and there illumined by pale lights. If I had not known I was in Venice I should immediately have recognized her, seeing her rise as if by enchantment from the waves, balance herself between the surface of the water and the liquid air, without visibly touching the earth in any part —a floating city, a nomade maritime caravan, presided over by some god of the waves taking a temporary refuge in the tranquil bosom of the blue Adriatic. What beauty of colors, notwithstanding the night! The stars seem to tremble in the undulating light; the marine vegetation gives some sombre touches to the scene; a light-house contrives by its reflections to make serpents of topaz; the oar of a boat throws up a shower of brilliant flashes of phosphorescent light; already white stars (like those of the Milky Way) show themselves in the heavens; on one side are the shadows of the houses, darkening the twilight, extending festoons of jet across the water; while on the other side a cloud lost by chance, and which, like an aerial sponge, absorbs the last rays of the absent sun, letting them fall on certain points in a rain of purple —all varied by the gases and the strange reflections which the vapors of the air and the changes of the lake give to this almost ideal world of most enchanting beauty.

At last the train stopped. The formalities of giving up the tickets and collecting the baggage excited in an incredible manner our natural impatience. One would wish to be a bird or a fish, to arrive in Venice through the air or the water without being annoyed with trunks and umbrellas, which our human weakness makes necessary. At last, however, you tread those shores eternally kissed by the waters. A long row of black gondolas, light and elegant, await you. Mechanically you enter the first, without troubling yourself either as to your destination or the price of the voyage, as if all the conditions of economic life were upset there, where all the conditions of vulgar life in ancient and modern towns are also reversed. Giving, in answer to the gondolier, the address of your hotel, you feel by an almost imperceptible movement that you glide along the waters. The soul is weighed down by a profound sentiment of sadness. The gondola, ill-lighted by a little lamp placed at the end, and conducted by two men, one standing at either extremity, appears sometimes a coffin, sometimes a whale, sometimes a black swan, sometimes a glow-worm, or the transformed corpse of one of the ancient citizens of the Adriatic, which draws you onward to the dark caverns of the profound bosom of the ocean. As you are dazzled by the brightness of the resplendent lagune, you seem to enter into the region of darkness. The waters have a wonderfully sombre color, looking as if thick and really bituminous. The great walls of the high buildings deepen the night. The lanterns, placed at long distances, only serve as a slight contrast against the general obscurity. Venice has her streets of land and her streets of water. The streets of water are not lighted. Only the white phosphorescence of the track, or the feeble brightness of a window, or the faint ray of the dull little lamp from a silent gondola which passes beside you, or the reverberation from some distant corner, illumine and animate that curious and tortuous labyrinth of stones and iron gratings, of bridges and of posts for attaching the gondolas— a sort of stunted aquatic trees, but without branches, without leaves, sad and withered. The city appears uninhabited.

From time to time some living beings pass over the arches of the bridges, looking as unreal as the shadows of shadows. The silence is sepulchral. You hear only the cry of the gondolier, who warns his comrades to prevent a collision. This cry, repeated all around, is sharp and shrill, like the note of wild sea-birds. The green slime which swims on the surface of the canals floats at intervals and looks like dead bodies. The gate of a palace turns slowly on its hinges, some persons descend silently by the marble steps and enter a gondola. They resemble the inhabitants of a pantheon who go to repose in a coffin. Moving onward you enter the Grand Canal, and breathe an air more fresh and free; you see by the light of the stars shafts of twisted columns, plinths, and pedestals, which mount above the water, Gothic roses, arched, arabesque, and Byzantine windows, arches of the Renaissance; but floating by all these, the gondola loses itself anew in the maze of narrow, watery streets, and all the beautiful decorations disappear from our view, as the rapid hours of pleasure vanish in the long sadness of life.

The way was extremely long from the station to our hotel. The gondoliers continued on foot at each end of the gondola, propelling it with their two broad oars and repeating their sharp cries. At every step a corner, at every corner a bridge, at the foot of the bridge and at the corners of the houses flights of marble steps; over the last white step the green water, and under the arches of the bridge and joined to the marble stairs the black gondolas covered with large dark cloths, resembling those of a bier. The most necessary object of Venetian existence is the gondola, and the gondola is also the most melancholy. Imagine an ellipse of black wood, with various relievos; at one of the extremities a great halberd cut deeply with teeth, whose steel shines ominously, and at the other end a kind of little twisted tail; in the centre, like the ancient Venetian *Tartanas*, or small, light coasting-vessels, is the place of repose, lined inside with black velvet, covered with black cloth, with silk embroidery; full of soft cushions of morocco leather, provided with four windows, of whose glasses, curtains, and blinds you can make what use you please; all is dark, melancholy, mysterious, and romantic, all inviting to adventure, and leading the imagination to legendary stories, one or the other of which remain as the natural consequence of all around, and above all of your inseparable companion, the silent gondola. Each city has its characteristic. Thus Rome is the sublime city, Naples the pleasant city, Florence the academic city, Leghorn the mercantile city, Pisa the dead city, Bologna the musical city, Milan the civil city, and Venice the romantic city. The Moor and the Merchant of Venice of Shakespeare, the Angelo of Victor Hugo, the dramas of Byron, have all been inspired by these shadows, and have here, in these gondolas, their mysterious cradles.

To-day Venice unites to the poetry of her arts the poetry of her recollections, and to the poetry of her recollections the poetry of her sadness. Her palaces are crumbling to decay, her statues fall in pieces from their pedestals, the smiling figures of her pictures vanish as the butterflies at the rude breath of winter. The blow which occasioned the variation of human movement toward other regions, as a consequence of the apparition of America in the world, and the discovery of the Cape of Good Hope; the wound which ruined her commerce is not of a nature to be cured by her recent liberty, because liberty can not balance or undo geographical fatalities. Venice is dying. Only in place of dying as an outcast in an Austrian dungeon, she dies like an honored matron in the bosom of her home and surrounded by her children. Venice fell at the foot of the cradle of America, like Iphigenia at the foot of the cradle of Greece. The paths of humanity are strewed with victims, and progress is not exempted from this law of necessity. Life is nourished upon death. But on this account it is not the less sad to see a city perish—a city whose Doges had the imperial crown of Byzantium so often in their hands, and repelled it by the Phrygian cap of the old Republic; to see a city fall whose standard terrified the Turks, and awakened the powers and energies of labor and commerce; to behold the death of a city whose liberties are the most ancient of the Christian era, and who alone has been the England of the Middle Ages; to watch the slow decay of a city who in her cups of crystal, in her bacchanalian banquets, in her sensual songs, in her coral garlands and sea flowers, brought to our hearts and imaginations the immortal aroma of the Renaissance. How I regretted in that voyage through the streets of Venice that I was not a poet or an orator, or a writer of any merit—that I could not lament with eloquence the death of that city unique in the world! Ideas of mourning and desolation only were inspired by those floating coffins, those sombre palaces, the magnificent half-ruined windows, the tortuous labyrinth of narrow streets and gloomy canals, the shadows outlined on the high bridges, the broken steps of marble kissed by the wavelets, the murmur of the water like tear falling on tear, and the cries of the gondoliers, which sounded like a wail repeated by another lament.

We stopped at a hotel on the Grand Canal, opposite the Church of Santa Maria della Salute, where we purposed remaining, very near the Square of St. Mark. At this point the breadth of the canal is that of an arm of the sea. Its waters are as clear as the sun-illumined daylight, and the phosphorescence left by the oars and keel leave around broad white ribbon-like bands of moonlight. On coming out of the narrow canals into that broad expanse, many gondolas were being directed toward the Rialto, lighted by Venetian lanterns, to be compared only to garlands of luminous flowers. This magical illumination showed vividly in the obscurity of the night, and was repeated in the transparency of the waters. From the gondolas came a solemn and most harmonious choir, accompanied by excellent instrumental music: a mysterious melody, increased and softened by the sound-conducting properties of the air and of the lagunes. After having made that strange journey, after having threaded that strange series of winding canals, in which Venice seemed one of those mystic towns painted by the artists of the Middle Ages on the walls of cemeteries to represent Inferno; seeing myself in the Grand Canal, among that great crowd of monuments rising from the limpid waters under the transparent heavens, showing the white marble churches illumined by the starlight, and looking like mountains of snow; beholding the gondolas rapidly gliding along, a floating festival consecrated to art; drinking in that music, that delicious harmony in the waves, of the wind, and of the lagune, I believed myself in ancient Venice—in her who brought to her shores the riches and the colors of the East; in her who listened to the serenades of Leonardo di Vinci; in her who lent the shades of the rainbow to the palette of Titian; in her who loved laughter and merriment; in her who put the Empire of Constantine at her feet like a slave, and as a companion at her side, Greece, the land of poets. But the serenade died away in the distance, the lights were lost in the windings of the canal, the lagune sunk again into profound silence, and the turrets of the neighboring churches rung out the hour of nightfall with elegiac melancholy.

It seemed too long to wait for the daylight that I might see Venice. Of the arts, I confess that in my opinion the most wonderful and impressive is that of architecture. The stones of Venice, shaped by design as the notes of a piece of music, or the parts of a discourse, where beauty and harmony are both expressed, give pure and intellectual pleasure. The great lines, the broad spaces, the ambitious arches, the aerial cupolas, the columns with their adornments, the galleries with their perspectives, the court-yards and their cloisters, force upon the mind profound meditations, and always express the genius of the age with its symbolical character. I admire greatly the Grecian architecture, its soberness, its severe simplicity, its infinite gracefulness, the facility with which it expresses great sentiments with small means, and attains to beauty without doing violence to form, putting a light frieze, squared, on four fronts of intercolumniations, the whole being in perfect harmony and proportion. I also admire the Romans, who placed, one over the other, three kinds of architecture in their monuments, as they placed one above another the three ages of history in their code of laws and in their civilization. And I shall never forget the great dome of the Pantheon where Paganism expired, nor the triumphal arches and magnificent gates of the new age of the world. Above all, the sentiment with which ancient art always inspires me is a profound admiration for simplicity of form, and for a resemblance to nature in expression. But this enthusiasm for ancient art does not prevent me from doing justice to all the bold and striking beauties of architecture. Nothing is more illiberal than the exclusiveness of art. The architects of the past age —those destitute of refined taste—in their great dislike of the Gothic, succeeded in erecting some grand buildings, not such as could speak to the imagination, but dumb, severe, rigid with all the stiffness of death. There are styles of architecture distinguished by the knowledge they express, by their complete subjection to the laws of harmony and proportion —such are the Greek and the Roman. Over these centuries have passed, and other things more destructive than ages—the unthinking and devastating rage of men; but that has been unable to prevail against their imperturbable strength and stability. Doubtless there are architectures distinguished by their expression, such as the Oriental and the Gothic. Venice appears in Granada, because Venice has an exclusive and suitable architecture, born of her peculiar historical circumstances, and representative of the ministry exercised by her between the East and the West. In like manner the people of Granada, always preserving that Moorish character which arrived at perfection in the mosque of Cordova, approached the Gothic; the Venetians, preserving the Byzantine and Gothic styles, general in the Middle Ages, flung over them like a golden veil the rich jewels of the East. Thus Venice has created this series of monuments that are the wonder of wonders by their variety and their riches. If you go and examine them with Vitruvius in your hand, with the rules of Vignola in your mind, taking with you a square and compass, submitting them to a rigid mathematical examination, demanding from them a blind obedience to the laws of proportional harmony, ready to feel indignant if you see a gallery supported by ironwork, or a heavy column placed upon a slender one, as if ridiculing the general principles of gravity—if you see that a mass of marble weighs like a mountain over the delicate tracery of a light aerial gallery—if you place mathematics over all and above all, you do not appreciate those edifices of the Middle Ages, that above all and before all place the wealth of expression, the riches of greatness, far-fetched and hyperbolical perhaps, but at the same time extremely beautiful. Whenever the arts unfold themselves, they strongly influence their surroundings. Venice is a magician, who obliges artists to follow her, and impresses her kiss of fire on their foreheads. The artists of the fifteenth century built severe edifices in Rome, at the same time that the florid Gothic expanded its open-work roses in all Europe as the first flowers of the April of the Renaissance; and the Venetian architects at the end of the sixteenth century and the beginning of the seventeenth, when the classic art had subdued it, without failing to follow it, crowned the friezes of their monuments, the cusps of their towers, the roofs of their palaces with ornaments and enameled chiselings, always of the Oriental and Venetian character.

Let us go then and look at Venice. Our gondola glides over the Grand Canal, the waters are of an emerald green, the heavens of a turquoise blue, the banks of sand are tinged with gold, the houses on the neighboring islets are bright and many colored, and the marble churches are so transparent that they look like churches of crystal; the sun gilds all objects with its rays. The beauties of nature and the soft breeze perfumed with the aromas of spring, with the saline exhalations of the sea, fresh and invigorating, invite you with their voluptuous caresses to the infinite joys of existence. We have time to admire this Grand Canal which the Venetian painters reproduced in all manners, from the dawn of the school with Carpaccio to its extinction with Canalletto, and have impressed indelibly on the retinas of the lovers of art. It is easy to see with a rapid glance that from the heavy Byzantine buildings to the more elegant structures of the sixteenth century, and from those of the sixteenth century to the motley edifices of the decadence, in company with all kinds of Gothic constructions, ornamented with Syrian and Arab garlands—the history of the art is displayed in two broad marble walls on one and on the other side of the canal, illumined by the reflections of the water and by the tints of the sky.

In every town you first look for a monument or point whereon to fix attention. In Seville, the Cathedral; in Granada, the Alhambra; in Cordova, the Mezquita; in Rome, the Coliseum; in Naples, Vesuvius; in Pisa, the Campo Santo; in Florence, La Piazza della Signoria, and in Venice the Square of Saint Mark. We arrive at the foot of its magnificent flight of steps—we remain there in delighted astonishment. It is not possible to describe Venice. Our language has not words enough to paint so rich a picture. At least I can not attempt it. One must see and feel and admire, and steep the eyes in those colors, and absorb that beauty in all the pores—and then be silent.

I must confide in the goodness of my readers, and hope they will excuse me for so ill describing this place. There is indeed a superb panorama before my eyes and a feeble pen in my hand. In the first place, the lagune, splendidly illuminated by the heavens, and the sun which borders it with his rays; at the north is the mouth of the Grand Canal, with its rows of palaces. At the extreme right of the mouth is the marble church of Santa Maria della Salute, whose white cupolas are outlined wonderfully in the lustrous air. Before the church, elevated on a graceful tower, is a great sphere of gilded bronze, with an angel of dark bronze on the top. At the left side of the canal is a terrace, blooming with gay spring flowers and butterflies; near is a little square and the palace of Sansovino, sculptured like a work of Cellini, and surmounted by a group of statues. The palace of the Doge at the other end, resting its mass of red and white marble on a double gallery of Gothic arches, interlaced by a capricious arrangement of oriels, and adorned at the upper part of the columns with Byzantine sculptures, which harmonize and mingle admirably with the diadem of sharp triangles and the airy belfry above. Before these two monuments, the two columns of Oriental granite, two colossal monoliths, and, above, the crocodile of St. Theodore and the lion of St. Mark, which seem to exhale hot breath from their open mouths; in the background, to the left, the Campanile, light and elegant as our Giralda, paved by a marvelously sculptured tribune, and crowned by an angel standing on a point and raising his wings on high. Farther on, at the right side, the Basilica— Oriental, Gothic, Greek, Byzantine, Moorish—a mixture of all orders of architecture, an epitome of all epochs, its blue arches sown with stars, its columns of different colored jasper, its statues and its fantastic bell-towers; the four horses of Corinth above the door, mosaics of Venetian glass in the recesses, from the golden groundwork of which wonderful figures of all colors detach themselves; the cupolas above, small copies of those of Santa Sophia, like an apparition of Asia; and in the vast proportions of that panorama, the *Riva degli Schiavoni* filled with vessels, realized by the picturesque costumes of the Turks and the Greeks, by the great Venetian population continually passing in that wide street.

Beyond the isle of San Giorgio, with its church of red and white marble; the Giudecia, with its buildings of all the colors of the rainbow; San Lazzaro, with its Armenian convent, whose Oriental towers look like the curled sail of a huge vessel; the Lido, with its groves of trees which touch the Lagune with their branches, the nightingales filling the air with melody, the gardens like floating islands, or gigantic bouquets flung upon the water, all crossed by the blue stripes of the canals, all varied by colors, and gilded or silvered by the sand-banks, all diversified by the contrast between the white lateen sails and the black Venetian gondolas which glide around, all lulled by the waves of the Adriatic; the Alps in the distant West, resembling an army of celestial pyramids, and in the far East, like an eternal music, the wind which comes from the shores of Greece. It is unequaled in the world!

How many lovely cities there are in Italy! Each one contains a marvel, and each marvel has its particular character. When going from Rome to Naples, you do not find yourself in another land, but in another planet. The cemetery of Pisa and the cemetery of Bologna are both magnificent; but there is as great a difference between them as between the Pantheon of Agrippa and the Cathedral of Milan. You travel from Florence to Pisa in two hours, from Pisa to Leghorn in half an hour, and between each of these towns, their streets and monuments, there is an abyss of difference. The magnificent leaning tower of Pisa seems to have been constructed at a thousand leagues distant from the place which contains the divine rotunda of *Santa Maria dei Fiori* at Florence. Each of these cities has its especial school of painting, and its especial kind of architecture. Each of them has produced a genius which it unfolds, in exchange for the present of existence—the gift of immortality. Pisa boasts of a Nicolas, who adorned the Renaissance by two ages of anticipation, making marble obey the efforts of his chisel; Bologna had her John, who delayed for a time the decadence of sculpture; Fiesoli a Fra Angelico, who painted angels with the same graphic facility with which Plato described pure ideas; and men kneel before the Virgins produced by his pencil between the limits of two such ages as the fourteenth and the fifteenth centuries, which are the limits of two worlds, symbolizing the end of the mystic ages. Venice is the mother of Titian, Verona of Paul Cagliari, Florence of Michael Angelo, and Rome may call herself, by the Transfiguration of Raphael, the Sibyls, the Galatea of the Farnese, the Madonna of Foligno, and the Isaiah, the city of Raphael. From whence has arisen this greatness? From the decentralization of governments, from the liberty of republics, from municipal independence. There is only in history one epoch superior to that epoch, one people more illustrious than her people—Greece. But the secret of her greatness is the same as that of the greatness of Italy. Michael Angelo is one of those Titans who raised broken and calcined masses, placed them one above the other to scale the heavens; his foreheads show the wrecks of the tempest which have crossed them, searching alone and by solitary paths the regions of the infinite.

When Michael Angelo saw the liberties of his country expire, he carved a most beautiful and melancholy figure, gave it the Grecian perfection of form, and Christian sorrow in the expression; closed its eyes, extended it on a bier, and called it "Night." The loss of liberty was the death of Venice, the death of Milan, the death of Pisa, the night of Italy. Every where liberty or the absence of liberty moulds society, as God is visible in the relations of the planets.

Chapter VII.

ON THE LAGUNES.

It is light at last! At length we have that fluid only comparable to thought, which illuminates and vivifies. How I reveled in the ether from a cloudless heaven, reflected by a lake without shadow! I wished to see my own mind, to be able to comprehend my own being, under the new and strange aspect flung over all things by this Oriental splendor. We ourselves are the darkest and most incomprehensible of existing creatures. Why is not my reason as clear as the sun? After all, the light of the great star would be lost, as inaudible music, if it did not brighten the human face. Why is not my spirit as diaphanous as those celestial waters, in whose limpid surface are repeated with all their Asiatic beauty, with all their Grecian elegance and proportions, the palaces of Venice? After all, the universe would be like a blank or a closed book if its pages were not filled with human sentiments. Why was not the horizon of my thoughts as vast as the horizon before me? All things would be but the shadows of shadows if they were not animated by a soul. Take the spirit from the planet, and then tell me for whom warble the birds among the trees, whose leafy branches touch the water, and for whom do these flowers, which now drink the delicious juices of the spring, exhale their incense? Things would be without meaning if destitute of vitality—hieroglyphics without readers or interpreters. The universe without a spirit would be, at the least, a theatre without actors. But the spirit—what interior light has it?

I know not in history any epoch so serious and important as ours. The beliefs created and fostered by five centuries of faith and martyrdom have fallen in three ages of analysis. Many and great changes are perhaps drawing near, and we know not what another day may bring forth. The bell which now sounds the hour of vespers, the organ which now accompanies the litany of the monks, the image now venerated by the mariners of the Adriatic, will soon pass away, like the hymns of ancient Greece, like the bass-reliefs of the Parthenon: objects of artistic admiration, but not of religious worship. Here is heard rising from the waters an elegiac lamentation, only comparable to that of the sirens of old, when they heard from the lips of the Nazarene that the world was called to a new faith, the evidences of which were macerations and penitence. The god-Spirit saw rising against his power and against his word clouds of new ideas as menacing as those which dethroned and destroyed the god-Nature. What interior light has the spirit in this supreme crisis?

Such thoughts as these arose in my mind one evening in the month of May on the splendid shore of the marvelous lagune of St. Mark, before the mouth of the Grand Canal of Venice, on the Isle of St. Lazzaro, at the gate of the Armenian Convent. The sun was just sinking behind the Giudecia, and gilded with his last rays the spires of the churches and the Oriental domes of the Great Basilica; the black gondolas, skimming along the blue waters, moved rapidly in all directions like fantastic living creatures; in front were ranged the magnificent Venetian palaces, enameled and beautified by the arts; on one side stretched the Lido, like a floating garden of luxuriant vegetation, blooming with flowers; and all around rose the islands, in which the trees seemed to have their roots in the water, and between their foliage were glimpses of beautiful and stately buildings, looking as if anchored in that sea of indelible recollections and of eternal poetry. One must have beheld all that loveliness to be able to comprehend the effect of the sunset on the lagunes; now the waters are illumined by white phosphoric tracks, now rose the first stars of the evening, and now the first lights appeared in the windows and the streets of the city; now these lights were tremblingly reflected in the canals; now the last strokes of the vesper bell sounded in the sweet air and mingled with the love songs of the gondoliers and the psalmody of the convents—the voices of the spirit in harmony with voices of the universe in the heavens.

While absorbed in the contemplation of so much beauty, a monk approached me to say that the hour drew near for closing the gate of the convent. That seemed reasonable, but did not reconcile me to departure. I felt an unconquerable desire to remain there, the closing time had not quite arrived, and my gondola was ready to carry me to the town, about three kilometres distant from St. Lazzaro. The Armenian monks sell Oriental curiosities and works of art; I am not quite a stranger to their language, and I made use of my knowledge as a contrivance to prolong my stay in so delightful a spot.

Immediately the monk forgot the gate, and began to talk about study and literature. By degrees the conversation took a religious turn. I have always felt an insuperable impetus to diffuse my ideas and opinions among the masses; but I never fall into the temptation of endeavoring to convince or persuade those with whom I speak in private. As I draw a broad line between ordinary language and oratorical language, I draw another line between the numerous hearers and the one hearer with whom I try to keep up a conversation. But I have observed that if I never attempt to convince or persuade in ordinary life, many of my acquaintances, I know not wherefore, fall into the error of trying to convince and persuade me.

The person with whom I was conversing was a young man, a Turk by birth, by religion a Catholic, by his sect an Armenian, by enthusiasm a monk; Oriental in his language, which was shown with glowing images, a Venetian by tact and hospitality; in the depths of his conscience a mystic, like an Arabian sectarian, but in his intercourse with his fellow-creatures extremely tolerant, and perfectly in harmony with the character of our age. He was ill, very ill, and was quite aware of his approaching death. This knowledge produced a natural melancholy, visible in his ideas, which were as severe as morality, as solemn as worship, as poetic as the land where he was born and the earth on which he was about to die, and gave him an infinite perspective of eternity. The conversation I held with him made so lasting an impression on my mind that I can not forget it, and will repeat a portion which much interested me. Many of his thoughts still strengthen me in my internal combats, and increase my hope in a moral renovation analogous to social renovations. The discussion between us made many doubts vanish, which had heretofore passed like shadows through my soul.

"Do you believe," said he to me, "that our moral condition will continue? Do you think we could for so long a time have borne a dead faith in our consciences? All dead ideas must kill the spirit which contains them, as the dead embryo would destroy that which incloses it."

"I have already said so several times," I replied. "I do not believe that the conscience can be maintained alive in the bosom of a faith which is completely dead. The spirit is analogous to nature. And nature does not annihilate—it transforms; it does not kill—it renews. The spirit must be renovated in the renovation of society."

"Renovated!" he exclaimed. "And how will you attempt to create a new religion? Where should you find the apostles who preached, the martyrs who died, where the necessary doctrines, the indispensable sacrifices to a religious transformation? The tree of faith is watered with blood. Humanity, in our epoch, holds labor as a vocation; it does not consider martyrdom a vocation, as it did in the time of our Redeemer. You may drain off even to exhaustion the vital power spent over the machines of labor, you will not find one drop of blood before the altars of faith. The people of to-day appear athletes full of physical energy, but wholly deficient in soul.

"Miracles will not be performed if people do not feel within them the germ of great sentiments. They have ascended the heavens and have snatched the lightning, for they have sufficient moral stature to touch the clouds with their heads. The times of decadence neither create nor invent nor labor. Discouragement and decrepitude are felt in all spheres of activity and in all manifestations of life."

"But I have heard it remarked that people do not grow if they have no ideal."

"It is true. But I think that the ideal should not give birth to fancy and sentiment alone, but to reason. Your ideal is for the imagination only. And, in times of reflection, ideals which are but the offspring of fancy and custom die, as the flowers in the season of fruit."

"You do not believe in miracles?"

"We do not speak of our individual opinions," I answered, "for then our debate would be a dispute; we speak of something higher—we speak of the crisis which at this time is passing over the human spirit. Our own ideas are of less value in comparison with the infinite soul of humanity than the drops suspended from this oar are compared with the immensity of the ocean."

"Very well, but our age does not believe in miracles."

"It is right. Its acquaintance with natural laws has convinced it that these laws can not be for a moment interrupted.

But here is the root of my thesis. You must neither invent nor maintain a religious ideal in absolute opposition to science. The lowest of our faculties—sensibility and fancy—are moved at the sound of the bell, at the sight of the sacred images, at the echo of the organ which raises a hymn to the heavens, at beholding those wonderful Basilicas, like that of St. Mark, adorned with mosaics wherein color exhausts its shades, and crowded with works in which art exhausts its inspirations—monuments in whose vaults have been heard the supplications of ten centuries, and under whose pavements repose the bones of innumerable generations; but, though you may be a poet, though you be moved at these things, reason penetrates through dreams and harmonies; they shall vanish with their cold but incontestable affirmations, leaving you in a perpetual struggle between sensibility and understanding—a struggle which must terminate if we are to be sovereigns of nature, submitting only to truth and science."

"The struggle, oh! the struggle shall be terminated by faith."

"But faith can not contradict probable or evident truths. The ancient gods smiled on the heights of hills crowned with temples and myrtle groves on the shores of seas which seemed to sleep under their protection, among choirs of poets, over an artistic and believing people; but one day science demonstrated that those divinities were contrary to reason, and, in spite of having heroic and invincible peoples, like the Romans, to support them, they all died together at the breath of a new doctrine."

"But with those divinities died the societies that personated them."

"They did not die; they were transformed. Did the Roman law die? Did that classic literature die which is still the model in our academies? Did those plastic arts die which we so often imitate and repeat? Did even those languages die to whose wise combinations we owe all our scientific nomenclature? The only thing which perished was the only thing which believed itself imperishable, the god or the gods of that world."

"And how many tears, how much blood it cost to found the new faith!" replied the priest. "The world reveled in vicious orgies. That Rome, once so powerful, let fall the sword of battle to hold the cup of bacchanalian festivals. The veins of humanity were inflated with the cancerous wine of all concupiscence. To cure such evils nothing less was necessary than the irruption of barbarians and the dethronement of Rome."

"See where you go with the implacable logic of your deductions: to weep the death of Paganism, you, a Catholic priest! Surely in no part of the earth is the soul of the artist so much moved at the disappearance of those beautiful beings, imagined by the poets, and in the marble enriched by sculpture, as here, in this country, at the murmur of the waves of the Adriatic under that heaven which reflects its beauty. But if organisms correspond to the chemico-physico condition of the planet, religions also correspond to the moral condition of the spirit. The world follows its own way and life independent of our abstract conceptions of this existence. And God exists independent of the relation established between His incommunicable Being and our spirits. At present we do not comprehend the world in the same manner as our fathers comprehended it. For them it was immovable; for us it revolves. For them the sun went round the earth; for us the earth moves around the sun. Has nature changed because our conceptions of her have altered? Neither has God changed because our conceptions of Him have been modified. The good, the true, the beautiful exist, independent of all the opinions people form regarding them. In order to approach the ideal, we have but to learn the true, in science as in conscience, and realize with absolute disinterestedness the good in every thing. Religions have served to educate humanity progressively. Their infinite hopes, their salutary terrors, awaken man from the bosom of nature in which he is sleeping to raise him to an interior life much purer and much more exalted. The fragile human spirit thus obtained the idea of the infinite, and felt thus the breath of the divine, as if creating it anew, and in a certain sense redeeming it. There is no reason to doubt it; if the religion of nature was a progress respecting fetichism, and if the religion of the spirit was a progress respecting the religion of nature, why, why imagine, why believe that this permanent revelation has become indifferent or has retrograded?"

"Do you suppose that there can happen any other or any further revelation? God, by an act of His will, by a breath of His nostrils, created the world without evil, and, in the world, man without sin; the guilt falls from the spirit made free upon nature made its slave, sullies the brightness of creation and absorbs humanity; children of men are born subject to sin like their fathers, and the sin is subject to the chastisement created by generations and generations of feeble beings, whose bodies are sadly destroyed by pleasure, and whose souls vanish as shadows of shadows in the abyss; till that same God, known only to one people, descends in mercy to redeem the iniquities of all men, and to reveal himself to all men; and henceforth the air is filled with guardian angels, saints are found for the altars, nature is regenerated by the purity of the Virgin Mother, the spirit enlightened by the divine Word, and the hopes of immortality, shining beyond the tomb, strengthen us with the energy of a life which expands itself into eternity."

"God forbid I should contradict any dogma. I respect them all profoundly. But I deny that they can be sustained by an external authority, powerful and coercive, in this age of liberty and reason. Faith must of necessity spring spontaneously from the soul. It must necessarily affect the conscience, and the conscience the will. Thus the sentiment becomes ingrafted in the mind, and the spirit mingles and diffuses itself with the life, and the life will be true and religious, and the standard of religion will be a living ideal."

"But you do not any where see this realized."

"No; I see, on the contrary, that while civilization most inclines to liberty, religious sects most incline to authority. I see that while the ideas of democratic equality take root most profoundly in the social sphere, they pretend more in the social sphere to deify absurd privileges, opposed to all that is fundamental in our nature. I see plainly that the reverse occurred in Christian times, in that God humiliated Himself even to repair the fallen nature of men; men, calling themselves infallible, aspired to exalt themselves, so as even to improve the nature of God. I see all pervaded by egotism and the utilitarian feeling, when it has become such a necessity for us that the ideal part of our nature, that upon which the heavens only look, should awake and live. Religious sentiments, which ought to be purely spiritual, seem turning to mechanical forces; and the priests, who should hold in their hands and reflect upon our heads the light of the ideal, are but simple functionaries of the State. I see all this with sorrow, for I would that in the aridity and desolation of our lives we should be able to shed some drops of celestial dew to moisten our parched lips, burning with thirst for the infinite."

"But the belief necessitates a definition which embodies it; the definition an authority which imposes and divulges it; the authority a personification which represents it. Faith should not be without dogma; the dogma would not maintain itself without definition; the definition without the church; the church without the Pope; the Pope without the Divine Spirit, which should communicate to him its own infallibility."

"Do you believe that God has chosen a person apart, and privileged, to communicate the truth? I am yet more believing. I believe that as He has extended His light to all orbs, He has given His reason to all spirits. I believe that as He has endowed us with vision by which to behold the external world—and as this vision can not be by any authority either replaced or substituted—He has given us a conscience with which to communicate with the interior world, and that conscience can not be replaced or substituted by any authority. I believe we all see the light, that we all acknowledge it; and that darkness of soul and understanding is as rare and exceptional as are those who have been blind from their birth. Creatures are immersed in universal life; planets and suns float in ether; human souls exist in the Eternal. I believe more; I believe that revelation is eternal, inherent, progressive through all ages; having for its organs all philosophers and poets, who have revealed a truth, and those martyrs who for a truth have died. Thus history illumines itself, life elevates itself to the infinite, the conscience becomes colored by absolute truth, as the iron in the fire. Thus our sentiments unite in all generations, and elevate us to the comprehension of things more exalted; thus alone we draw to our souls the human spirit, and in the human spirit refresh our souls. Thus alone we rise to God, and God communicates intimately with us. Thus only can we be true inhabitants of the Universe, true children of the Great Father, one and identical in all the succession of ages with the progressive development of the human spirit."

"In no way can I conform to your ideas. They appear to me contrary to all truths and justificative of all error. I believe that one people only knew the true God in the ancient world—the Jewish nation; and that only one society has preserved and propagated religion in the modern world—the Catholic Church. Beyond these two vast rays of light, extended through time as the Milky Way through space, I discover only darkness and obscurity which blind and stupefy."

"And the rest of human labor has been lost? And from the rest of the human conscience God is absent? What would you think of my reason if I should say that this goldfinch or this rose owe their life to the Creator, but not this fern or that bat? If we divide into divine and not-divine, we should deliver up the world to Manicheism; and the devil, with reason, would dispute with God a part of creation. If we divide humanity into elect and reprobate, we deliver up society to an arbitrary power more terrible than the antique Destiny. Nitrogen, oxygen, and carbon, which separately destroy, together form the vital atmosphere. So we can no more separate the various revelations of the true and the good, but all together compose the vital air of the human spirit. The prophets did not write in Judea alone — they alone did not drink of the waters of Jordan and Euphrates—they wrote also in India, and slaked their thirst with the waters of the Ganges. To form ideas Jews have contributed, as well as the Egyptian priests, the magi of Babylon, and the sages of Persia. The idea is as the sap, as the blood, as the light, as the electric fluid, as the juices of the earth, as the gases of the atmosphere, as the dew of the planet. The idea recognizes neither nations nor sects nor churches; it passes from the pagoda to the pyramid, and from the pyramid to the synagogue, and from the synagogue to the Basilica, and from the Basilica to the cathedral, and from the cathedral to the university, and from the university to parliament, with the celerity of the lightning which thunders, illumines, burns, and purifies. Christianity has been equally prepared and advanced by the mournful stanzas of Isaiah as by the philosophic dialogues of Plato. To the universal revelation each human race has brought its contingent. The Grecian people thought their life completely original, apart from all other human life, their gods purely national and domestic; yet their chaste Diana had temples in Asia Minor, and their Bacchus, who represented the exaltation and delirium of life in the universe, was intoxicated with the nectar distilled from Indian groves. When the Jew took refuge at the foot of his altars, thinking there he preserved his God and his religion removed from all Pagan temptations, Alexander went to disturb that sad monologue of a people, and to drag behind his war-chariot the Greek divinities to the triumphal music of cymbals and Phrygian flutes—once awakeners of Hellenic gayety—in the bosom of sad, immobile, and pantheistic Asia. The expectation of the Messiah was not a Hebraic hope only, it was also a universal hope. The Sibyl of Cumæ conceived it in her grotto, by the shores of the voluptuous Tyrrhene Sea, in the days when Daniel counted on his fingers the weeks of years wanted to make up his number. And in Posilippo, under the shade of the tall elm-trees, festooned by vines, in sight of the foam-crested waves, from which rose the sweet voices of the Grecian sirens, among the bacchanalian dances, hearing the flageolet of the god Pan, and surrounded by the chorus of virgins who twined garlands of flowers upon the altars, smoking with the fragrance of myrrh—Virgil announced the universal redemption at the same time that the Baptist declared it, clothed with camel's-hair, mortified with sackcloth, in the grand desolation of the desert. Athens with her arts, Rome with her laws, Alexandria with her science, have contributed as much to the Christian revelation as Jerusalem with her God. Do not forget that these are evident truths, confirmed by all history. Be not as the Jew, who shuts himself up in his Bible, and believes that since the creation of the human race not one single religious truth has been added to the Judaical doctrines. Christianity, more human, and at the same time more divine, has taken all the Bible, and has added to it the Gospel. Why shall not we add to the Gospel the Renaissance, Philosophy, and the Revolution, which have raised in the social sphere these three Christian words —Liberty, Equality, Fraternity? Leonardo di Vinci painted Bacchus and the Baptist in his pictures, which represented the spring-time of that modern spirit. Raphael depicted in the lineaments of the Grecian goddesses the inspired and holy soul of the Christian virgins. Michael Angelo placed the two choirs of sibyls and of prophets on the vault of the Sistine Chapel. The human spirit is like the universe; one like God; and God, Nature, and the Spirit are the eternal Trinity which illumine the pages of history. Let us not separate from them—neither from the Spirit, nor from Nature, nor from God."

These words, if they did not convince, at least moved my companion. I had excited myself in an extraordinary manner by the warmth of my own expressions. So I took the hand the young priest extended to me, pressed it, and left him absorbed in his own reflections. The night was calm and serene, the stars shone in the heavens and the phosphorus in the water, the breath of spring refreshed the ambient air, and wafted the echoes of the town and country to the broad expanse of the lagune, inviting me to meditate on this evident truth—that nature continues tranquil, immovable, and beautiful, regardless of the disputes or discords of men.

H

Chapter VIII.

THE GOD OF THE VATICAN.

Do you really believe that Paganism has been rooted out and destroyed in this land of Rome? Near my lodgings stands proudly the Pantheon of all the gods. The Catholic genius has not been content with exalting it and binding it as a diadem to the Basilica, mother of all Christian Basilicas, but has also converted it into a temple of all the saints. Prayer is there hushed upon the lips. There enters too much light by the large unroofed circle which crowns the rotunda to suffer the soul to give itself up to meditation and preparation for spiritual exercises. Consecrated, full of altars, converted into a church; like the great mosque of Cordova, it protests against innovations, and sighs sorrowfully for its ancient worship.

Every thing is thus in Rome. Paganism has been transformed, but has not been destroyed. The months of the year and the days of the week preserve the numbers of the ancient divinities, of the ancient Cæsars, of the ancient Roman numeration, and we have not dared to take the calendar of the French Republic, which appears to have been conceived in the bosom of creation. The two solstices of summer and winter we still celebrate with festivals analogous to the classic festivals. Adonis is born, dies, rises again, when the corn is sown, shoots, or is in ear. The feast of Candlemas, dedicated with many tapers to the Virgin, like the festivals of Lupercal, is consecrated to light. The Romans wave torches under the government of the Popes, just as the Pagans waved them under the dominion of the Cæsars, and chanted hymns to the light, which have changed their form, but the essence of which is unaltered. When the Pope, seated on his chair of state, is carried on men's shoulders, enveloped in magnificent brocades, his head crowned with a jeweled tiara, in his hand the precious crosier, at his feet a mitred crowd, gay with many-colored mantles—one returns to the days of ancient story, when Oriental customs and Oriental luxury, introduced by the Cæsars, came from Syria to the Eternal City.

I certainly do not speak of this in order to deny or combat the virtue of the Catholic faith. What I purpose is to deny that originality which all those attribute to it who are ignorant of the working of the antique spirit on Christianity, which was partly the cause of its continuation, and, up to a certain point, of its purification. The apotheosis of heroes has been replaced by the canonization of the saints. Any one might believe he was listening to a Catholic poet when he hears Lucanus say before the tomb of Pompey how the faithful went to pray over the dead who refused to offer incense to the gods of the Capitol. Is hell not a Pagan creation, as the demons were an invention of magic? Satan has passed through Deism before passing through Christianity. Christ is the fundamental conception of the Christian faith. The expectations of a Messiah were not the exclusive hopes of the race of Israel in the age of the coming of Christ—they were universal aspirations. When St. John wrote the Apocalypse, the Stoics also wrote theirs, and words of despair were uttered by two choirs at the same moment, and in Pagan heaven and Christian heaven alike is found religious terror at the speedy termination of the world. We have not banished from us the number of gods worshiped by the ancients. The gods have been converted into angels, says St. Augustine—

"*Deos quos nos familiarius angelós dicimus.*"

Why then so much antipathy for the antique world, to those same ideas which are the heraldry of our nobility and the genealogy of our ideas? Why, do we not even receive holy water? Do we not collect votive offerings in our chapels? Have we not processions according to the Greek custom? Do we not on the vigil of St. John kindle bonfires, after the fashion of the Rhodians, the Corinthians, the great founders of the Hellenic colonies? Our personality has not come by a sudden creation; it is, like the planet we inhabit, the slow work of ages, the work of generations in their turn. So, when I see passing beneath the triumphal arches of marble, whose succession composes the Vatican—when I look upon the majestic form of the Pope, amid so much luxury and the acclamations of the people—I can not help acknowledging to myself that Papal authority, so great and so universal, does not proceed from the Christian doctrine, so democratic, especially in its early ages, but from the superiority which antique Rome exercised by her power and her conquests over all the cities in the world.

What domination can there be like the empire of Pius IX.? It no longer is extensive on the earth. Revolution has divided his possessions, and has reduced them first to Rome, then to the Vatican. But no one can supplant him—no one who in the exaltation of his own faith could believe himself with power pre-eminent over the human conscience, and sufficient authority to interpret on the earth the sentiments and the will of the heavens. No Pope, but this one, has been bold enough to separate himself from the Universal Church, from the Œcumenical Council solemnly convoked, to proclaim a new dogma of faith, a dogma so transcendent as the dogma of the Immaculate Conception of Mary, and, moreover, to except a creature from general human laws, to add to Christianity—that veiled in such a manner the pure deistic idea of the Bible—another religion which exalted a creature to the heights where alone can shine the Creator.

Pius IX. has reigned many years. His predecessor, the aged Gregory XVI., notwithstanding all his divine power over consciences, had not an equal authority over nature, and at a feast of the Ascension was seized with a severe constipation which rapidly brought him to the grave. Rossi thought he described this Pope in three words, calling him "an Austrian patriarch." But the election of a Pontiff appears to move the lips to murmur prayers, to surround the altars with clouds of incense, and to lead men to ask God in all manners for His divine light, indispensable to a suitable election; and, notwithstanding, for the election of Pius IX., regiments of artillery moved in the Marches, and vessels of the Imperial Austrian Marine on the waters of Ancona. If the maritime and land armies were moved, so perhaps were the angels of the celestial court. Not less in commotion were the embassadors, whose character of double-dealing and duplicity, if it gives them great aptitude to discourse with kings, ought not to be useful to them in communication with the heavens. Among the embassadors, those of great and exceptional influence were the embassadors of the courts of France and of Austria; the one too timid, the other too daring. The Count Broglia spoke in the following terms to the Sardinian Government of the representative of Louis Philippe in the days of the Conclave: "The Count Rossi is of a feverish activity, and imagines himself to have very nearly the power of the Holy Ghost." The French embassador opposed his veto to all the cardinals marked by their attachment for the Jesuits and for Austria; in the same manner as the Austrian embassador opposed his veto to all the cardinals stigmatized by an adherence to France and to the modern spirit. Among the number of those that Austria was disposed to prohibit was counted the then Cardinal Mastai, now Pius IX. If the prince of the Church, charged to give this veto formally, had arrived in time at the Conclave, there never would have been a Mastai Pope.

On the 14th of June, 1846, the cardinals directed their steps toward the Quirinal. Gregory XVI. had been buried but a few days previously, his corpse insulted, and his memory reviled by the people. The Conclave preferred the saloons of the Quirinal to those of the Vatican, because, while it hoped for the inspirations of the Holy Spirit in every place, it feared that in the palace, *par excellence* Pontifical, divine inspirations would not sufficiently counteract the effluvias of the fever. In the procession from the church where the Conclave was assembled, to the Quirinal where the Conclave was to sit in council, the cardinals were altogether deficient in the respect they owed to each other; and as a few drops of rain began to fall, they entered the palace without order and without any composure. At length the hour for voting arrived. The Conclave was divided. There were various indispensable examinations. In none of them resulted the number of thirty-seven votes necessary to enable a Pope to mount the throne, and from thence to interpret the will of Heaven. The last scrutiny took place after long delays. Pius IX. was the examiner, and on him it devolved to read in a loud voice the numbers of the voters. Accordingly he drew forth the scraps of paper, unfolded and read them; his strength failed, his voice faltered, tears fell from his eyes, profound sobs convulsed his throat, until, at the end, fearful of fainting, he gave up the examination to another cardinal, and, retiring to a place apart, covered his face with both hands. At the conclusion he had the thirty-seven votes indispensable to his proclamation as sovereign Pontiff. Before he was officially proclaimed, he turned to the cardinals, one by one, and begged, prayed, and insisted that they should remove that cup from his lips. He seemed to have been taken with a secret presentiment that he would be the last king on the temporal throne of St. Peter. The Conclave did not dare to accede to his desire, and confirmed him in his high dignity. Pius IX. accepted, and, after having done so, he prostrated himself before an altar, and murmured many fervent prayers for the space of half an hour. Afterward he returned to the Sacred College, and the Holy Ghost descended on that head as its nest upon the earth.

In times of decadence, power always searches for minds of a niggardly temperament, the undecided, and above all those who have passed their lives in a sort of twilight, without being able to determine for any of the bolder measures. Innocent III., in an epoch favorable to the Pontificate and to his own power and authority, imperiously ruled the world; but in a period unfavorable to this same power, the firmness, the resolution of Innocent—reproduced in Boniface VIII.—only served to bring upon the cheek of the Papacy the rude buffet of Nogaret. Feeble and obscure, his debility and insignificance enabled Mastai to keep apart from the great differences which had on a thousand occasions divided the Sacred College and the Conclave. His had been a varied existence. From being an armed soldier, he became a spiritual warrior. His abode in Chili was worthy of a prophet, worthy of a martyr. But his ideas had always continued in the uncertainty of the dawn. If we examine his conduct after the manner of Espoleto, Pius IX. was a Jesuit; but if we scrutinize character, as would Imola, Pius IX. was a Liberal. This contradiction of ideas and character served him admirably to obtain the suffrages of the College, and to exalt himself to the highest religious authority that can be exercised in our age, and which, notwithstanding its evident decay, serves yet to express its ancient splendor.

If the Cardinal Mastai desired the tiara, he did not demand it of his colleagues. Not one supplication, except to be allowed to reject it—no word which was not a renunciation and withdrawal. So it is not strange that some have compared Pius IX. with Sixtus V. There were relations between the ancestors of both Popes; rivalries in Rome, and rivalries much dreaded between the embassador of France and the Spanish embassador; emulation within the Sacred College, and an almost warlike rivalry between the family of Medici and that of the Farnese; inquietude and fearful apprehension in all Italy; peculiarities that, if they coincide with and are analogous to the circumstances of the election of the reigning Pontiff, do not go so far as to confound two characters truly opposed and contradictory; for the one was imperious and despotic, even to the constituting a Cæsarian Papacy, and the other humble even to be the docile instrument, perhaps against his will, at all events against his conscience, of Jesuitical depravity.

Sixtus V. mounted the throne when the Renaissance was expiring, and the great Catholic reaction was approaching; Pius IX came to the Pontifical dignity when the reaction of the Holy Alliance was expiring, and the world was returning to revolutionary ideas. In the election of Pius IX., as in that of Sixtus V., that cardinal was successful whose triumph seemed the most improbable. None of the colleagues of either had thought of them on entering, and although Pius was elected simply by a majority, and Sixtus by unanimity and homage, both were able to pacify the adverse spirit in the Roman Conclave and the rivalries of European politics. But here ends the analogy.

Sixtus V. was educated on the mountains; Pius IX. in the court; Sixtus was the son of a gardener, and Pius the son of a noble; Sixtus had adopted in his youth—almost in his childhood—the habit of a monk, and Pius the uniform of a soldier; the youth of the one was passed in the severity and retirement of the cloister, the youth of the other in the freedom of society; the former Pope was of a pure Sclavonian family, which took refuge on the shores of the Adriatic on flying from the Turks; the present Pontiff is of a pure Italian stock, which, by the modest aid of retail commerce, by connections, by political ardor, and by warlike enterprise, raised itself to the dignity of the nobility; Sixtus V. was a preacher; his eloquence showed the temperature of his character, which was sanguine, bold, and unpolished; Pius IX., too, is a preacher; his eloquence is also abundant, but melodious and mellifluous; the consciousness of power held possession of the mind of the great ancient Pope; the habit of submission is the essential characteristic, of the reigning Pope, implacable before all powers, unyielding with all sovereigns when they are opposed to his opinions, and now completely submitting, after some feeble resistance, to the will of the reactionaries and the Jesuits.

The mother of young Mastai gave him an excellent education. But a most terrible infirmity—epilepsy—prevented his education from bearing all the expected fruits. It was in the time of the wars of Napoleon and of his victories when Mastai began his youth and embraced the military career. But he loved adventures better than battles, and cared more about the color of his uniform than the temper of his sword. He loved poetry to excess, even devoting most of his time to its study; and in poetry it is certain, from his character, that he preferred Metastasio to Dante. At last he renounced the military service, entered the Church, and applied himself to the duties of a preacher. His attractive figure, his majestic air, his prominent features, sweetened by a smile of the purest benevolence, his nervous and impressionable nature, the rather sickly sensibility of his temperament, the liveliness of his poetic imagination, the tone of his voice—the most mellow and sonorous I have ever heard, when, for instance, he intones the mass in St. Peter's, or gives the benediction in the Vatican—all these qualities secured him undoubted advantages as an orator, as one to be listened to and beloved by the multitude. Some still remember his nocturnal sermons in the public square, half-illumined by torches, with a great crucifix on his shoulder; before him a discolored skull, on which was burning a yellow candle; in his hands, at one moment the benediction of the Church, at another the malediction, with truly tragic gestures; and on his lips an eloquence which charmed the Italian people because of its sentiment and poetry. These brilliant gifts made him much admired in Chili, where he was attached to an apostolic mission. But in Chili his words could not excite souls as in Italy, because he was deficient in a profound knowledge of the Spanish language, and in the mastery of its accent. Yet he speaks Spanish fluently, and to Spanish ears his accent sounds as if it were American. I have only heard him speak in Latin. He presided over two great dioceses, and in both he observed a different administration. In the first diocese he disinterred the body of a Liberal: conduct which drew upon him the odium of those districts, and he had to fly at the time of the first revolution, which burst forth in 1830-1; but in the second diocese he yielded to the influence of his family, all of them Liberal, and was tolerant and benevolent to Liberals. Such were the principal events of the life of the Pope before mounting the throne of the Papacy.

Pius IX. still preserves the poetic passion of his youthful years. He loves the fine arts, like almost all the princes who have sat on the chair of St. Peter. There is much grace in his conversation, great sweetness in his face, much benevolence in his character, and in his voice all the charm of music. But his sudden impulses are dangerous, as they force him to rapid and inconsiderate changes—such as the flight from the Vatican in 1848. He sometimes acknowledges that he has lost himself by his impetuosity; but he does not repent, believing, reasonably enough, that repentances which come too late tend to nothing. In such times he reproves himself with expressions of bitter irony, which fall from his lips on his oppressed heart. Irony and mockery are very remarkable in the conversation of Pius IX., touching even upon religious subjects. A Spanish embassador wished him on a certain occasion to canonize a saint of his country; and, in order to persuade him, he told of numerous miracles the saint was reported to have performed. The Pope for his only reply asked one question—"Could he put the head on the shoulders of one decapitated, and make him speak and walk again?" "No, Holy Father, no, that would be too much." "That," rejoined the Pope, "seems to me the only miracle that would be truly great, and I ought to tell you that as yet I have not happened to see it."

Like all lovers of art, Pius IX. loves great emotions. His popularity and his triumphs delight him. I have beheld the Pope radiant with joy and satisfaction when receiving the homage of Catholic delegates from all nations—with the same sort of eagerness with which one expands the lungs, after coming from a suffocating air, to inhale the freshness and oxygen of a healthy atmosphere. All pomp and luxury, tiaras studded with brilliants, mantles strewn with showers of pearls, rich and costly crosses, all the adornments of his exalted office, enchant him, as jewels and fine attire do a lady of high society. I shall not exaggerate this quality—as Petruccelli has done in his picture of Pius IX.—when I say that I observed how happy he looked when the crowd were pressing upon his steps and the Pontifical jewels shone on his majestic person. It is true that the wisest heads would be unsettled in such clouds of incense, at such servile adulation, the number of bishops which surround him, the Oriental court which attends him, the choirs which sing his praises, the varieties of music which fill the air with harmony in his honor, the pilgrims arrived from the most remote regions of the earth to hear the echo of his words—to catch the gesture of a benediction, the furtive shadow of a smile—the infinite homage which makes of the solitary old man of the Vatican more than a privileged and exalted mortal, a living god on the face of the earth!

To startle the world with great audacity in the religious and political spheres was always his desire; to leave an illustrious name among men, as well as among sovereign Pontiffs, has been ever his ambition. He had no great eagerness to reconcile the Gospel with liberty. The pulpit of the people was turning to Christ, the hope and consolation of the oppressed. The nails of His cross, the thorns of His crown, the gall of His cup, ceased to be the boast of the powerful, and became the true teacher of the humble. Democracy received on its forehead the sign of Christian baptism, and Christianity took the character of the great promoter of the democratic movement of this century. Joyous tremblings passed at the same time through the hearts of the pious, as well as through those of Liberal people. For those, it was impossible to believe in the durability of a belief, compatible with all the transformations of ideas, and with the numerous unfoldings of the modern spirit. For those, the liberty which necessitates moral restraints more than material restraints, holds a rigorous security in the evangelical spirit, a spiritual counterpoise to the perils which might be engendered by its successes. The thought of reconciling the Gospel to liberty was a great idea. But if Pius IX. conceives great ideas with facility, he also abandons them at the first obstacle; and then, when he encounters obstacles to liberty, he yields in his efforts for liberty. Great error! To renounce liberty because it may engender excesses would be to renounce the air because it is the element of winds and hurricanes!

The obstacles which restrained Pius IX. were principally those which arose in his court, and, indeed, among his courtiers. Thus it is that, in his Liberal tendencies, he found around him nothing but difficulties, and in his efforts at religious reaction every facility and assistance. The Jesuits, who swore war to the death against him, put themselves at his orders and surrounded his throne. The European reaction, which had not forgiven him his advanced policy of 1847 and 1848, delivered to him the direction of its thoughts and of its conscience. The Pope was raised to be the High-Priest of the Holy Alliance. But his ambition was beyond this. His ambition was to found new dogmas, to bring a greater volume of divine ideas to the Church, and of exalted piety to the faithful; to oppose with decided negatives the democratic and progressive spirit; to assemble Œcumenical Councils after the manner of pious ages; to create a new authority in the Church, and an absolute power over consciences which was not held in the preceding ages and will be unequaled in the future. Such was the desire of Pius IX.

It is easy to understand that he designed to compensate the defeat in the political arena by a victory in the religious world. But, in order to attain this victory, it became necessary to conform religious ideas to the spirit of the age, because ideas can not exist remote from the spirit of our epoch. An illustrious theological school had existed in Italy which treated of the harmony of religion and reason, of providence with freedom, of modern democracy with the ancient Pontificate, of the natural law with the revealed law—in a word, of Catholicism with progress. An illustrious priest, of talents, perhaps, as profound as St. Thomas, and of equal enthusiasm for a theocratic society, in which the direction of the world should be confided to moral force and to theological creeds, spoke with tears in his eyes, and with sobbing voice, of all the moral ulcers in the Church. The separation between the clergy and the people, on account of the dead language spoken by the former; the isolation of religious society, which flourished when supported by popular suffrage and free association; the subservience of the civil powers, which had converted the pure Christian spirit into instruments of tyranny with the higher classes and of vassalage in the lower; the tendency of the priesthood to close its conscience to the light of new ideas and its mind to the consideration of new social changes—all this and more he said; but he found the Pontifical Court always deaf to the voice of the popular desire.

Another priest, inferior in policy but not in greatness, wished to separate the Church of the State from sects, to elevate her to the true ideal of humanity. According to this man, reason and revelation were identical, and Catholicism universal, not only for what it embraces that is divine, but also for what it has that is human; the evangelical doctrines and the modern ideas are one in essence; the cause of the divorce between the Church and the age being the bad understanding caused by the conduct of the clergy, as well as by the turbulent ideas of the revolution. But this most eloquent priest would have applied energetic remedies to the evils of the Church: to the temporal power, the separation of civil life and ecclesiastical life; to the reactionary education of the clergy, a scientific education; to Jesuitism, which maintains a great number of mechanical springs and contrivances to move the people, the pure moral conscience which he directed toward absolute perfection; preaching on the ancient principles—truly evangelical preaching in the ears of the multitude and in the bosom of nature—taking his views from the living fountain of the moral conscience, and scattering them like refreshing dew on all spirits, to incline them to a religious transformation, analogous to that produced in the world by the first appearance of Christianity.

As some men, who were imbued with Rationalism, contested the impossibility of this reconciliation, on account of the incompatibility between modern science and the miracles of the Middle Ages, between reason and supernatural revelations, the philosopher replied that such sentiments arose from a false conception of miracles and prophecy, from considering them as real acts which actually occurred, when they were symbols of systems to come, of regenerative periods in the successive life of the spirit and of the planet. And what miracles and prophecies were really intended to explain is the arrival of an epoch in which natural revelation and religious revelation will mingle as the rapid and almost miraculous intuition will blend with maturity and profound reflection; as the sensible will be confounded with the intelligible, each one of our sensations being a thought; as, for the perfection of our language, ideas are confounded with words, in the same manner that Christ by His incarnation in our being mingled in His own person the divine with the human nature.

When a religion is separated from its time and from the progress of its time, alas! it perishes. It is impossible that a liberal age should harmonize with an epoch of absolutism in religion; an age in which the living conscience is progressive, and a religion drawn from departed traditions; an age of right, and a religion of compulsion; an age which unfolds itself to study all sciences, and a religion which closes itself against every thing which is not theological. In such a condition, in a crisis so fearful and supreme, either the people become fossilized like the Moors, who never change their fatalism, or religions decay and disappear, as disappeared the Pagan religion, when, on account of its sensual character, it could not satisfy the spiritual thirst awakened in the human soul by sad misfortunes and consciousness of having been deceived, and by the sublime truths of immortal philosophy.

How great would Pius IX. have been if, on feeling that his religious supremacy was incompatible with all political authority, with all political power, he had abdicated that authority, resigned that power, exchanged the purple of the Cæsars for the robe of the pulpit; renewed in the most exalted purity the faith of his ancestors; organized evangelically the Church of Christ; united the people in religious assemblies; exposed to the world the power of despots, the pride of aristocrats, and the avarice of the wealthy; if he had given to the wronged right, and to the slave his liberty, assisted the new birth of Italy, the resurrection of Poland, sent missionaries of the Spirit against the new Pagan sensuality, against the implacable selfishness of the governing classes, and maintained with profound conviction that Liberty, Equality, and Fraternity are not solely evangelical formulas, but also social truths capable of creating a new earth, and of extending above it new heavens of blessed and perennial radiance! Then had he been able to celebrate the new resurrection of the modern spirit; then had he raised his voice as a hymn of triumph; then had he seen by faith, at the gates of the churches of the Middle Ages, the angel clothed with white and resplendent with beauty whom the holy women beheld beside the sepulchre, announcing that Christ was not there, that he had risen indeed!

"*Resurrexit, non est hic.*"

The proof of how much he would have been able to accomplish with these great means is to be found in what he actually did with poor means, with timid reforms, with slight and very feeble palliatives. An amnesty which demanded the servile formula of a previous oath; a commission nominated expressly to study indispensable reforms; a consulting-chamber composed of a representative for each province, to appoint deputies, and to discuss the election of the Pontiff; a council of a hundred members, who were to nominate a senate of nine—all these timid announcements of social renovation awakened Italy; produced liberal codes of laws and reactionary principles, as those of Modena and of Parma; opened in Sicily the doors of her dungeons; gave a breath of liberty instead of the poisonous air of Naples; obliged strangers to retire from Ferrara before Pontifical protest; strengthened the arm of Charles Albert for the cause of independence; brought down Guizot in Paris, and Metternich in Vienna; proclaimed the five days of Milan, which were five days of saving martyrdom; cheered amid the deepest shadows of the lagunes the fainting soul of Venice; transformed with a new belief the hearts most closed against all noble sentiments; infused into the Italians their ancient valor; and in a few days, of the hundred thousand Austrians sent to oppress their country, four thousand were corpses, twenty-seven thousand wounded or useless, the remainder dispersed. Those uncertain words of liberty, uttered upon the heights of the Vatican, had poured new blood into the veins, new ideas into the conscience of heretofore lethargic Europe. The bells, which sounded for vespers, rang out also for the downfall of tyranny.

But in this supreme moment Pius IX. remembered he was a Pope, and a Pope after the old fashion. In a war between the Austrians and the Italians, although all the right was on the part of the one, and all the wrong on the part of the other, the Pope felt that both were Catholics. At the same time that the King of Naples abandoned the Italian cause, on account of sad territorial competitions, for the sake of a booty to be gained from the engagement to take arms, Pius IX. froze the blood in the veins of his nation by refusing to give the support of his troops or to bless the combatants in the most sacred of causes—that of Italy; and afterward convoked the Catholic powers, demanded their assistance, pointed out to them the way to Rome; beheld them, without emotion, destroy great monuments, immolate pious Catholics; and, amid ruined buildings and heaps of corpses, he was carried back to rest himself on his earthly throne, propped up by the bayonets of foreign legions!

From the day on which Pius IX. returned from the proscription of Rome, supported by foreign soldiers, he can not be held to have represented the evangelical spirit of the early Christians—he rather personifies the theocratic spirit of the antique Asiatic Pontiffs. And, nevertheless, those who profess the Christian religion with faith and sincerity are quite ignorant of that which can move the world when allied with liberty. In modern history it has happened that the strictest Catholics detest liberty, while those called Liberal Catholics are apt to fall into heresy; neither the one nor the other having found the means of reconciling the spirit of our age with the religion of our fathers; yet both the Old and the New Testament maintain republican traditions. It is known that in the organization of the illustrious tribe of Judah, the kings represented the incongruity of the Mosaic traditions with the ideas and ceremonies of the rest of the people—so much so that the prophet represented with austere republican vigor the pure idea of Israel. I repeat it, modern eloquence of the tribune may draw republican sentiments from the Holy Scriptures, as they were taken by the founders of the American democracy, whose renown, like that of all glorious consolidations, increases with ages. The people of Israel asked for a king, and God denied their request. Different warnings directed them to their true King, the God of Abraham, declared by the mouth of Samuel. A king will dishonor and oppress; will make you his soldiers, his grooms, and lackeys; will despise you, and mix his gall in the leaven of your bread; convert the people into beasts of burden, and make them forge instruments of war, as well as tools for agriculture; will cultivate without cessation for the royal advantage, grow corn-fields in the sweat of their brow, and with their blood water the fields of battle. He will take your children to divert him — to intoxicate him with their songs and flatterings. You will sow and he will reap; you will plant and he will gather; you will work and he will enjoy; your fields will be granaries for his courtiers, and your vineyards degraded by the orgies of his creatures; your gains will belong to him, and you yourselves under his sceptre will be but an assemblage of serfs.

The emotion that an ebullition of liberal tendency in Pius IX. has produced in the world, proves to what point progressive convictions would make way in the minds of the multitude if they were disseminated by the Church. But the heart saddens when it feels that, if the Pope can raise his voice against kings, he could also raise it in the name of principles more reactionary than those of monarchs—in the name of that theocracy whose tutelage Europe shakes off in proportion as the outline of civil rights is unfolded and human reason is matured. These monarchies have become odious, for they do not correspond to the present state of our culture and civilization — to the mysterious essence of the modern spirit; but one of the causes of the continuance of these institutions—one of the chief causes—is the tremendous opposition they offer to theocracy, to the predominant policy and rule of the sacerdotal power over human society. While the monarchy created civil principles, the theocracy sheltered itself behind its religious principles, and persisted in holding minds in serfdom. For this kings exist: because they struggle with Popes, because they dissolve bodies like the Templars, because they expel Jesuits, because they oppose civil life to theocratic life. The voice of the sovereign Pontiff, when it fought against the liberty of modern peoples—against the independence of Italy—against the secularization of European communities—was but a voice from the tomb, lost in the independent spirit of the nineteenth century, whose enlightenment never, never will accommodate itself with theocracy —with that spectre of the Middle Ages.

The man capable of dreaming of a Pontifical restoration— of that which is as contrary to kings as to the minds of the people—is Cardinal Antonelli, whom I saw for the first time on Palm Sunday, 1866, in the Basilica of St. Peter. I asked one of the noble guards stationed near me which was the Cardinal, and he replied that he would point him out to me when he passed. With much kindness, the recollection of which is fresh and pleasing, he passed me over to the other side, making way for me between the files of soldiers, where the Vicar of Christ was to stop, according to custom. A Frenchman near me, with an elegant and intelligent lady, shared in my desire to scrutinize the face of the Cardinal from that place, where either chance or intention had brought them. The Frenchman was very communicative, and made a thousand observations about every thing, some graceful, some flippant, all exaggerated—expressions carefully moderated by the lady with much ability. He had one idol in literature—Heine; and one hatred in politics—the Cardinal Antonelli.

The day was extremely hot, notwithstanding that it was early in April, and my companion, who had just crossed with much difficulty the great square of St. Peter, said, wiping his heated face with his handkerchief, "How hot it is outside, and how cool in the Cathedral! Heine was right; when, on hot and suffocating days like this, you enter a church, you can not do less than exclaim, 'What a beautiful religion for summer is the Catholic!' Coming here I met a peasant beating a scriptural ass, and he was saying to the poor animal, reminding me of Heine, 'Suffer, suffer, because thy parents ate forbidden barley in Paradise.' And Rome can not compare herself with the Paradise described by the great poet, where the sunflowers bear pastry, and the birds, ready roasted, come to you with salt-cellars in their beaks." I affected not to hear all this chatter, nor to observe the numerous sleeve-pullings of the lady, who vainly endeavored to change the conversation, and I said, "Are you personally acquainted with Cardinal Antonelli?" "I do not know him personally, but I can fancy what he is like. Morally I know him from memory—from having read Liverani."

"I do not know that author."

"He is a chanoine of Santa Maria Maggiore, a true priest; in his conscience he is a perfectly pious man; in his life an austere anchorite; in his origin a peasant, converted into a preacher. Agriculture is propitious to the prelates and dignitaries of the Church. Sixtus V. was not only a shepherd, he was the son of a gardener. And the Catholic Church occupies herself with such puerilities that she has tried to prove —as if it were a question of the highest importance—that he kept goats instead of pigs, and that the animals under his crook were not really his property, but belonged to his master."

"What trouble you give yourself, Henri," said the lady, "to calumniate Catholicism in her own Capital, and in her grand Basilica!"

In order to support the observations of the lady, I said, "One must see these great monuments with the mind full of the emotions awakened by each one of their stones. To see the Mosque of Cordova, you must be inspired with the spirit of the Middle Ages, and to see the Parthenon of Athens, with the spirit of Paganism."

The Frenchman understood the force of my remark, and became slightly irritated.

"If any thing proves to me with irrefragable demonstration the decadence of Catholicism, it is the extreme sensitiveness with which it bestows an anti-Catholic character to every ob-

I

servation more or less just upon the Pope and his court. He would have something to do who should seek to prove by dogmas the kind of cattle kept by Sixtus V.! Would the flock of goats be more ecclesiastic and orthodox than a drove of pigs?"

I, agreeing in the justice and even in the grace of this remark, changed the conversation, and inquired about the book of Liverani.

"It is dedicated to the Comte de Montalembert, who desires the restoration, that is to say, Milan and Venice under the feet of the Croatians; the Quadrilateral put as an Austrian horse-shoe on the Arms of Italy; and to see all patriots dispersed and wandering through the world."

"We have not been long in Rome," said the lady; "your imprudence will soon oblige us to leave."

"Do not be afraid; we can speak in French, and they will not understand us. A friend of mine, who lately left the Cardinal Antonelli, told me he speaks French detestably. And if Cardinal Antonelli speaks our language so badly, fancy how it is spoken and understood by the common people."

"Speak in French, then," I said.

"It is not extraordinary that Cardinal Antonelli expresses himself in the idiom of the Revolution, when he speaks equally ill in the language of theology. Father Liverani relates that in the Matins for the Nativity, in 1859, he heard him sing

'Erútus de potestate tenebrarum,'

putting the accent on the second syllable, when he should have sung

'*Érutus de potestate tenebrarum,*'
putting the accent on the first syllable."

Latin, when spoken by the French, is in our ears an almost unintelligible language; so I could not help laughing at hearing him criticise a grammatical error in the worst of pronunciations.

"What Antonelli understands profoundly is domestic economy. Sonnino, his native village, has been made the chief business city in the Roman States. It is a plantation of officials: Giacomo Antonelli, Secretary of State and Prefect of the holy Apostolic Palaces, native of Sonnino; Count Filippo Antonelli, Chancellor of the Exchequer, native of Sonnino; Count Luigi Antonelli, *Conservador* of Rome, native of Sonnino—you could write a whole litany of Antonellis. As Diocletian was Cæsar, Diocletian Pontiff, Diocletian Tribune, Diocletian Consul; so Antonelli is Administrator, Antonelli Chancellor, Antonelli Diplomatist, Antonelli Soldier, Antonelli Cardinal, Antonelli enemy of modern civilization, Antonelli monopolizer of the Holy Ghost, Antonelli Pope of the Pope."

I began to observe that the garrulous talk of the Frenchman was compromising me, and as there was a sudden movement among the people, I withdrew from the spot, when a noise and murmur among the crowd foretold the approach of the Holy Father. Cardinal Antonelli came close to me, pausing for some minutes just in front, forming part of the procession of Cardinals and Bishops which partly precedes the Pope and partly surrounds his chair. Antonelli appeared to me to be tall and strong—a huntsman rather than a Cardinal—a mountaineer, but no courtier. Eyes dark as night, a prominent nose, full lips, a lemon-colored complexion, a rude and rugged physiognomy, a daring character, a robust constitution; and his attitudes and gestures—according to my impressions—proclaimed a man long habituated to command imperiously, and to be obeyed without resistance. But I should also declare, he seemed to me to be a person of extreme vulgarity.

I recalled my historical lectures, remembered the list of those illustrious Cardinals, of those Pontifical Ministers, described in the admirable history of the Popes, during the sixteenth and seventeenth centuries, by Ranke—a work which deserves great praise from the most devoted Catholics. I thought of Gallio di Como, who directed political power with so much ability in two consecutive Pontificates; Rusticucci, as severe in his life as in his morals; Santorio, firm in principles, pure in habits, energetic for his friends, inflexible toward his enemies, superior in his exalted solitude to human passions; Madruzzi, the Cato of the Sacred College; Sirlet, so learned in all sciences, and especially in philological science, who conversed equally with doctors and with children, who bought fleeces of wool from the little shepherds on condition of teaching them the Christian doctrine; Carlo Borromeo, a saint whose memory will never be effaced from Milan, and from the mountains near the Lago Maggiore; Torres, who concluded a league against the Turks, and whose victory was called the battle of Lepanto; Bellarmino, the first of controversialists and of grammarians; Maffei, the historian of the conquest of the Portuguese Indies by Christianity; Felipe de Neri, the founder of the order of illustrious orators, who seemed called to restore religion in the European conscience; when the great Sixtus V.—always alive to improvement—fertilized the Roman hills with flowing waters, making their gardens bloom with flowers, and erected stately monuments; when Fontana raised the obelisk before St. Peter's, terminating it with the Christian Crucifix; when Patrizi harmonized the Catholic theology with philosophical traditions, and reconciled Moses with Hermes; when Torquato Tasso breathed the last accents of the Catholic Muse, and Guido and Domenichino showed the exquisite beauty of painting; and to the echo of the sublime music of Palestrina the spiritual worship—already nearly extinguished—was rekindled, and received new vitality.

Grün compared Cardinal Antonelli to the prelates of Benevento, judged with so much harshness by Montesquieu, and who, while Pope Benedict XIII. prayed before the statue of St. Vincent Ferrer, ran from monastery to monastery, kissed the hands of the friars, performed extreme penance, despising all pleasures and all earthly pomps, gave themselves up to ambition, to wealth, and the follies of the world. The character of the Pope is a radical contradiction—most radical—to that of the Cardinal of Sonnino, as the character of Benedict XIII. was a radical contradiction to that of the Cardinal of Benevento.

Pius IX., whose election was so unexpected, imagined himself called by God to work miracles and do all sorts of wonders; and from the first day of his Pontificate he was ambitious of doing good. Extremely sensitive by natural temperament, epileptic by constitution, incapable of violent hatred, without strong passions, moral from habit, of a lively fancy, gifted with flowing language and a clear and sonorous voice; easy and eloquent in his improvisations, quiet in his gestures, sweet and benevolent in appearance, mystic even to ecstasy in his prayers and praises, majestic on the throne, an artist before the altar, a rigid formalist in religious ceremonies, a lover of human pomps, devoted to a historic destiny and to his exalted ministry — believing in his greatest errors and equivocations that God inspired and guided him, and that he interpreted His thought and expressed His will on the face of the earth.

He does not enrich his own relations, nor hoard up treasures, nor measure out charity, nor does he refuse to give an audience, no matter how inopportune and troublesome. He puts no lock on his ever open heart, never bites his lips, which are always slightly apart, and often gives the impression that his thoughts are far distant. He has no very profound knowledge of human nature, understands more of outward formalities than of secret motives; of his power, more of the pomps than of the prestige; of his authority, more the display than the strength; and accustomed to live surrounded by those who treat him as a god, he feels pleasure in being called every day, "holy, holy, holy," in breathing the smoke of such incense. But in this exalted position, when he promulgates doctrines of faith, when he assembles Œcumenical Councils, when the entire Church declares him superior to human errors, when to others his thoughts seem divine as those of the Word, and his lips sacred as oracles—at such times a passing cloud, the electricity of the air, the rapid and frequent changes of the Roman climate, affect his nerves, which are extremely susceptible to atmospheric influences; his nerves act upon his temper, and force him to bursts of ill-humor and impatience which contradict his natural amiability, and prove how this demi-god—this great and supernatural being—is subject, like all other mortals, to the sins and infirmities which arise from the imperfection of our nature and the laws which govern the whole universe. And under the dominion of this Pope, who aspired to evangelize the world, to Christianize the democracy, the Pontifical authority has been converted to an absolutism which was impossible under the empire of the most absolute monarchs. The soul trembles on considering how our Church has moved inversely to our civilization. An institution of the very highest pretensions, a ministry which professes to redeem the human race, should be the light and the warmth of souls, as the sun is the light and warmth of our bodies. And in order to be the light and warmth of our souls, the Church should unfold over the head of the man stamped with the seal of divine election the ethereal wings of a truly superhuman ideal, spiritualistic and celestial. In a mysterious manner the Church conquered the Latin world and subdued barbarians. By her tendency to act on the imagination, she assembled councils, like the

Council of Jerusalem, where Jews and Pagans were reconciled, always heretofore separated in history, and Christianity progressed till it became the religion of humanity. By her mysterious tendency to the ideal, she formalized that earliest Greek theology which diffused the creating breath of the divine into the human understanding. In the same way she raised slaves to the dignity of religious beings, and impelled the Cæsars to assist the Nazarenes to elevate man; to educate him in pure idealism; to make his conscience as a sacrifice consecrated to the Divinity on the altars of the universe, was a worthy, a most worthy ministry of a religion which will triumph by its radical opposition to Pagan sensuality with all its cancerous putrefaction. The Church in the three first ages was a democratical federation. The Church from the time of Charlemagne has been an empire; yes, an empire according to the Roman fashion, while Europe has tended to federation. The Roman Bishops desired to be more Cæsars than Popes; they wished to perpetuate, under the protection of the Cross, the subjugation of the world. At the foot of the new altars, as at the foot of the ancient shrines, Rome only, of her own authority, consented to confine the new barbarians in her Basilicas, as she had confined the old barbarians in her Capitol. For this object she had armies that, instead of arms, carried bells to summon to prayer, and instead of bucklers wore sackcloth—she had the monks. She had her jurisconsults—the canons; she had her code of laws —the false decrees of the Popes; she had even the title of Cæsar left to her by Constantine; and she had her emperor

—the Pope. But the Popes had not always to boast of this, for during some centuries they served democracies.

The religious movements in Rome can be always explained by political interests. Rome is among ancient cities the most faithful to the Pagan religion, for she believes that the Pagan religion is the most favorable to her power and greatness. Rome, in the deluge of the invasion in which her gods were overthrown, embraced Catholicism with ardor, not because it was the truest religion, but because it was the religion most opposed to that of her conquerors, which was Arianism. So Rome excited the Italians and the world to rebel against the imperial barbarian, supporting herself upon two great and capital principles, upon Catholicism and Republicanism. To the unity of Lombardy was opposed the Roman democracy. The city not only gave up her soul to the Pope, but she humbly implored the help of Constantinople; and by means of the divine virtue of enlarged intelligence, by means of the geographical position of the Peninsula, she unites in the isles of the Tyrrhene Sea, in the lagunes of the Adriatic, behind the Apennines, in the defiles of the Abruzzas, all the shipwrecks that have preserved the antique ideal and the ancient Italian worship.

It is impossible to comprehend how the Popes have been supported by the world, without understanding the political situation of Italy in the sixth and seventh centuries. The Byzantine unity, that is a shadow in Ravenna; the unity of Lombardy, that is a sword and sceptre in Pavia; the federal unity, that is a religion and a democracy in Rome. The Eternal

City could not protect herself nor protect the Republic. She found herself, after five hundred years of empire and five invasions of barbarians, among the ruins of her temples and the ashes of her power; she was no longer defended by dictators, by consuls, by Cæsars, by the ancient magistrates, but by bishops; for it is evident that now bishops are the defenders of cities, the chiefs of the plebeians, the new tribunes of the democracy; those only who find their own words of faith and enthusiasm enough to create armies of plebeians, where are formed legions of martyrs to the battle and to death. But those who imagine that the power of the Popes in this supreme crisis was solely to be attributed to miracles of faith, are much deceived. They are strong, because they have had devoted to them the warrior nation—the French people. The French are the soldiers of Catholicism. While we struggled for Catholicism in its old age and decay, the French did so when Catholicism was youthful and vigorous. It is always useful to serve a progressive principle. The French increase, and we degenerate while supporting the same principle. But they helped it when the Church was educating humanity, when the Church was a religious body and a republican federation, while we assisted it in Europe after we had finished our wars with the Moors—we who from the thirteenth century represented for the house of Aragon the civil principle opposed to the theocratic principle—we served it in Europe when the Church in Germany, in Holland, and in England opposed herself to the education of humanity. The patriarchs of Constantinople aspired to be, through the viceroys of Ravenna, the directors of the crusade against the Lombardians. But the bishops of Rome showed the federation of bishops at whose head they appeared—the multitude agitated and bewildered by Catholic doctrines and the miraculous lances in the hands of the French, whose valor was invincible, ready to pass the Alps and the Pyrenees, the Rhine and the Ebro, to defend the priests and their new religion. This is the singular means by which the Pontificate became the head and centre of the world.

Afterward, in the crisis of society, the movements of the human spirit conspired in the first period of the Middle Ages to strengthen this precedence. The people of Lombardy were converted to Christianity, embraced the religion of the vanquished in Italy, a century after the Goths embraced the same religion in our Spain. From that moment the Pope, who had no longer any need of the Emperors of Constantinople, turned against her, combated her Monotheism, her iconoclasts, her viceroys, her embassadors, whom he wished to secure to his own interests, refusing her the sanction of all Pontifical authority over his religious power, and exciting the Catholic conscience against the heterodox sentiments of Constantinople; and the Italian patriotism and the Italian federation against the re-appearance of the ancient empire, in a rival city, an enemy of "Eternal" Rome. But while he separated from Constantinople and acquired moral independence, he wished to overcome Pavia and to attain material independence also. It was of no avail that the people of Lombardy had been converted to Catholicism; they had not been changed into republicans, and the Pope was at the same time the High-Priest of the Catholics and the Chief of the federation. During this age—the eighth century—the Italian people abhorred monarchy, and even preferred theocracy. All the sea-port towns demanded of the Pope that he would liberate them civilly from the tutelage of a king as he had liberated them morally and religiously from the authority of the Emperor. The Pope could not attain so great an object unassisted, but was able to do so by counting on his faithful and select people. The French San Leon would not have felt the anger of Attila if the French had not previously disarmed the great exterminator in the Catalonian fields. To overcome the Lombardians, it was necessary to repeat the same story, to act over again the same programme—the French were to wound and slay, the Pope to bury the dead.

In vain the best Italian patriots cursed that period in the history of their country, in which fell the civil and monarchical unity, to be replaced by the theocratic unity of the world. Perhaps when the kingdom of Lombardy conquered, the Italian people became more warlike, nationality more united and powerful ; but it could not be the nation of theocracy, which nourished and educated Europe for so many centuries; it could not be the first nation in modern culture ; it could not be the country of so many free and independent municipalities and of so many republican towns ; it could not be that universal school of music, of painting, of sculpture, in which the mind has been developed and cured in adversity, consoled in sorrow, keeping always before it a bright and living picture, and like the aroma of flowers, like the warble of the birds, like the rustling of the groves, like the incense of the fields, diffused through the celestial immensity, giving to Christian Europe the illustrious name and the enviable ministry exercised by immortal Greece in ancient Europe.

In the year 800 Europe rose against the first idea of the Pontificate after the treaty with Charlemagne. The Pope delivered over to the French the old kingdom of Lombardy, and the French made over to the Pope the new patrimony of St. Peter. Exalted on this feudal soil, the Pope, after having disposed of his enemies—after having separated his city from Constantinople, from Pavia, from Ravenna, which all eclipsed Rome—gave himself up to all his spiritual ambition, to all his supposed sovereignty over souls; to be a creature apart, almost a God; to dictate moral laws superior to all written laws; to extend an authority over a dominion that knows no limits, over the dominion of the human conscience; to place his own moral codes higher than all others; to set his Church on a more lofty pinnacle than all societies, his voice where the ancient oracles had never dared, his person above the gods of antiquity; to destroy the lineage of the priesthood conceded to whoever demanded it—to make celibacy impossible for them by making it into a hereditary dignity; to oppose moral force to so much material power, religious unity to the numerous divisions of feudalism, the democracy educated in monasteries and universities to the military aristocracy that dwelt in fortified castles; to transform the world, the earth, as reality is always transformed by an anterior and superior transfiguration of sentiments. It imported little, very little, that the Popes now fell into the mire of vice—that they became demented from pride and power, and passed, under the tutelage of their courtiers, to the greatest depravity; their power did not lie in their characters or habits, but in the belief of the people; and they ruled the world by the magic of their doctrine; by the sorcery of their relics; by their miracles and legends; by their numerous pilgrimages; by the power of their bishops, almost omnipotent in feudal territories; by the commentaries of their jurisconsults, who invented numerous laws and falsified many old writings; by the necessity, above all, that the world has in its childhood, the spirit in its innocence, of a theology which is at once its nurse and its mistress—which attracts it with fables, like that of the near destruction of the world in the year 1000, and holds it by these legends subject and submissive. The chief work of the Middle Ages will remain: the treaty of Charlemagne, a Pope sanctioned by the Emperor in the centre of Italy, an Emperor crowned by the Pope in the centre of Germany, and crowds of feudal bishops around the two great stars of the Middle Ages—around the Popedom and the Empire.

The bishops, possessed of so much influence, enjoy a supremacy which Popes and Emperors wish to keep under their respective domination. Hence there is a struggle between the Italian element and the German element within the Church; hence the celebrated litigation of the Investitures. The German Emperors succeeded in having German Popes in Rome; and the German Popes were almost all sacrificed in Rome. At last the Cæsar of the Pontiffs mounted the throne —Gregory the Seventh. He anxiously desired the free election of the Popes, the independence of the bishops; to be able to unite and administer all ecclesiastical properties; to make of the Church a society superior to the world, and separate from it; to get back by all means the Holy Sepulchre, in a war whose symbol should be the Cross, with an army whose general should be the Pope; and, to emancipate himself completely from the Germanic Empire, he invented the fable that the patrimony of St. Peter was the gift of Constantine, and obliged the Emperors, clothed with sackcloth and camel's-hair, to hear tremblingly on their knees a word from those Pontifical lips that could raise or subdue nations—a benediction from those hands which could appease or irritate the powers of Heaven.

If the Popes had been suppressed, Europe would not have been educated by the civilization of the Middle Ages. If the human intellect had completely submitted to the Pope, Europe would have been to-day a stagnant empire, Asiatic in its character—an ecclesiastical empire, having its Grand Lama in the Eternal City. Fortunately the principle of contradiction sprang up to obviate the sad and imperfect absorption of all human nature by one of its elements. Great opposition arose against the Pope, reminding him of his dependence upon the civil power, and of the recent accession of authority, for which he was solely indebted to the Western Emperors. Neither the war nor the peace of Investitures cleared up the numerous difficulties. Notwithstanding the humiliations of Henry IV. and the schemes of Pascal II., nature desired the prolongation of this struggle, and the continuance of this uncertainty, that neither of the two principles striving for the mastery should be able to predominate and overthrow the other. Thus the Church preserved her moral character and her theological reputation, while the idealistic element entered the soul; and the Empire preserved its civil and political character, forbidding the theocratic authority to enslave the whole of our being. By this struggle the Western World constituted unity in variety; tranquillity in the midst of war; equilibrium between opposing and contrary forces. All the harmony of the Middle Ages arose from this enmity between the Popedom and the Empire. Without the one Europe would have become a military camp; without the other Europe would have been turned into a monastery. Thus mutual opposition completely saved the culture of humanity.

Such was the spirit that overflowed in Europe; and the East arose to receive with eagerness the advance of human thought, and the monks preached, and the towns were moved, feeling a new life awakened in their bosom; crosses were erected on the wayside, and the multitude neither knew from whence they came nor whither they went, but were aware that some mystery enveloped and sustained them, and believed that every town was Jerusalem, that each monument was a sepulchre, that each wild rose was the desert, till a great part of the ancient ignorance disappeared, and a great part of the modern equality came from the common struggle and the common troubles, revealing the identity and the unity of nature in each man and in all human beings, which begins by being the slave of the theocracy and of feudalism, and goes on seeing freedom and determined to attain it; which goes from Europe blindly believing, and returns, as it were, from the desert, with the doubt of Job upon the soul, disposed to enter into another phase of civilization, more human and progressive. The Pope imagined that he could preserve the faith by upsetting and agitating Europe; this very commotion awakened Europe to reason.

Commerce is a new force of civilization and culture. Like all social power, it engenders political organisms. Labor and commerce are united. Commerce and labor are the commencement of the emancipation of those who pay taxes. From thence arose the tribunals of commerce in Italy, the municipalities in Spain, the communes in France. The Pope understands that this invoking of nature will make the fictitious part of the Catholic religion disappear; and that these invasions of the democracy will destroy theocratic aristocracy. As the universe, which may be turned into a fountain of life from having been a fountain of evil, labor turns from its original curse to be the means of continuing the creation; commerce is ended with the isolation of each man, of each people, which engenders penance and superstition; yet it communicates with Catholics and infidels; sackcloth, camel's-hair, and serge are bartered for gauzes, for brocades, for glistening silks. This appearance of nature in the midst of all the pretensions in the world, takes possession of religious terror, appears to the Church like the work of Antichrist, and darts its lightnings against the transfigurations of the life and conscience.

But Abelard thought. And thought, when put into words, becomes history. And history makes men. And the man who represented Abelard was Arnoldo de Brescia, a monk and a soldier, a tribune and an ascetic, a philosopher and a mystic, a most eloquent preacher and a consummate politician, a bright apparition of the democracy before theocratic altars, capable of suspending for a moment the political authority of the Popes of Rome, and of demonstrating that excommunication is powerless against reason, which emancipates; against heresy, which takes its convictions from nature; against labor, which elevates; against commerce, which binds the people together, and isolates the Church. The Pope may triumph for a time, but the seed sown by Arnoldo remains in the soil of Europe. The time will come when it will spring up.

The wound in the heart of the Church is open. She has lost the prestige of the Crusaders; two Christian armies struggle for supremacy, while the cimeter again takes possession of the Holy Sepulchre and the True Cross; pilgrims set forth for Jerusalem, and wait by the way to lay waste and pillage Christian cities, like Palermo and Constantinople; Frederick II. wished to renew the exploits of King Godfrey in the Holy Land—far from receiving the benediction, he drew upon himself the Papal anathema; heresy reigns in the territories where modern culture prevails, Languedoc and Provence, and kindles a civil war; the kings of Aragon, who previously submitted to the Church, quarrel about the Albigenses; an unbridled democracy, half composed of demagogues and beggars, the professed enemies of order and of all property, enter with the Franciscans into the Church, which, surrounded with troubles in that insurrection of the kings against her power, in those continued outbreaks of heresy, calls on the Inquisition, and kindles the flame to scatter terror with the Franciscans on kings and aristocrats, and with the Dominicans on heretics and on the people.

How did the Pope issue from all these upheavings of the human spirit? He was the head of Christianity, and the chief of a party—the Guelphs. He was also a legislator, and wished to see ecclesiastical legislation united to Roman and imperial legislation. He was the master of religious houses, and shared the supreme power with kings. The universities called upon Popes and royal personages to educate a class, that of jurisconsults. These would have removed the diadem of divine right from the head of the Pope to that of a king. The Church will, to a certain extent, accommodate herself with colleges; but in the college there will be more of Aristotle, more of Averroes, more of the Greek philosophers and of the Moorish commentators, than of the Fathers and early Christian writers.

At the end of the thirteenth century the real decay of the Pontificate began. And this decline did not consist, as superficial writers have supposed, in the character and reputation of the Popes, but in the change of ideas and opinions. Innocent III., who represented the greatest power of the Church, is the first of the Popes of the decadence, as Marcus Aurelius is before Commodus a great character, who sustains and elevates by his own force a very powerful institution wounded to the death. Neither valor nor intelligence nor virtue are sufficient to fortify institutions which have become enfeebled, to save institutions which are expiring. Could Probus sustain imperial Rome by his virtues, when she was already in her last agony? Few men will have in history so great a name for daring and force of character as that earned by Boniface VIII. He was not exceeded in valor by St. Leo, nor in activity by St. Gregory; in deeds of daring he surpassed Hildebrand, and in coolness Innocent III. He blockaded the feudal and Ghibeline family of the Colonna in Rome, which had opposed the Popedom for many centuries, and always been allied with its enemies; he pursued it with fire and sword through the fields and on the mountains; shut it up in Palestrina, and there executed a most cruel chastisement, without leaving one stone upon another in the city that guarded the most precious records of the antique, and of the most beautiful works of art of modern genius; a town whose destruction will be eternally deplored by both Latin and Christian muses. But Boniface VIII. was never deterred from any project or design from any respect for humanity. Recovering Poland and Hungary, he ruled over Italy without heeding either the Empire or the Emperor; made public rejoicings which enriched the Eternal City with hundreds of pilgrims; excommunicated and deposed civil magistrates, as if the

Cæsars had been born anew under the tiara; he defied France, and conspired against Germany. But his enemies, collected together in armed bands, came to search for him, ravaged his capital, attacked his palace, slaughtered his followers, drew near to him whom they found awaiting them on his throne, with the serenity and steadfastness of a god confident in his own omnipotence, the triple crown on his head, the Papal mantle on his shoulders, the crosier in his hand; one of the invaders struck him a violent blow on the cheek with the iron glove of feudalism, after which affront it only remained to the Pope to fly, to conceal himself, to deliver himself up to another lordly family, the Orsini; and between epileptic fits and angry maledictions, to die a miserable death, in the frantic sorrow caused by his rage and helplessness. The life and death of Boniface VIII. confirm the true pithy saying of the Roman people: "One arrives at the tiara like a fox, governs like a lion, and dies like a dog."

But his Pontificate will always mark the decay of the theocracy, till then ruler of Europe. Then the Papal party was divided: the Guelphs into white and black; the theologians into the disciples of Scotus, nominalists, and loyalists; the Popes themselves into Popes of Avignon and Popes of Rome; the Catholic nations into schismatics; scientific bodies into sects and heresies; councils into revolutionary assemblies; the poets into satirists, who disturbed the peace of the soul with their doubts, and persecuted the faith with their subtle irony, obliging the human mind to seek elsewhere than in Roman Catholicism its indispensable aliment. The Order of the

Templars, which rose in the happy times of the Pontificate, which struggled unceasingly for the Church in the East—sovereign of Cyprus, defender of Jerusalem—submissive to the Popes, is dissolved by the great slave of Avignon, by the French Pope; who submitted to the Kings of France and had their property confiscated, and their fortresses ruined and occupied by royal troops, and their knights burned by slow fires in their fields and cloisters, all bearing witness to the glory and power of that illustrious army. Even the great inspired theological poem, living temple of the Catholic spirit, consecrated not to passing battles of heroes, but to the journey of souls to eternity, to the unfathomable kingdom of the dead, touched them not. In the last circles of inextinguishable fire and of perpetual punishment, in the depths of hell, almost in the mouth of Satan, stand the Popes as the enemies of the greatness and of the independence of Italy.

What spectacles! The son of the poor laundress and obscure tavern-keeper, Rienzi, interpreter of Roman inscriptions, bringing to memory with true eloquence ancient recollections, saw himself proclaimed and honored by the people, who convey to him the homage of patricians, of cardinals, of kings, of emperors, of Popes, and personating for some days the genius of the Eternal City, till his head, giddy from such exaltation, falls rolling from the heights of the Capitol to the shop of a butcher below. And the world saw masqueraders of tribunes fill the Pontifical palaces; and bloody schisms and strifes rending the nations; so that men of genius, like Petrarch, turned with sorrow to the antique Paganism, asking again its courage and inspiration; so that there was a Pope in France, another in Italy, another in Aragon, in the sad Peninsula; so that the Emperor Sigismund took upon himself the ecclesiastical power to convoke the universal Church; and the chieftainship of the Catholic world passed from a simoniacal Pope to a pirate, from a pirate to a madman, from a madman to an epicurean, who succeeded in the decay of the empires; that the councils alone were able to kindle souls, to subvert the people, to unchain wars; that the flames consumed men of rare faith and genius like John Huss and Jerome of Prague; that the body of Wickliffe was disinterred and thrown into a river because he had desired the purification of Christianity; that the soldiers of the democracy, preceded by a blind general, called together by the beating of tambourines made of human skins, destroyed all before them with fire and sword, receiving the Holy Sacrament with the priests in the two elements of bread and wine; that the reconciliation of the Latin and Greek Churches—the work of one moment—was broken in another moment; that kings put themselves over the bishops, and the Church declared herself superior to the Pope;. that the devil fled before knowledge, and nature recovered her rights, antiquity its prestige, and conscience its voice, while the world lost its ancient faith, and the sovereign Popes their domination over Catholic humanity.

In fine, this movement of the human mind arrived at length at the true conception of reform. Thus Christianity has not been a sudden and miraculous apparition, the work of a moment, a singular inspiration, but the result of all the ages.

In like manner the Reformation was not brought about by the impulsive courage of one friar, the cry of a rebel risen in spiritual arms against the Church, the intuition of one soul alone, moved partly by its own passions, and partly by the historic hatred of its race ; but by the precise corollary of the doubts sown by the poets, of the ideas scattered by philosophers, of the politics imposed by kings, of the pretensions emanating from councils, of all the impulses that have been given to the human spirit by the action of society and the incontrovertible progress of things, to which each step of our history testifies.

Every man himself aspires to be a priest ; every generation wishes to interpret the doctrines of faith which affect it the most, and succeeds in transforming the dogma previously held to be definitive and unchangeable ; revelation seems to enlighten all minds, to be the patrimony of all humanity ; the book falls from the hands of the people ; the sacerdotal lineage disappears, and democracy invades the sanctuary ; the monastic orders, dedicated to maceration, the worship of holy relics, the exorcism of demons and indulgences, give way to the severe doctrine that extinguishes purgatory, exalts hell, and attributes the salvation of man to the divine mercy. From this time the predominance of the Pontificate in Europe has really disappeared—that influence which contributed so largely to our culture and education. It is true that Protestantism will be repugnant to the nature of our race and to the character of our history ; that if the Pope loses his hold on Europe, all America will arise to spread his name and to receive his baptism—America, which was discovered and conquered by heroes who were always Catholics, and who finished in Spain its war against the Moors, and then undertook on the opposite shore of the Atlantic a crusade against the Indians, going and returning in her ships, traversing immense countries, and then offering a continent as a holocaust before the altars of the Church.

It is evident that the Church works her greatest miracles and performs her most astonishing actions when she sees herself surrounded by snares and perils. No one can tire of admiring her action during the sixteenth century. In the person of Giulio II., the warrior and conquering Popes of the Middle Ages were restored—those who were disposed to make souls submit to their words as well as to make fortresses yield to their swords. During the Pontificate of Leo X. the spirit of antiquity was awakened; history repeated itself; Christian doctrines were diffused; the beautiful mystery of the plastic art was discovered in ancient monuments; statues were brought to light whose lips seem to tremble with the classic hymn of Greece. The soul of Plato arose over the sensuality of Aristotle; the glowing language of the ancient rostrum was revived; bronzes and marbles became animated, and the heavens of art were opened; the Titans of Michael Angelo and the Virgins came to captivate and to beautify our planet; life and pleasure returned to exhausted and macerated nature; the Renaissance was founded, and competed with the most glorious ages of humanity, and inspired troops of artists, who, laying aside petty jealousies, became united by the magic of genius, which flung a golden halo of illusions over the universe, softening the corroding cares and sorrows of existence.

Catholic was the marvelous magician who returned to depict beings fantastic and beautiful as in the days of the gods, creatures natural and spiritual, animated by the sublime inspirations of a poem; Catholic was the profound thinker who discovered the laws of the revolutions and reactions, who showed the deep abyss of crimes and hatreds caused by the repression of the human intellect; Catholic was the sweet Spanish poet who gave his voice to the groves, his melody to the streams and breezes, his incense to the flowers, his living eclogues to the fields; Catholic was the young painter, unique in the annals of history, who was able to evoke the beauty of ancient Greece, and, instead of scenes of cruel flagellation and penance, to transform in his pictures and embellish the human organism; Catholic was the architect, the sculptor, the miraculous designer who crowned with the dome of St. Peter the temples of the Renaissance; Catholic was the immortal music in which the lament of Jeremiah and the plaintive accents of David seemed to issue from the abyss of past ages; Catholic was every thing beautiful and artistic produced by the sixteenth century.

And the strength of Catholicism was so great that it brought about a real reaction in the seventeenth century. The Jesuits disciplined themselves as an army, and undertook to bring souls to the Pontificate; Catholic soldiers inundated the whole of Germany, demanding—as says a great writer—the lands of the living for the dead; William of Orange falls wounded by the hand of a fanatical Catholic for the crime of having founded the republic of Holland; Carlo Borromeo establishes a pious league in the Cantons of Catholic Switzerland against Protestant Switzerland; Charles and James Stuart think they have succeeded in banishing Protestantism from England; the revocation of the Edict of Nantes occasions in France a series of reactions against the humanitarian Treaty of Westphalia; in the Spanish Empire the pencils of Velasquez fall from his hand, and the fantastic dreams of Calderon are buried in an abyss more profound and obscure than the tombs of the Escorial, falling into the enchantments of Charles II. Rome puts herself at the head of all European cities with her religious doctrines, with her epopees like those of Tasso, which celebrate a sepulchre, and a sepulchre in the hands of the infidels; and any one would say that the world is changing, that the spirit returns to the temples and to the altars of the Middle Ages. But none of these reactions could restore the Pontificate. Behind them came the spiritual philosophy of the eighteenth century, which denied even the great excellences of Christianity, and was irritated at the mention of the truth of its past history. And the spirit of this age produced the cyclopædia which brought philosophic ideas to the level of the common-sense of the people. And these philosophic ideas not only descended to the intelligence of the common people, but they rose even to the thrones of monarchs.

The Jesuits, who had been, like the Templars, soldiers of

the Church, the permanent army of Catholicism, were dissolved by the Popes of Rome and by the sovereigns of Europe. The new philosophy took strong hold in Austria, which had been like the axis of the whole European reaction; and in Spain, which had supported Roman Catholicism in its most important crises, and had given it a New World in compensation for the Old World. What more could be done? The philosophic theories ascended even to the throne of St. Peter, spreading itself there like new sap on an old trunk. Philosophic speculation took possession of consciences, consciences engendered new institutions, new institutions changed the face of society; the right, which had previously been perpetuated in isolated families, in privileged orders, spread itself among all men; democracies replaced the aristocracies, the revolution replaced immovability; and the Popes, who had vainly on their knees supplicated the Emperors of Germany, dreading a royal revolution, fled from Rome, and made a compact with the French Revolution by anointing the head of the soldier of fortune who was elected as sovereign.

The Pontificate then represented itself in the world as one of those institutions, heretofore great, become disorganized by the active efforts of society. And when one of these organisms is upset and disordered, no new social element — not any—can recompose it. Even the power which engendered it has been destroyed. The spirit which produced it has been devoured. The world loses its faith and confidence in it by one of those intimate convictions which neither struggle nor contrast, but which come from the continued efforts of thought and reflection. During four centuries after the death of Marcus Aurelius the human mind employed itself in upsetting the ancient world. Who reconstructed it? When the barbarians came they only met the great corpse. The souls had fled to another institution. And the hereditary institution of the ancient spirit is, in the modern world, the Pontificate. To the Pontificate is due the first force of cohesion employed in reuniting modern societies, the highest authority, and all our most ancient discipline. But from the thirteenth century the Pontificate has been falling into gradual and irremediable decadence, which has brought it to its present extremity. Now the Treaty of Charlemagne is broken. The grant of Pepin has disappeared. The dogma of the Papal Infallibility has augmented the number of the enemies of Rome. Internal struggles distract the Church, which do not result in schisms because of the want of sufficient force and ability to sustain them. And Europe learns in this great disorganization in what manner and for what reasons the most rooted institutions expire, even when they are also the most powerful; when they have accomplished the ministry for which they were created by society, which exists by continually producing and devouring organisms.

But Pius IX. believed himself the one chosen to restore the Pontificate! What then?—did it not receive new life and new blood from many Popes? Did not Giulio II. restore it up to a certain point by his power? Leo X. by his artifices? Sixtus V. by his traditions and discipline? And can not he revive it also?—he, elected to his exalted position by a miracle? But what path to choose? Two are equally open to his thoughts and his perception. Take which he will, both are strewn with dangers. The one leads to the idea preached by Rosmini—the re-animation of the ancient spirit in the Church; to the result foreseen by Gioberti—of the intellectual and moral supremacy of Italy over all other nations by means of the Pontificate. The other road was that of Jesuitism. The Pope believed, and with reason, that the first way had been closed against him after his misfortunes of 1848. The Pope thought there only remained to him the path of radical opposition to all modern institutions, and immediate re-establishment of ancient ideas. With this impression, he began by exalting into a doctrine of faith in our time that which our time has rejected and destroyed. For this he continued proclaiming a dogma of faith without assistance from the Council. For this he flung into the midst of the afflicted Church the dogma of his own infallibility—that is to say, the germ of quasi-divinity for himself and of eternal slavery for believers. Thus to deny God, to ignore His law, to deaden the voice of the conscience He has given, to disrespect public morals, to acknowledge no more the Creator of the universe, is an error as great, but not greater, than to deny the Pope, to ignore his infallibility, to be deaf to the voice of his ecclesiastical oracles, even in those points which do not touch the faith. These apotheoses, these deifications to which the ancient Pagans raised their vain-glorious Cæsars, accord precisely with the blasphemies of a celebrated Roman Catholic writer who maintains the following thesis: "There are three adorable beings for the true believer—God in the Heavens, Christ in the Host, and the Pope in the Vatican." To such extremes extend the dogma of Infallibility!

We are never tired of repeating that the dogmas promulgated in our time, and the spirit which has presided over them, converts Catholicism into a religion of sects; consequently the Pope is the chief of sectarians. That ancient human feeling which assimilated itself to philosophy and history is altogether lost. Before our philosophy, before our revolution, he has only scorned or receded or cursed. And this right of property is claimed in ideas which are almost extinct, of systems in decay, shutting himself up from all the emancipations of modern improvements, from all the progress of society — ideas and progress which in better times they nourished and strengthened. Catholicism assimilated itself to Pagan philosophers like Aristotle, and to Mussulman philosophers like Averroes. That power of assimilation supported its progress. And the Mohammedan religion, which was not able so to conform itself—which translated Aristotle and produced Averroes, without the ability to combine them with their fatalistic and monotheistic dogmas—by degrees ceased to be the creed of one single human family, the religion of one race, the soul of imperious soldiers dead as quickly as engendered. God will not protect those religions or those doctrines capable of losing in their maturity the reason and signification they had in their youth. Each new movement of time will believe itself divine; each revelation of the conscience will believe itself supernatural. And not being able to lift itself to comprehend nature and spirit combined, it will lose with the knowledge of life the reason of former ages. Each sect incloses itself within its own party, and does more than ignore the history of its opponents — it does more, for it calumniates them, dishonors them, curses them, thinking it realizes an eternal good. Imagine what would be the history of Christianity related by a Jew! Imagine the history of modern Judaism told by a ferocious inquisitor! The Roman Catholic scarcely comprehends the faith and doctrines of Protestant peoples. The Protestant calls the Pope Antichrist. Read a Greek orthodox work, and it will demonstrate to you that these Byzantine notions, which we hold to be the extreme of moral decadence, would have saved the world by their metaphysics, if the world had not fallen into the power of the Jesuits and the Roman Canonists. How blind is the sectarian spirit! We remain in ecstasy before the Venus of Milo. Her beautiful severity, her majestic chastity, the purity and harmony of her features, the grace and serenity of her brow, the complete possession of herself indicated by that spirit looking through her immovable eyes, and ruling her thoughts and passions, the calmness of that perfect type—beautiful ideal of the plastic art—transports and absorbs us in mysterious adoration. But to a Christian of the early times, fanatical in his new-born belief, that loveliness seemed hideous, and in her he beheld indistinctly the wicked and deformed effigy of the Devil. Nothing in the world illuminates like the sun, nothing vivifies like the air, nothing is perfumed like flowers, nothing refreshes like fruit — charms like the murmur and the aroma of the fields, nothing absorbs like the waves of the sea; and, notwithstanding, mysticism has even been able to engender in man an indifference, a hatred for the universe.

Is it surprising if each individual, shut up in his egotism, each sect in its tradition, each tradition in its dogma, each dogma in its Church, each Church in its intolerance, and each kind of intolerance in its cruelty, never arrives at the comprehension of the overflow of the human spirit in all human works, various, multiform, contradictory at times, without ever losing its fundamental unity? And those who look upon life from one side, upon time from one age, upon science from one system, upon art from a single school, the doctrines of one religion, society from one party, history from one phase, humanity from one people, will never understand the human mind; which, as it can not separate itself here, in this planet, from its first organism, the body, with which it is combined, no more can separate itself from the hearth nor the temple, nor art nor science nor society, which are parts of its life, organisms of its being, intimate and perpetual revelations of its essence, degrees in its progress, but in whose total we virtually exist, and in whose unfolding is the expansion of our own life. We have been with those who *were*, we shall be in those who *are* to come. Do not let us believe then in one sole Church as depositary of the whole absolute truth, nor in one people as alone representing the spirit of humanity!

I argue against Catholic sects and parties because they only understand one part of life, our historical life. They consider only what we have been, they do not think of what we are, nor upon what we shall be. When philosophy reveals every day a secret of this human organism—abstract of the universe; when chemistry has divined the powers of the decomposition and the recomposition of nature; when astronomy puts us into direct communication with the Infinite; when wonderful discoveries have delivered to us the lightning, which we make to vibrate in our hands as in those of the ancient gods; when the earth upon which we live has counted its age to us by means of its geological revolutions, and the heavens which surround us have revealed by the solar spectrum the fundamental unity of Cosmos—in this growth of human nature and of the human mind, joined to the growing conviction of the fundamental equality of all men, and joined with a science which declares the fundamental equality of all beings in Cosmos, do you think a religion can satisfy us whose two last dogmas, instead of spiritualizing the life, of idealizing the faith, teach us to believe in the exceptional privilege of two human creatures; a privilege and exception incomprehensible by the intelligence, and opposed to the universality of nature?

So society, science, and life go by one road; and Catholicism goes by another which is totally different. The Pontifical Court only feeds itself upon tradition. The Catholic science is Archæology. In Rome, in Pontifical Rome, the wail of an elegy is heard around. The nettle and the buttercup bloom upon the material ruins, and over the weeds spring the moral ruins. Good Friday is like the last day in this singular city, the day in which the heart is desolate, the sanctuary deserted, the lamps extinguished, the altars stripped and veiled, and the lament of Jeremiah sounds mournfully in those temples of tears and sorrow. I remember on that day, after having been in the Sistine Chapel in the morning, I was on the Via Appia, the road of ancient monuments, in the evening. I stopped a moment to contemplate the entrance to the Catacombs, and to gather blessed inspirations from their ashes. It seemed to me that the souls of the martyrs were reborn at my conjuration, and accompanied me through that path of sadness and desolation. Sometimes I involuntarily turned my eyes to the city, where I saw outlined the formidable ruins of Pagan times and the aerial domes of the Catholics. Rome behind, the Sabine Chain in front, the desert around, aqueducts in all directions, broken and interrupted, the road of past ages beneath my feet, the heaven of continued prayers above my head, four leagues of sepulchres open to my reflection, the monk or the shepherd interrupting the journey with their picturesque presence or their religious salutation—make one feel one is really descending the region of shadows, the abyss of history, and one looks for the guide of Dante to accompany the journey. To the right are the Catacombs of St. Sebastian, where the martyrs repose; and at the left is the Circus Maximus, where the martyrs were immolated. A few steps in advance is the tomb of Cecilia Metella, which records the last days of the Republic; a grand mausoleum, being a kind of fortification, on which another age has raised a new fortification, as new laws have been formed over the laws of that time, and new institutions over those of past ages. The stones forming this monument, embrowned by the ardent sun of the Campagna, have resisted the storms of centuries and the passions of men, as the Republic has resisted all the political movements of history. On all sides are the broken stones of glorious monuments, in beautiful relief, the remains of tombs and temples, the relics of past civilization; as if the ground had been a battle-field, where fought in ancient times, not armies of men, but worlds and planets. Going on a little, you see the tomb of Seneca. Tyranny does not like to hear the complaints of its victim, and art has derided tyranny, leaving in bass-relief a protest, repeated by ages, against the cruelty of tyrants. I, who had been trampling the dust of the Catacombs, could do no less than put my hand on the stones of that sepulchre. How many ideas of the ancient Stoics, and how many ideas of the primitive Christians form the foundation of our faith, of our code of morals? What soul has conceived the law to whose empire I find myself submitting? What apostle or what martyr has raised the altar of my belief? Useless questions. Ask not of the cloud where it has been formed, nor of the lightning where it has been kindled, nor of the molecules which pervade your organism how they have been created; the universe is the laboratory of life, and the universal conscience is the laboratory of ideas. Thus some engender them, others express them, these preach them, those die for them; and even those who oppose and combat them aid in their development, till they pass into the common-sense of society.

Mausoleums, above all those of ages widely apart, preserve cold ashes; but they also preserve living ideas. Along the Via Appia, not far from an ancient circular tumulus, terminated by a small tower of the Middle Ages, is the grove of Cluilius, where tradition, since confirmed by Dionysius of Halicarnassus, puts the field of battle between Alba and Rome, consequently the tomb of the Horatii and the Curatii. Primitive inhabitants of this neighborhood, at the sight of so many ruins, which appear like skeletons, naturally love to record the glorious days of Latin festivals, when they congregated upon the mountains of Albano to offer sacrifices, and from thence went to the grove of Albano to listen to the songs of the Fauns, and from the grove to the grotto of Tivoli to question the prophetic sibyl; and while the women celebrate in the bright days of spring, when the heavens smile and nature revives, festivals in honor of the god of the sheepfolds, girded with foliage, crowned with garlands, drinking between religious canticles the yet warm milk in cups just cut from oak-trees, you would acknowledge the nature around you, and see that nature in other times had not another life and other forms. And perhaps the creeds that will be substituted for yours may not sufficiently remember that nature is living and immortal. To-day the Grecian vessel bringing merchandise and knowledge is not anchored in your ports, the laughing and singing gods no longer sport in your fields; the desert has encroached upon their hearths and temples, the battles have spared but the mute and motionless inhabitants of the tombs.

Good Friday, consecrated to the dead; the Via Appia, the road of tombs; Rome, the great necropolis; all, all spoke to me of the departed. And all invited me to reflect upon this great mystery. We imagine ourselves absolute monarchs in nature, and we live under laws we do not comprehend. Why this interruption of death? Why this dark stone of the tomb rolled from an unfathomable abyss to the dim border of another unfathomable abyss? Let us be comforted. The natural dynamics are not interrupted. We leave the corpse in the grave; and we return, grief-stricken, to mourn over the death of the one beloved; but the corruption of the body is but a new form of existence, a new function of life, a new germination of beings. The want of nutritious juices in the stomach, the want of blood in the veins, the want of oxygen in the air, can these destroy man who proclaims himself lord of immortality? Each organism is a little universe in the midst of the total, of the moral and material universe. By food, by respiration, by the continual change of atoms, we absorb the life of nature; as by synthesis, by generalization, we expand the concrete and individual soul in the human spirit. As light and color are identical in the universe, as the grave and the sharp tones combine in harmony; as the carbonic exhalations of animal respiration, and oxygenic exhalations of vegetable respiration in the atmosphere, so life and death combine in our being. From these oppositions result the highest of life's pleasures. Unsatisfied desire is a pain. Love is a desire unsatisfied, inextinguishable; and love is a felicity. When the desire is accomplished, the passion which gave rise to it is no more. And satisfied desire is no longer desire. Then to preserve desire is to preserve love, to preserve pain is to preserve happiness. To preserve death is to preserve life. Death is a resurrection.

I understand all the sublimity of the symbol of the Church on the celebration of the Resurrection. It is a day of universal rejoicing. It happens in the season of the earth's resurrection. The warm and reviving breath of spring covers and renews the wearied earth. The snows melt and send down their clear waters to the rivers. The fields are clothed with verdure, the verdure with flowers, and the flowers with butterflies. Apple-trees and almonds, orange and lemon trees look like so many bouquets. The birds give themselves up to music and to love. The buds swell with sap, and the larvæ become transformed into painted insects. The ant comes forth from her nest and the bee from her honeycomb. The bells, which were silent for three days, ring out joyfully. The peasants all wear their festal costumes. The Virgin Mother, heretofore weeping, is decked with garlands to meet her divine Son, and, in the Easter procession through our fields and villages, all intone the canticle of the resurrection: Hallelujah! Hallelujah! We seem to behold the Crucified rise from his bed of marble, burst his shroud, break the stone, and return to life in resplendent glory. The poppies wore a deeper red, the flowers of the almonds had a more rosy blush, the orange blossoms were more fragrant, the song of the birds was sweeter on that day when our souls were touched with holy mysticism. Nature was most beautiful. The internal vision did not withdraw me from the external world. Pious travelers have assured me that they have heard in crossing the ranges of the Andes mysterious sounds from the birds which imitated the human voice. Let us convert the universe into the expression of our thoughts, the echoes of the words murmured by conscience in our ears. Holy joy of the Resurrection Morn, blessed, blessed art thou! I understand that the doctor of the German epopee, after having felt all the griefs and miseries of humanity, after having experienced all the disenchantments of science, being himself distracted by doubts and tortured by anxieties, thought to purify the poison; and only dashed the fatal cup from his lips at the sound of the bells which announced the resurrection — of the hallelujahs which announced the Easter—those sacred rejoicings which can reconcile despair with nature and with life.

On Easter Sunday in Rome I followed all the appointed religious ceremonies. I listened to the gay ringing of the bells, went to the Basilica of St. Peter, and, crossing the great square, heard the murmur of the two fountains, throwing upward their jets of water; I looked at the obelisk of Caligula, brought to Italy by the largest ship of all antiquity; I mounted the majestic flight of marble steps leading to the church, and went into the interior with my feelings affected by the remembrance of my old impressions and illusions on the same festival. I was without the desire to criticise which attacks most of the visitors to the church of the Vatican. As fabulous riches have been expended there, as the first architects in the world have contributed to its embellishment, few can resist the temptation to criticism. "How absurd," some say, "was the idea of Bramante, who proposed a still greater cupola than this!" "What a pity," exclaim others, "that the design of Raphael was not realized—the Greek cross, which would have allowed us to see the rotunda from the entrance of the Cathedral." "Variety and decoration cleared Michael Angelo from the suspicion of opposing the plan of St. Galo," say some, "for he renounced the Gothic in his pyramids and his cupolas, which was abominated in Pagan Rome;" while many observe that optical illusion alters the effect of the church; that its vastness can not be comprehended at the first glance; that the immensity of its dimensions damages its artistic beauty; that, from the extreme end, the door looks as if shrouded in a sort of mist; that it is necessary to walk two hundred paces along colossal pilasters, supporters of the immense lantern, in order to know by analysis the magnitude of this unique church; that the wealth of the bronze and marbles is astonishing, but not overpowering; that the statues in violent attitudes show the epoch of sad decay, as also the great altar with its gilded columns, and the Holy Roman seat with the colossi in gilded bronze, representing four fathers of the Church, whose mantles seem to be filled and blown about by a tempest, and the Holy Ghost appearing amid transparent yellow crystals, which is like a dove falling on a gigantic fountain of well-beaten eggs.

We need not in the church of the Vatican look for the mysticism which pervades our Gothic Cathedrals; that religious expression perceptible in the faces of the statues and effigies, which emanate from purely Catholic spirits; the soft beauty of those rays of light filtered through many-colored windows. No; the classic genius, the classic spirit, raised the Roman temple to ideas separated from the fervent Catholic spirit—to Pagan ideas; and the grandeur of the arches resemble the antique triumphal arches; and the elevation of the gilded vaults, and the dimensions of the marvelous cupola; of the richness of the marbles, whose shades vary from pearly white to opal, from opal to rose, from rose to lilac, from lilac to amethyst, and the glitter of the bronzes brilliant as native gold; and the beauty of the mosaics, which represent in stones of lively colors the most precious pictures; and the altars in all their display, and the statues in their gigantic niches, and the angels with expanded wings, and the Popes extended on tombs of so many different forms and periods—constitute in reality, if not a Catholic temple, one of the grandest monuments in the world.

The Pope passed through the Basilica. The ostentation with which he was accompanied on Palm Sunday was increased on Easter Sunday. The number of bishops and archbishops was much greater. Pius IX. wore a snowy mantle embroidered with rich jewels, on his head the golden tiara, surmounted by three crowns of brilliants. Conducted to his place, he intoned High Mass with a melodious voice; and after the mass he adored the holy relics with extraordinary devotion. This being accomplished, he ascended to the great window of St. Peter's, and showed himself to the multitude assembled in the great square. His arms were extended as if he would embrace them all; his voice was full of feeling and intensity;

and Rome and the entire world were blessed by his words and his hands. I, in the midst of the exclamations of the vast concourse, of the ringing of bells, the roar of cannons, the sound of thrilling music, the joy painted on every countenance, thought how truly that benediction would spread through the entire world; how it would extend from the frigid regions of the North to the sunny lands of the tropics; and how it would be welcomed among all people, even among those who believe themselves most emancipated from the Catholic Church—in Britain, by the Irish; in Russia, by the Poles; in America, by the States of the South; in Germany, by the Bavarians; in the whole world by the ancient Portuguese and Spanish Colonies, which have sown Asia, Africa, and America with churches, and have displayed the symbol of Nicæa both to the Indians of the Old Hemisphere and to those of the New.

If, with all these ceremonies, it is intended to prove that Rome preserves her ancient predominance over the world, the consequences are marvelous. No other city possesses this power. Benedictions are not sent from Parisian palaces to Patagonian cabins. No other city can exhibit her first magistrate blessed in all tongues, adored in all regions, borne to the height of a real and true divinity; no other can say that her laws are the moral code of a considerable part of the world, or that her sovereign reigns in the consciences of peoples scattered throughout the globe. The bishops are true prefects, empowered to maintain the moral superiority of Rome over all nations. We are tributaries—tributaries like the ancient Roman provinces—tributaries of the spiritual Cæsar, who blesses or curses us at his pleasure from his immense sanctuary of the Vatican. Formerly the various churches opposed some check to him, the different nationalities kept up the rich variety of life though under the same Pope. Now he has no curb whatever. Now he declares his infallibility; the Pope is the whole Church. In vain the bishops, assembled in council, warned him of the enormous risk to the unity of Catholicism; in vain the prelate of Orleans, an enthusiastic friend of the Pope, designated the new dogmas as dangerous innovations; in vain the eloquent Strossmayer, who so energetically protested against the rupture of the Austrian Concordat, made his thrilling words vibrate in the ears of the Episcopacy, to save them from a shameful abdication; in vain Döllinger appealed to science to demonstrate that nothing so monstrous had ever been attempted, except by the Councils of Lateran, true ante-chambers of the King of Rome; in vain Father Gratry proved that Pope Honorius had been condemned in the Sixth Œcumenical Council for declaring the heresy of those who denied the two natures in the person of the Redeemer; in vain Cardinal Schwarzenberg reminded them that after the pretensions of Boniface VIII. to absolute dominion over the world's conscience, there came dissensions, religious wars, schisms, submissions on the part of the Pontificate; all in vain. An assembly restrained by servile regulations, pushed forward by continual decrees of the Pope, placed under the influence of the invader Jesuitism, incapacitated from sustaining the moral unanimity indispensable in the proclamations of dogmas; then a hundred and forty bishops, the most eloquent, the most learned, and of the most enlightened dioceses, opposed it. An assembly under these circumstances, among violent protests, after the departure of the most illustrious and the most celebrated councilors, arrived, one stormy evening, which was like a premature night, at the deification of Pius IX.! From thence he alone upon the earth was superior to all humanity! Like a god wandering through our lower regions, he was above the errors and weaknesses common to our limited and most frail nature!

Antiquity has also its apotheosis. The man who attained the dignity of Cæsar was not content with being Cæsar, he aspired to be God. The senate assembled and decreed divinity to its tyrants. Consuls, priests, vestals, flocked around Cæsar, crowned him, placed him upon an altar, wreathed him with garlands, decapitated victims in his honor, with sacred songs and offerings of odoriferous myrrh, celebrated his birth and his immortality with innumerable festivals.

But the equality of life, the impartiality of death, the implacable justice which shows us all to be but children of the earth, subject to identical laws, denied these apotheoses; and far from raising a man above the level of his fellows, such supreme arrogance depressed him even to placing him below our nature. Sorrow and labor, pain and error, necessarily exist in the limited conditions of humanity, and consequently the men-gods fall quickly—very quickly—as fell the Pharaohs and the Nebuchadnezzars. And it happened that the ages of the apotheoses were the ages fatal to Paganism. When men entered into heaven, the gods retreated. The people left off going to the temple of Delphi, from whence they saw the summit of Parnassus, where was heard the murmur of the fountain Castalia, of which the Pythoness speaks in verses which contain the secrets of the future; where were celebrated the Pythian games and the popular assemblies, where Apollo scattered light upon the head of the mother Greece, and inspiration on her soul. In vain a man of genius, a philosopher, orator, poet, warrior, hero, and artist—Giulio—wished to restore, idealize, and renew the old dogma with the new metaphysics; the sacrifices had been interrupted, the altars were destroyed, Paganism was extinguished, because having commenced by the deification of the natural forces which rule the universe, it ended by the deification of the Cæsars and of the Pontiffs.

Easter Day in Rome! After having been at the Catholic mass, at the Pontifical benediction, I asked myself if in reality any thing has been recuscitated in these latter days upon the earth, upon the earth of the resurrection in the sixteenth century, upon the earth of the Renaissance. Here is Galatea, there Psyche, yonder are the muses dancing around the ancient Parnassus; on one side the schools of Athens, more living and more beautiful than they ever were in reality; on the other side the sibyls raised to the height of sublimity to make known the oracles. In one compartment is Diana, with the half-moon upon her forehead, the bow in her hands, followed by her nymphs, and greeted by the woods; in another, Aurora opening her gates to the eternal day: all around are triumphal arches and beautiful statues, from which the ancient art of sculpture was reborn in all its serene perfection.

But the Middle Age has had no resurrection; for, while the political supremacy of the Holy See has been sustained, the predominance of the clergy over the other social classes, the direction of European politics by the Popes, the religious and feudal character of the ancient patrimony of St. Peter, the inquisition for the conscience, the censure for the thoughts, the mixture of temporal and spiritual authority in one person, the anathema, against which there is no appeal, over the State which is independent, over the laic schools, over civil matrimony, over religious liberty and printing—the Middle Age has not only not arisen, but could not have arisen in Rome. Oh, Popes! the gods you have wished to annihilate have arisen, if not in the heaven of religion, in another heaven, which is more beautiful—that of art; while the spirit of the Middle Age, which you intended to revive, sinks every day more into the past! All that you have cursed is born anew; all dies which you desire should exist. Does this say nothing to the infallible Pope; nothing to the god of the Vatican?

But I will not be exclusive and intolerant. The eighteenth century, in its work of destruction, and looking upon life from one aspect only, may have believed in the necessity of destroying all the Middle Age. The nineteenth century, in its work of reconstruction, of reconciliation, can not deny that ten centuries, a thousand years, have been useless to human progress, and have left nothing in the foundation of our civilization and culture. That spiritualistic tendency, that idealism of the Middle Ages, ought to be renewed in our age, without its exclusive character, reconciling itself with nature and with science. In order that our civilization should be perfect, we must of necessity kindle upon it the clear light and purifying fire of true idealism. Miracles are repeated every day in the natural sciences, in the exact sciences, in the physical sciences, in all that has for its object the material and the sensible. We know how to observe and to calculate better than any other age; but do we know with equal perfection how to feel? do we know how to think? We understand the sun: we are sure that his bulk is one million four hundred thousand times greater than that of the earth, and that, moving at the rate of seventy kilometres an hour, it would take us two hundred and seventy years to arrive at his burning surface; and that this mighty star, if put in one scale of a balance, would require three hundred and fifty thousand terraqueous globes like ours in the other scale to preserve the equilibrium. We know all this of the sun, which is at such an immense distance from our vision, and we scarcely know any thing of our own consciences, of that internal sun which we carry within us and possess forever!

The marvels of physical science are not interrupted. At one time we discover in the Milky Way phenomena which almost evade the power of our dynamics; now we know the changes which twenty years have made in the nebulæ of Orion; we see the course of ages in the planet, the appearance of the first species of animal and vegetable life, the awakening of the infusoria on those sea-banks formed during the oceanic epoch, the causes of the wondrous vegetation revealed by buried carbon; while astronomy connects us with the universe, and geology evokes recollections of the historic world, chemistry reveals the secrets of existence. Priestley discovered oxygen, Lavoissier analyzed the atmosphere, and found therein the gas which favors, and the gas which threatens human life. He detected virtues, before concealed, in different minerals which assisted agriculture; as he found a great number of alkaloids, till then unknown, which gave new acids to medicine. Electricity came to add to these wonders.

From the mysteries of Cagliostro we come to the clear experiments of Galvani, who lent movement and apparent animation by his electric sparks to the limbs of dead animals. From the rudimentary and imperfect experiments of Galvani, we arrived at the knowledge of the electric fluid and its laws, thanks to Volta, who placed mechanically a piece of damp newspaper on his lip, between thin plates of zinc and copper, and found their wonderful relation; so that in perfecting these discoveries he arrived at the great fountain of electricity through the means attained by the Voltaic combination. Morse—a man belonging to the race of Franklin, the first whom nature thought worthy to hold the lightning in his hand, till then reserved for the Deity—Morse invented the telegraph, and put the electro-magnetic fluid, the soul of fearful tempests, under the dominion of man.

The human thought, notwithstanding its infinite intensity, wants power to follow all the advances made from steam, magnetism, electricity, the discovery of new gases, and the composition of chemical substances, the explorations of telescopes in the heavens, the discoveries of travelers on the earth, the ascension in the atmosphere, the descent into mines and into the depths of the sea, the classification of dead as well as of living species, the progress of physiology which regards our bodies, and the progress of the cosmogony which studies the universe.

But can we boast of equal moral and equal physical greatness? Do we not err by excess of materialism, as did the ancient classic world? Do we not sin by forgetting the soul we bear within us, and the God who animates the universe? It is indispensable to raise a grand ideal before the eyes of this materialistic civilization. I know how much exclusive vocations are opposed to this. Thus, as there are ears which can not perceive the harmony of music, eyes which do not see the beauty of landscapes, so there are souls which do not feel the necessity of religion. But human societies can not be exclusive; human societies always contend, as in the law, as in art, in science, in labor, as in that other end of the serious part of life—religion. But in proportion as the material progress is great, the spirit religious, the inspiration artistic, it should hold more tenaciously to idealism. And the god of the Vatican—that species of material idol, clothed with brocades, crowned with diamonds, enveloped in clouds of incense, intoxicated with the adulation once offered to the deified Cæsars of antiquity—does not respond to the necessities of our epoch, nor slake with his theocratic doctrines the inextinguishable thirst of our spirit. In Rome, under the shadow of so many temples, in that labyrinth of altars, at the sight of the innumerable cupolas, from whence have ascended as by a mysterious stair countless prayers to Heaven, over the ruins heaped on those sacred plains by devouring ages, the recollections of dead gods are scattered to the winds, and the heart is raised to the living Jehovah, One, Absolute, Eternal; that Being, Essence, Truth, Good, Perfection; the God of Nature and of the Spirit, elevated above all the changes and transformations of history, and who communicates to our souls the ineffable hope of immortality.

This great idea grows with the growth of the conscience, and is purified with its purification. Revelation is not over, no, though some believe the fountain is exhausted. The age of reason commences, and we know not what light and heat reason will bear in her bosom. The Indian Zeus, born at the foot of those high mountains, perfumed with the aroma of those leafy groves, received in his cradle of palms the light which spread from nation to nation and from generation to generation, till it reached the summit of the Greek Olympus. And one day, among the people protected by the Holy God, burst forth the revelation of the unity of the human conscience, a necessary completion to the unity of the divine nature which was revealed among the lightnings of Sinai. And these two most grand ideas grew and were spiritualized in the dialogues of the Academy, at the magic influence of the eloquence of Plato, as an infusion of the Deity into the veins of man; and when thought, extended and enlightened, was able to reduce metaphysics to morals, and from morals passed to law, it became essential to universalize it in the minds of the multitude, to give it to the people, that so much labor should not be lost, that so many revelations should not remain as ideas without reality and without form in the vague abstraction of the schools. The belief in its generality, in its pure abstraction, seems to be a spirit without a body—it neither agitates minds nor alarms the interested. But a new conception, preached in the free air, told in the ears of the people, clashes with the general feeling of its time, and provokes the wrath of superstition and ignorance. For this the Redeemer was wanted; the Redeemer born to diffuse the truth and take it to human hearts, to speak it as an incessant prayer on His most eloquent lips, to spread it among the people, who kindled the anger of the old idols and strictest sects, who gave His life in fearful torments for the weak, for the humble, for the oppressed, for the disinherited of the world. And the religion of the Redeemer became embodied in a Church at first believed to be the work of one sole people, of one single sect; but afterward opened to the invasion of all races, to the influence of all doctrines, by means of the genius ever found in the virtue of innovators, the elevation of philosophers, the eloquence of apostles, the heroism of martyrs. And revelation has not been interrupted. Some have brought to it the Judaic and Shemitic spirit; others the Hellenic-Latin; others the Alexandrian. Those four mysterious cities which hold in their hands the web of European civilization—Jerusalem, Rome, Athens, Alexandria—spoke; and their words were preserved and raised to heaven by the divine Word. And the infinite series of revelations has not been interrupted; because there came the revelation of art in the Renaissance, the revelation of science in philosophy, the revelation of the right in the great revolutions, whose electric current has created man anew, and brought, in tongues of fire, a divine spirit to the conscience. Alas! there are sects and dignitaries of the Church who believe their exclusive spirit, their narrow doctrine, their egotistical feelings to be the spirit, the doctrine, and the feeling of humanity—of that immortal being whose conscience is as the space inclosing all great principles; whose thought is as the sun enlightening the worlds; whose spirit is as the air giving life and vigor. Ruins are skeletons accumulated by ages. Doctrine arises from some altar and moves ceaselessly onward to others, reborn continually from its ashes, transforming itself into an infinite series of developments, as a perpetual renovation of the earth, and a never-ending holocaust which sends an eternal cloud of incense toward the heavens.

Chapter IX.

THE GHETTO.

From the greatest height to the deepest abyss—after the Vatican, the Ghetto! The district inhabited by the Jews in Rome is called the Ghetto. A population within another population astonishes many, but not the Spaniards. It is nearly four hundred years since we expelled our Jews, reserving to ourselves the right to burn all those who imitated or followed them—all Judaizers; even yet we have in our cities well-known quarters where Jewry dares not enter. Remember Toledo! The Church of San Juan de los Reyes, on the hill-side near the Cambron Gate and the Bridge of St. Martin; also the Church of the Transito, with its arched windows, its rich inlaid work, its vaults of cedar incrusted with gold and marble, the psalms written on its walls in Hebraic characters, like the Church of Santa Maria la Blanca, with its octagonal columns, its Syrian capitals, its horse-shoe arches; both these churches are ancient synagogues, and show that there dwelt the Children of Israel—those tenacious worshipers of the one true God—those pursued by the Goths who revenged their affronts in Guadelete, the wealthy merchants, the untiring workers—those who disseminated the teaching of he Arab schools of Cordova, of Seville, of Toledo, through the south of France, and through all the regions of Italy—those who demonstrated to Don Alonso VI. that they had no part in the death of the Saviour—those who aided in the labors of Don Alonso the Wise—those wounded by the sword of Enrique de Trastamara—those spit upon and beaten by the eloquence of San Vincente Ferrar—those expelled by the piety of Doña Isabel, the Catholic—the Jews of Toledo.

These Israelites are truly an extraordinary race. We ourselves have swallowed innumerable successions of gods. The divinities of the Phœnicians, of the Greeks, of the Romans, joined to our aboriginal deities, have fallen into the depths of our consciences, and have in time passed from our consciences. Even now the great Catholic theology, but lately cherished like the essence of our spirit, is passing away. Our soul is changing because it is progressive. Among Western peoples, those who think often neither pray nor believe—those who pray and believe do not think. We pass the second half of our life destroying with our reason the creeds inspired by the education and the faith of the first half. No, as a people, we are not religious! And these Jews still speak like Abraham, sing the same psalms as David, keep the idea of God treasured as the manna of souls in the desert, obey the law given from Sinai, overcome the captivity of Babylon, the cajoleries of Alexander, the irresistible sceptre of Rome, the dispersion exacted by Titus, the maledictions of the Popes, the mandates of Kings, the rage of the people, the flames of the Inquisition, the intolerance of all sects; and between the currents of ideas which ceaselessly move and transform those around, they, as if they were beyond time and change, rebuild in their hearts their ruined temple, where they preserve unaltered their ancient faith and their consoling hopes.

Guided by a double sentiment of compassion and curiosity, I went to visit the Jews' quarter in Rome. Cleanliness is unthought of in the Eternal City. Heaps of dirt surround you at every crossing. The clear streams which flow along gigantic aqueducts and through monumental fountains are wasted, neither cleansing the heights of hills nor the depths of the valleys, as if they were lost under the earth. The Tiber is truly the river of the sewers. Its yellow waters look like a flow of gall. The Eternal City is a dirty town. To say truth, one must hold his nostrils to inhale those spiritual aromas which intoxicated the soul of Louis Veuillot. The Jews' quarter is filthy and disgusting. The feet sink in those revolting streets, which resemble ill-kept pig-sties. Half-naked children, so incrusted with dirt that they look as if covered with leprosy, play in all directions. Old women with wrinkled and yellow complexions, gray hair, watery eyes, and a sinister expression on their withered lips, stand at the doors of the little shops, which look like rat-traps. Each of these dens emits an insufferable odor. With the Jewish race there are mingled some gypsy families, fallen from a higher position, and living now under the same malediction. Some of these poor women, whom the Inquisition would have burned for cheating, robbery, and above all for witchcraft, invite the stranger in an almost unintelligible guttural to have his fortune told upon the cards. Several groups of people, seated on stones, play cards, the games being much like those in use in the southern parts of Spain. When any difficulty, fraud, or dispute arises, they utter cries which are heard all over the Ghetto. Some gnash their teeth, others clench their fists, pour forth threatening words, and gesticulate as if about to engage in a pitched battle. The children add to the noise and confusion by screaming around the circle. The women look out of the windows, participate in the general emotion, and take sides in the quarrel, being guided, not by truth and reason, but by their feelings, which tell them their nearest relations are in the right. Hear them, but beware of mixing yourself in the fray, or you will probably be beaten and bruised by the excited and angry crowd. In the Ghetto you must limit your observations to the squalid and filthy streets, the hideous dens, the yellow and miserable-looking population, the rags hanging from the windows, and the thick atmosphere of pestilential vapors which surrounds that pandemonium, where dwell the representatives of the race which above all others keeps true to its belief in its ancient history and religious principles.

The keeping up of old ideas is a virtue beloved by the Popes, but the Jews have never found favor under the Pontificate.

However, the condition of the Israelites has considerably improved under the present Pope. The iron chains which separated them from the rest of the population, and kept them prisoners, have fallen, thanks to the liberal views of Pius IX.

There is no longer any necessity for them to bury themselves in their dens after nightfall, and they are free to go where they will about the city. The tribute of fifty centimes per head, formerly exacted from the Jews, has not been demanded from them since 1848. They rarely take advantage of the privilege of being able to live in any part of the city, on account of the great difficulty of finding quarters as cheap as those of their own district, where rent and taxes have been mercifully fixed at a low rate by some old Pontifical decrees.

But how these Jews have suffered! Tacitus made them the subjects of his bitter invectives, and Lucian of his contemptuous mockeries. They were most cruelly treated by the Emperors, who on many occasions flung them as food for the wild beasts of the circus. They were also persecuted with the Christians, even though they abominated the novelties brought by Christianity to their belief. They were ill-treated by the barbarous nations recently converted to the Christian faith. They were isolated and shut out from the rest of the world by the Popes. And, notwithstanding all this, there are countries where the persecution was still more implacable against the Israelites than in Rome—countries where the records of them remain only in history. Let us admire their faith and firmness. For one of their religion who abjures his faith, vast numbers retain it. The deepest of their thinkers believe that the human race has wandered because it has admitted with Christianity the metaphysical ideas of the Greek school, in the theological dogma of the unity of God, and in the severe and sublime decalogue of Moses. They believe that the Jewish people will renounce their supremacy as a sacerdotal people, as a Levitical people, the day that their brothers, the Christian sectarians, renounce the anthropomorphic ideas of Greece. And humanity, united in the same spirit from which right only is derived, will be enabled to purify its conscience in the great principle of the divine Unity, and its will in the strict precepts of the Decalogue. These ideas do not circulate through the minds of the poor Jews of the Ghetto, whose imaginations have been compressed into the narrowest compass by persecution, but the cement of a solid faith binds them to all of their own religion.

I can not understand how some religious writers wonder at this Jewish steadfastness. Why then does not all Roman life participate in the same immovability? Is there any other part of the world whose history is so eventful? Still the nymph Egeria is heard in the grotto of Numa; still the shades of the tribunes wander on the heights of Aventino. On descending to the Catacombs, imagination brings back the Christian Agapæ; and when coming through the Via Appia, after having visited the sepulchres, fancy conjures from the past a funeral of ancient Rome. The desolation which the wrong doings of the patricians produced on those majestic plains exhales to-day the same deadly vapors. The Cæsar-Popes still inhabit the gardens of Nero. The architecture of antiquity still overawes the Catholic spirit. The Roman aristocracy shows still the debility contracted in the times of the Empire, when the perpetual dictators who succeeded to Cæsar laid down their arms, and with them all their dignity. The clergy close their eyes to the voice of reason, struggle against all progress, oppose all reformation, just as the priests of Paganism, when crowned with verbena, waved their sacrificial wands of gold over the invading legions of the Goths, and forbade the proclamation of Christianity as the religion of the Empire by the Senate of Theodosius. And if you attentively examine the lower classes, you at once perceive the features of antiquity, not only in the Grecian profile and in the Roman muscle, but in the mixture of pride and indolence; like a people accustomed to be amused by all others, and who are at the same time supported and taken care of by a ruler.

The Jews show a wonderful tenacity of conscience and religion. And what cruel attacks have been made against this tenacity. The same repugnance exists against them in Rome as against the Chuetans in Majorca. In this age of religious tolerance, of democratic institutions, we have seen expelled from a public ball in Majorca those citizens who belonged to the race of Chueta, that is, those descended from Israelites. The Roman Catholicism of these people, raised to the most extreme exaltation, has not exempted them from the consequences of their original error. There are towns in the island which consider it a glory never to have admitted a Chueta within their precincts. And some of these Chuetans signed in the year 1854 several reasons against religious liberty, although the *quemadero* is scarcely yet cold on which the bones of their fathers were consumed in the fire. I have been unable to ascertain if those observers of the Catalan rites, now in use among the four synagogues of the Ghetto, will have any dealings with the accursed race of Majorca. Never have I beheld such love of country as that manifested by the Spanish Jews. So much injustice, so much cruel oppression, has not been able to inspire them with a mistrust for their mother country, which has been for them a step-mother. I knew in Florence a Jewish couple who had come from Damascus, and were traveling through Europe. The wife was the Oriental type of most perfect beauty. Her pale complexion, toned by the lustre of her large black eyes, half veiled by long and shadowy eyelashes, appeared between the rich curls of hair, fine and brilliant as silk. Her nose was Grecian, as that of the Venus of Milo; her lips rosy as the bright carmine of the pomegranate blossom. My attention was drawn to so much loveliness, and hers was attracted by the language of my country, which I was speaking with some Spaniards and Americans. Immediately she turned to her husband and said some words to him in Spanish. The national language, spoken in a foreign land, vibrated in the ears of the exile, overcame and transported him like the most harmonious music. Being unable to restrain my emotion, I said, "Señora, are you Spanish?" Then she told me that she was a Jewess, born in Leghorn, and married to a Greek residing in Damascus; that she had learned Spanish in the synagogue of her country, and that she was accustomed to speak it with those of her religion in the East, many of whom had preserved it as a pious souvenir of their origin, as a glorious stamp of their nationality. The most lively affections are always those arising from contrasts.

My love of country, intense as it is, seemed but feeble compared with the love of this race for Spain, which persecuted them as if they had been savage beasts, insulted them by all kinds of affronts, rooted them out of their national earth, dispersed and exiled them for four centuries; yet toward which they turn the loving eyes of children, still speaking her language, as the Israelites of old intoned the songs of the prophets on the banks of the Euphrates, under the weeping-willows of Babylon.

Thinking and feeling thus, I saw as in a magnetic vision the political movement which is to break the chain of ancient traditions in my country, and I vowed if I should at any future time obtain the confidence of my fellow-citizens in the exalted post of legislator, to make ceaseless exertions till we were no longer in the modern world a monstrous exception to other nations by our intolerance, and to open the doors of our country alike to all sects, to all peoples, and to all ideas; to hold as a sacred right, compared to which all other rights are as nothing, the right to open the mind to light, and to adore in public as in secret the God who lives in our conscience.

How much I was influenced in the accomplishment of this promise, given by my heart and my intelligence, by the recollection of that pale and miserable Jewish population of the Ghetto, steeped in ignorance and poverty! And as on entering the Pontifical States we are forced to compare their prohibitive custom-houses with the free commerce of the Swiss Republic, so, on seeing the filthy quarter of the Roman Jews, we remember the religious liberty of Geneva, the full right enjoyed by all there to worship as they desire, the supplications addressed to God by the Children of Israel in the republican language of the prophets that He should preserve to Switzerland her free institutions, where the light of different consciences shines like stars in the immensity of the heavens.

Truly the Jewish people have admirably preserved their religion in the court of the chiefs of Roman Catholicism, where the Catholics have persecuted the Jews, tortured and proscribed them. But if this is a proof on one side of some tolerance in the Popes, on the other hand it is a proof of the remarkable tenacity of the Jews. They have preserved their identity and their religion, it is true, but they have done so in great misery. The prohibition to acquire landed property condemns them continually to commerce. And commerce is unfruitful without frugality, and frugality is unproductive unless it is transformed into property. For this reason, as soon as the Roman Jew by his industry has been enabled to gather together a sum of money, he leaves his poor abode, and goes in search of milder laws than those of the Eternal City. So in the dens of the Ghetto you only find those hungry and wretched Jews who traffic in old lumber of all kinds, and who gain barely sufficient to sustain their feeble lives and to warm now and then their melancholy abodes.

No one can deny that Pius IX. has considerably improved the condition of the Jews. But the latter still feel the power of tyranny and the scourge of theocracy. To be able to comprehend this position, one must study rationalistic and revolutionary authors, one must read the works of Catholics on this subject. At first sight it is extremely difficult to discover the truth among the contradictory judgments pronounced upon Rome by those irreconcilable schools—the Catholic and the Rationalistic. The times are past in which the clergy, like the Archprelate of Hita, and Catholics like Hurtado de Mendoza, tyrannized in Rome. Already for great numbers of Catholics, their religion is no longer a religion, but a political party. And consequently its doctrines are not so much dogmas which require explanations, as polemics which demand dates and arguments. On the other hand Roman Catholicism is for many a domination which should be destroyed at all costs, as galley-slaves should at all efforts break their fetters. Some see only in the Eternal City the virtues of Catholicism, others only see its abominations. It is difficult to deduce the truth from these contradictions, which influence even the most trifling details. A Liberal journal will tell you that there exist in Pontifical Rome two thousand women devoted to the perilous office of models; and a religious paper will declare that the perfidy of their enemies has falsified the number by two ciphers. The *Journal of the Debates* relates the following atrocity:

"The Romans are brutalized and degraded to such an extent, and are so blood-thirsty, that it is their custom to shut themselves up in a large hall, and there, after having extinguished all the lights, to satiate their desire for butchery by mutually wounding each other with daggers. This frightful slaughter is called by the name of *cicciata*."

A Roman Catholic, an apostolic prothonotary, in speaking

of this gives the following explanation, which I copy literally:

"Father Caravita founded not a hall, as the Voltairian journal declares, but an oratory. This Father Caravita was a Jesuit of the ancient order. He assembled in the oratory people of good life and morals, to ask in common of heaven the conversion of sinners. This pious society soon took different denominations, and became extended over the whole of the Christian world. It was open alternately to men at night, and to women in the day-time. From the commencement of the ceremony five or six priests were seated in the confessionals and received the confessions of the sins committed, which they pardoned in the name of God. They counted in a year fifty thousand absolutions of prodigal sons, who, conquering their human scruples under the shades of darkness, came to purify their consciences and to find repose. While some confessed or prepared themselves for confession, others kneeling on the pavement recited the litany to the Virgin and chanted psalms in choir. The prayers concluded, a priest descended from the great altar and distributed among those who demanded them flexible cords, with the extremities well prepared. Then all the lights were extinguished, and in the midst of total darkness a priest in a loud voice exhorted the congregation to penance and contrition. Affected by his address they prostrated themselves, and, when he had finished speaking, they lashed their shoulders with repeated blows during the whole time of the chanting of the Litany and the *Nunc Dimittis*, till the words *lumen ad revelationem*, when the tapers were again lighted."

Reading and comparing both these relations, one can easily arrive at the truth. I read in an author worthy of the *Index* that the Popes compel the Jews to go every week, at least once, to hear a Catholic sermon directed expressly against them and their doctrines, in order to touch their hearts and to attract them toward the true religion. At first I did not believe such an enormity. Could there be a greater outrage to the inviolability of the human conscience? Is it possible? I believe that such a temple is a shadow instead of a light; that such a service is a superstition instead of a sacred ceremony; that such a doctrine is an error instead of a truth; and I oblige myself to enter these temples, to be present at this worship, to hear these doctrines torturing my soul and her belief with miserable agitations. The most offensive and insufferable of all tyrannies is that imposed upon the thoughts, for, without offending in any way, I am permitted neither observation nor reply; arguments are brought forward with insults more or less painful to my religion—that which constitutes the soul of my soul, the blood of my heart, the very essence of my spirit, that intimate faith under whose protection I live and hope to die, that religious belief which is my national law, the tie which attaches me to life, my hope for all eternity. And I can not picture by any force of imagination what would be the sufferings of some pious persons whom I know and esteem, if they were compelled to go every week to a temple where they would hear evil spoken of Christ and His mother, where that Scripture would be denied which renews their strength and fortifies their souls. To me it appears that such a proceeding ignores altogether that evangelical maxim which obliges us to do unto others as we would they should do unto us, the peace of our hearts and of our souls, the inviolability of our consciences, and the comfort of our lives.

It is impossible to understand why the Jews should be outraged in this manner—impossible. Even polemics are difficult between them and Christians. We believe all the principal Jewish dogmas. Their God is our God, their law our law, their Bible our Bible. We have added the Gospel to the Old Testament; to the monotheistical God of the Shemitical desert, the word and the spirit of Grecian metaphysics. The great difference is that we believe the Messiah has already come, and they look forward with hope to His appearing. For us redemption is consummated, for them it has yet to be accomplished. They can not comprehend that the prophecies have been fulfilled, when they have a national signification, and Israel is notwithstanding dispersed, and the temple of God is still in ruins. Go and tell them, if their own inspiration does not persuade them, that the poor Nazarene, born in a lowly station, without other army than His apostles recruited on the shores of Tiberias, without other arms than the words confided to the winds, without other throne than the cross, without other glory than death and the gibbet, is the all-powerful Messiah come to redeem His chosen people from serfdom. You would offend, but could not persuade them, and they will depart from the temple more wounded than edified by your teaching; and, as a natural reaction, a hatred and blasphemy against our faith will become almost a necessity to their souls.

And, nevertheless, it is impossible to doubt of this ancient custom, when the apostolic prothonotary Gaissiat, in his work entitled *Rome Avenged*, not only mentions but glories in it. He exults in narrating how the preacher explained and commented upon the Psalms read and chanted by the rabbi during the past week. He asseverates that he never heard in those discourses offensive words from the lips of the Israelites, which, if it does not arise from terror, proves a degree of prudence unfortunately not copied by their masters ; and he adds that, at the conclusion of the sermon, the Jews went to congratulate the preacher, though doubtless astonished at the bitter attack upon their most deeply rooted prejudices. Be it said in honor of Pius IX. that under his Pontificate this custom has been abolished, but little importance having been attached to these pretended conversions of persons who, as regarded their own belief, were greater royalists than the king, more papistical than the Pope. And if this custom, so opposed to the religious spirit of the Gospel, ever existed, we can not doubt of the existence of other customs, such as bringing a Bible to the newly elected Pope, near the Arch of Titus, which records the destruction of Jerusalem, and the abolition, in 1848, of bringing the tribute of blood, the tribute of the stranger, every year on the eve of the Carnival to the Roman senators, hearing in exchange some offensive and contemptuous formula.

Let us try to be guided by strict truth and impartiality. The proof that the legislation of the Popes is made up of incomprehensible cruelties is to be seen in the celebrated history of the Jewish boy, secretly baptized through the officiousness of a fanatical maid-servant, torn from that divinely appointed authority, the natural and unreplaceable guardianship of his father and mother, and shut up in a convent that can never be a substitute for home education, and which, being contrary to all the established ideas of right, can not be blessed by God. When this boy arrives at maturity, if he has then a mother, if he meets her, if he feels in his heart toward her the natural promptings of filial tenderness, and he hears her say how much she has suffered from being divided from the object of her sacred affections, from that inseparable part of her own being, from the child of her hope and consolation—will he not curse and forswear that religion which has made his mother shed tears of bitter sorrow?

After this example, I, for my own part, have no scruple about believing similar stories referred to by revolutionary authors, and which prove that under the pretense of converting to Roman Catholicism the Roman Jews, after the manner of the ancient Moors of Spain, they break without remorse the most natural authority, such as that of parents; and ignore the strictest duties, such as those of the family, not only in the civil sphere, but in the moral sphere, there especially where a priestly government should be most scrupulous.

It is time for all persecutions against opinion to be abolished. I condemn the Roman Government when it oppresses the Jews, and the Government of Prussia when it proscribes the Jesuits. I assert that to persecute doctrines is like the persecution of light, air, electricity, magnetic fluids; because these escape all persecution, and are placed above all power. If I can not conceive the persecution of opinions, still less can I comprehend the persecution of associations, when they have for a definite object the unfolding of a principle, a system of religion or of government. Ideas by their own worth become organized into societies. Both combined form a perfect union like that of soul and body, of light and heat. But if I can neither understand the persecution of ideas, nor of associations whose object is to explain and divulge them, still less can I conceive the persecution of entire races, of human families, under the pretext that one act mentioned in the history of those races has condemned them through all the succession of ages to be accursed. I know all the defects of the Jewish people, I know all their unrestrained love of money and all their egotism. But their misfortunes more than overbalance their errors. And above all they do not deserve the oppression which has weighed upon their lives and consciences so many ages for having put to death a religious reformer. For them the Redeemer was not one alone. In the history of humanity there have been many friends and helpers. This one has enlightened the conscience, that has instructed the reason, the other has saved from labor. And almost all these liberators have died before their work, immolated legally or illegally by tyrannical sects, by intolerant churches, by barbarous institutions, against which the protest and doctrines of innovators have arisen. What people have not brought upon themselves some crime similar to that of the Jews in their own eyes? What great man has not been the victim of the laws, or the object of human ingratitude?

The Greeks sacrificed the revealer of the human conscience; the Romans, the tribune of social reform; the Florentines, the precursor of modern revolutions; the Britons, the prophet of religious tolerance; the French, the Titan of democratic principles; the Spaniards, the discoverer, almost the creator of a new world in the immensity of the ocean. The Jews sacrificed the Christ. But tell me, how many prophets, how many reformers have not the Christians sacrificed when they preached against their Church as Christ preached against the synagogue? how many have attempted to reform or complete the law of Christ, as Christ reformed and completed the law of Moses? And for the Saviour, there was the bloody sweat in the garden of Gethsemane, the traitor kiss of Judas, the prison of shame, and the examination of the tribunal; the anguish in the prætorium; the smitings on the cheek, and the blasphemies cast upon His name; the way of sorrow where He fell three times under His burden; the nails which wounded His hands and the thorns which tore His temples; the gall and vinegar which steeped His lips; the sharp spear which pierced His side; the agony on the cross; the words, the bitter supplication, laden with that terrible agony; the death cry, at whose echo the graves were rent asunder—these should be the eternal epopee of religious liberty!

Let there be no more accursed races upon the earth. Let every one act according to his conscience, and communicate freely with his God. Let thought be only corrected by the contradiction of thought. Let error be an infirmity, and not a crime. Let us agree in acknowledging that opinions sometimes take possession of our understandings quite independent of our will or desire. Let us be so just as to be enabled to see even to what degree each race has contributed to the universal education of humanity. These Israelites, cursed by Christian legislatures, are they who have given to us the doctrine of the unity of the Creator — they who have brought the decalogue which is stamped on the heart of our families and in the sanctuary of our homes—the children of the ancient prophets—the descendants of that David whose Psalms we still sing under the roofs of our churches—the subjects of that Solomon whose Proverbs constitute the basis of our common belief—the redeemed from Egyptian bondage by that Moses whom we count among our legislators—those taught by Isaiah, by Jeremiah, whom we place among our prophets —those who have contributed most to form the essence of our ideas and the leaven of our lives. "How much would Catholicism gain in this supreme crisis," said I, while trampling through the filth of the Ghetto, and seeing in the faces of its inhabitants the signs of moral and religious debility, "if the Christian conscience would but consider the services lent to the education of humanity by all races and by all institutions?"

Chapter X.

THE GREAT CITY.

Naples is now not only the first among Italian cities on account of its numerous population and its great dimensions, but it is as certainly one of the principal towns in Europe. When looked down upon from a height, the eye is scarcely aware of that space which separates it from the adjoining villages, and then it appears to be as large as London. So much was I deceived as to its size, that, comparing my recollection of the panorama of Paris seen from the Pantheon, and of Naples as it appeared from Posilippo, Naples seemed to me to be very much greater than Paris, by one of those optical illusions to which the light and brilliancy of the southern sky so much contribute.

I shall never forget my arrival at the most beautiful capital of the ancient Two Sicilies. In a foreign land the smallest accident or inconvenience irritates and oppresses. Vexation soon becomes pain, and pain grows into suffering as homesickness increases. It appears as if the whole human race should abhor you, since you became wearied of your country; that all society should renounce you, since you have renounced the society in which you were born. When you meet a citizen who speaks about political subjects in the midst of his own people — the father of a family who goes into his home or walks out with his children—you feel yourself the most miserable of mortals, and think your bones are destined to lie solitary and forgotten among strangers. Above all, if the government—if the policy of the nation in which you hoped to find a safe asylum—molests you, the heart becomes doubly sad, and you ask yourself the bitter question, "If every where I am to be persecuted, why, oh! why have I abandoned my country?"

While I was in Rome I devoted myself altogether to study and meditation. For me the antiquities were alone interesting in that city, and the works of art rising majestically among the ruins. I almost completely avoided society, and spent my time in the museums, in the churches, in the Catacombs—in the great world of past ages. Every day I found something new among the old, and bound together these discoveries with history and laws, in the same manner as the naturalist confirms his classifications and his varieties with the discoveries of new or repeated specimens. I found myself calm and contented in that city where all great sorrow can find a refuge, for it can have there a consolation. The desolation of the Roman Campagna harmonized well with the loneliness of my own soul. The self-forgetfulness which the spectacle of so many ruins procured for the lacerated heart could not exist, could not be attained in any other city in the world.

How often I thought of detaching myself from the ties which bound my life to Paris, as the centre of my banishment, and of remaining there in silent contemplation of the monuments, in intercourse with the arts, in the continuous study of history.

True, neither my philosophical ideas nor my political opinions would be acceptable to the then ruling power, but what could be done against the Government by a poor unfortunate without home, without country, without family, without connections in that society? One, too, who desired to seek forgetfulness from his sorrows, and to devote himself to the study of dead institutions, buried in the tomb of that vast necropolis as sad as my own heart.

I was thus thinking one lovely spring morning when a waiter from the Hotel Minerva entered hastily into my modest apartment, and, without drawing breath or wishing me good-day, said to me in a terrified manner—

"Why did you conceal your rank from me?"

"My rank? I had none to conceal; for I am of no position in the world."

"Your importance?"

"I am not of any consequence."

"You are a distinguished person."

"I celebrated! Bah! are you mocking me?" I demanded.

"I have kept the police from coming to your chamber."

"The police?"

"Yes; the police would have been here before this if I had not dissuaded them by saying I would communicate to you their order."

"What order?"

"The order to leave Rome immediately."

"For what reason?"

"You have given much reason."

"But may I not be informed what reason?"

"They say that the books written and published by you are condemned by the *Index*."

"It is true; but if all the authors whose works are condemned by the *Index* are forbidden to inhabit this literary Rome, truly you will be visited by very few literary people."

"They say you are a friend of Garibaldi and of Mazzini."

"It is true."

"At all events you are very brave."

"Why?"

"For coming to Rome with such antecedents."

"But I ought to assure you that I did not come to Rome for any political purpose. You must have noticed that I neither make nor receive visits."

"They say more than that."

"What do they say?"

"That you have been condemned to death.

"For what offense?"

"For taking part in a revolution."

"For being a Liberal—a Democrat."

"And you know," he said, mysteriously, "the very cordial relations existing between the Government of the Cardinals of Rome and the Government of the Bourbons of Spain. It is to be feared that, you having been sentenced to death in Spain, the Roman police will arrest you and take you a prisoner to Civita Vecchia, then send you on board the military frigate anchored in the bay. There they will hang you."

"What an opinion you have of this Christian government!" I exclaimed, with astonishment. "This danger is altogether imaginary."

"But the real and great danger you are in at this moment is to be imprisoned if you do not leave Rome by the first train."

"Imprisoned! I have already endured confinement with resignation in my own country. The thought that I was among my own people, the acknowledgment that I merited it as a conspirator, probably softened my troubles. But the prison here terrifies me. At what hour does the earliest train leave Rome?"

"At ten o'clock."

"What time is it now?"

"Half-past nine."

"Where does it go?"

"To the south."

"I am neither ready, nor have I been able to make any preparation. But no matter."

I summoned my traveling companions—a Mexican landed proprietor, and two young Spanish gentlemen who were studying in the College of Bologna, and who were going through Italy during the Easter vacation—gave my luggage into their keeping, set out in one of those little carriages which do not run but fly, arrived at the station, took a ticket, and installed myself in a carriage, with the travelers' guide-book in one hand and the *Roman Journal* in the other.

On setting out the train skirted the Via Appia, and we beheld the tomb of Cecilia Metella. These grand monuments always inspire me with deep melancholy. An exile, one condemned to death for the crime of professing certain political opinions, was it not one more ruin among many ruins—one more shadow among so many shadows—one more death among so many dead? No fear or inquietude should be felt by that immense power whose name is daily invoked by millions of beings at the foot of their altars all around the globe. They had driven me not only from my country, but from that city which appeared to have the eternal right to be a refuge. A corpse is never denied a few feet of the earth, but it is refused to a living man. To draw my mind from such painful reflections, I turned my eyes upon the newspaper and saw the following notice:

"The Pope offered a residence in Rome to the King of Hanover, who was dethroned and proscribed; for Rome is an asylum, an eternal refuge for all the unfortunate."

I smiled bitterly, and seemed to taste gall upon my lips. With such sad thoughts I left the city of eternal sadness.

What a contrast between the Campagna of Naples and the Campagna of Rome! In the one is unity and in the other variety; in this is the sublime and in that the beautiful; here the majesty and there the grace; in Rome is heard the melody of a lament like the harmonious psalmody of the Biblical prophets, and in Naples the choir of the ancient Greek divinities. But if the contrast is great between country and country, how much greater it is between city and city. Let the sworn enemies of Pontifical Rome say what they will, it appeared to me, when compared with Naples, a severe — a most severe city. At least there reigns in Rome sadness and silence. Its inhabitants seem to look upon darkness. Their faces have a certain solemn sadness, like that of a sovereign but a dethroned race. The innumerable convents, the multitudes of monks, the chapels which arise on all sides, the statues which ornament the corners of the streets, all show that the Romans are a people submissive to theocracy; while the cries in the streets of Naples, the continual vociferations, the gay groups standing around, the universal gayety, the dances on one side, the open-air concerts on the other, the concourse of people to the water-stalls and cafés, show you are in a civil city where life is a continual festival. And there is no longer the same number of religious pictures as formerly. For the image of the Saviour they have substituted the portrait of Garibaldi. To worship is a necessity for the Neapolitans—to worship fervently whatever be the object of their adoration; to worship devotedly among blows and outcries, with huzzas and shouting, with all the exaltation common to highly nervous temperaments, and with the fanaticism which accompanies the excitement of southern passions kindled by the intense heat of the climate. There is something of Vesuvius — something of its burning fires, something of its eruptions, something also of its changeableness—in the fickle and ardent nature of the Neapolitans—of those degenerate Greeks who dwell, always with a smile upon their lips, upon the borders of death—threatened by their volcano with a doom similar to that which buried the cities of Pompeii and Herculaneum.

Many times when strolling through the streets of the great cities of Northern Europe, and observing the silence and gravity of the people, I have thought of the effect which would be produced by so vast a population as that of London, or even of Paris, were these capitals situated in the south of Europe. What a stormy sea would all these people make under one sky! What an uproar would arise in the streets! A town of the south is like a grove of the tropics whither the people resort for recreation. There is a life and gayety about them that you would seek in vain among the fogs of London or Paris. From the heights of Montmartre or from the cemetery of Père la Chaise, I have never heard at the fall of day the same noises I have heard at the same hour from the gardens of the Retiro. One could fancy Madrid a larger town than Paris. But, when compared with Seville and Valencia, Madrid is a silent city. What nights those are in Seville! The children play and shout; the young men sing and touch the guitar; families, seated at their ease, listen to the piano in the open air of their *patios*, among bright flowers, aromatic plants, and jets of murmuring water. What days are those of the festivals in Valencia—above all, those of summer! The ringing of the bells, the music in the streets, tambourines and trumpets keeping time to the dances, the fire-works exploding like little cannons, the interminable row of small petards upon the ground, and the sky-rockets flying through the glowing air!

Well, then, I tell you that Seville and Valencia are quiet towns compared with Naples. True, Naples contains six hundred thousand inhabitants. But the difference does not arise from the greater population. No! Our southern temperament is restrained by our Spanish gravity. There is even in more southern Spanish towns something of the abstraction and of the religious silence of the Moors. Neither the Andalusians nor the Valencians throw up their hands, gesticulate, or shout like the people of Naples. Even our peasantry, in the midst of their chatter and their festivals, have all the Spanish dignity. The Neapolitans are noisy and loquacious as Greeks. What confusion in the town! How much more suitable to the state of my feelings was Rome, with all her melancholy sublimity; the Miserere of Palestrina, the walk along the Via Appia, bordered with monuments, the continual contemplation of the desolate Campagna, the philosophical meditations over the weather-beaten stones, among the ruins of the Coliseum, under the shadow of the Cross.

Those who are fond of clamor and bustle throng to Naples. The foot-paths all support a traffic. Upon all these are little shops and movable stalls, sometimes sleeping people, as motionless as corpses. A thousand small organs, harps, and violins distract the ears. Crowds of puppet-players, rope-dancers, and conjurers, with their corresponding circles of wonder-struck admirers, throng the thoroughfares and embarrass the movements of passengers. The workmen sing or dispute with each other in loud voices.

The idle, when they have no one to speak to, talk noisily to themselves. The coachmen or cart-drivers who pass vociferate energetically, dashing along in all directions and throwing up clouds of dust. Every mule wears hundreds of buttons and little jingling bells. The carriages creak as if creaking was the object of their construction. The sellers of newspapers, and in general all itinerant traders, shout in the most astonishing manner. Every tradesman at the door of his shop, or over his stall, makes a pompous oral programme of his rich merchandise, begging every stranger to purchase. The seller of scapularies, without knowing any thing of your country or religion, fixes his amulet on your neck; while the shoe-black, no matter whether your boots are dim or shining, rubs them over with his varnish, with or without your consent. The flower-seller, who carries bundles of roses and orange blossoms, adorns your hat, your button-holes, your pockets, without ever asking your permission. The lemonade-maker comes out with a flowing glass which he places at your lips. Scarcely have you freed yourself from his importunity when another tormentor approaches with a pan of hot cakes, fried in oil, which he asks you to eat whether you will or no. The children, accustomed to mendicity, although their plumpness and good-humor are indicative of proper feeding, seize you by the knees, and will not allow you to advance till you have given them some money. The fisherman draws near with a costume the color of sea-weed, barefooted, his trowsers tucked up and exposing his brown legs, his head covered with a red cap, his blue shirt unbuttoned, opening oysters and other shell-fish, and presenting them to you as if by your orders. The cicerone goes before and displays his eloquence, interlarded with innumerable phrases in all languages, and full of anachronisms and falsehoods, historical and artistic. If you dismiss him, if you say his services are useless, he will talk of the peril you are in of losing your purse or your life from not having listened to his counsels or been attentive to his astonishing knowledge. Do not fancy you can get out of all this by being in a carriage. I have never seen people jump upon carriages more quickly, or stand upon the step, or follow clinging to the back, or to any part, regardless of your displeasure. But if you have the air of a newly arrived traveler, they will not annoy you with their wares, but will force you to engage a carriage of their choosing. In half a second you are surrounded with vehicles, which encompass you like serpents at the risk of crushing you, whose drivers speak all at once a distracting and frightful jargon, offering to take you to Posilippo, to Baiæ, to Pozzuoli, to Castellamare, to Sorrento, to Cumæ, to the end of Creation.

The Sundays are enough to cause a vertigo. All the inhabitants of Naples appear without exception to have become insane. I have never any where seen such a bustle. I have never heard such a noisy bell-ringing, and should not like to return again in the midst of such continual uproar. In proportion to its size no city in Europe contains so many carriages as Naples. It is the custom for private carriages to go along the foot of the beautiful hills of the environs to enter by Posilippo on the Riviera di Chiaja. It is impossible to imagine more luxury or a greater number of elegant equipages. To the numerous carriages of the Neapolitan aristocracy are added those of many wealthy strangers, who are in the habit of visiting the city, and of remaining there during the months of spring and winter. But the carriage the visitor to Naples should see and hear is that used by the people on Sundays. It is the ancient *calesa* of Madrid, but rather lighter. The horses are thin, but are showily caparisoned. Ribbons, laces, flowers, tricolor flags, tinkling bells and ornaments, decorations embroidered with wool or bright-colored silks, even great squares of gauze are used to beautify them. They have always more than one coachman, generally two or three, who jump about like acrobats in the circus. In the carriage, on the coach-box, on the steps there are passengers; some ride on the old pony, cling to the stirrups or on the foot-board, balancing themselves in perilous positions, often more than twenty at a time—all shout and all move as if they were dancing. After watching several of these pass by, and being stunned by the fearful clamor, you feel giddy, the head swims, and the ears retain the sounds, as if you had been spinning like a peg-top in some infernal waltz.

Beware of entering one of those carriages, though you should hire it for your own party only. Any one who crosses your route and feels fatigued or desires to travel that way, jumps upon the vehicle as if it was his own property, takes possession of it, and goes on with his gymnastic exercises at your elbow, but without giving you trouble or annoyance further than that of his company, paying you many compliments, and friendly as if he had been acquainted with you all his life. The ascent of Vesuvius is made fearful with such people. If you have no guide you may reckon upon their sarcasms, on their snares, whistling, and insults; no one will point out your path or warn you of a false step. I shall never forget a poor Englishman without a guide whom I met near the crater. He attracted all eyes. But when you have a guide you become merely a machine. They give you a pony that will neither stop nor go on at your pleasure. Arrived at a certain point, four or five men take possession of each of your party : one fixes a cord about your waist, another seizes your right arm, a third holds you on the left, some begin to remove the stones from your path, or drag your body after them like a burden, upsetting you while seeming to give you support, till they have taken you to the top of the volcano. Then, after a short repose, they dwell upon the risk you run of dying like Pliny, drag you in giddy haste from the crater, on one side all covered with ashes, like a soul brought by the devil to the infernal regions. And all this after the establishment of constitutional laws, after the introduction of modern ideas and with them modern customs, after the disappearance of those traditionary lazzaroni who lived almost naked upon the sand, existing in the sun upon a little fishing and a great deal of charity.

The impression that the Neapolitan population does not labor appears to me extremely false. They shout, they sing, they gesticulate, they vociferate, they dispute, but they labor, and they labor with much toil and with little profit. There are poets in the midst of that dazzling light, under the influence of that enchanting nature, educated by the glorious beauty of the varied landscapes, supported and encouraged by the approval of their fellow-citizens, like lawful sons of the Greek Parthenope. There are many poets without culture, who improvise verses spontaneous as the flowers of the grove or the forest; many orators, who speak with inimitable eloquence of sentiment and of passion. Strength does not become exhausted in this eternal spring; the senses are not wasted in this life of emotions. The people are temperate as the ancient Greeks: a handful of figs, some slices of melon, a few cucumbers, tomatoes, and raw capsicums, with cockles from the bay, form the chief part of their nourishment. I know not if there is any truth in the observation of an English writer who laments that potatoes have diminished the intelligence of southern peoples by making them lymphatic. I remember in my own family an old servant who died some time ago under our roof at the age of ninety, and who would never eat potatoes. Our Englishman would have given her a prize, for he says that this vegetable is not like peas or beans, which contain phosphorus, and are therefore fitted to assist the unfolding of cerebral development, and that these should be restored as in the time of Pythagoras, who valued beans and recommended them as almost a religious nutriment. I can affirm that the people of Naples are remarkable for sobriety, and are not in any way addicted to wine or strong liquors.

If snow or fresh water should ever fail them, there would be a revolution in Naples. In this temperance they resemble their ancestors, the ancient Greeks; one of the finest Pindaric odes has a beautiful lyrical introduction consecrated to water.

Another analogy of the Neapolitans to the ancient Greeks is their love of living in the open air. The pearl is not joined to its shell, the spirit united to its organism, the artistic idea to its form, so completely as the Neapolitan is bound to his city. He rarely emigrates; for it is a necessity to live near that bay, on those lovely shores, under those smiling heavens, by the music of that sea, even under the threatenings of Vesuvius. The day that the volcano should again become extinct, as it was in the times of the Roman Republic, Naples would think something was wanting in her existence. Its dull roar in her ears, its frequent eruptions before her eyes, the white cloud of smoke in the sky, the reflection of the gigantic torch in those crystalline waters—man and nature harmonize and mingle in embraces.

There is a great deal of misery in Naples, and there are many poor in the city. But the poverty of Naples does not occasion the same wretchedness as the poverty of London. A poor person in London wears worn-out, patched, and soiled clothes, cast aside by one of the higher classes; a poor person in Naples, if he wears but little clothes, requires but little —he is warmed by that balmy air and bronzed by that life-giving sun. The poor of London must have spirituous drinks, animal food, coals to warm their habitations. The lower classes in Naples live upon the fruits of the field and on the fish of the sea—an easy and sober fare. To the poor of the great northern city all the public spectacles are closed—the aristocratic club, the theatre, the balls and routs of the nobility, the expansion of mind which comes from looking upon extended landscapes; while nothing can shut out from the poor of the South the continual festival presented by his beautiful country, the sight of the Apennines, the eruptions of Vesuvius, the chain of volcanic hills which encompass the city like a girdle of black diamonds, the florid and luxuriant vegetation, the celestial waters, the starry firmament, the melody of the waves upon the shores, the islets which raise their heads among the azure and fleecy clouds of the divine Mediterranean.

One thing in particular I noted in London and Naples. Liberty is more deeply rooted in England than in any other country, and yet there is no other country where the social classes are so sharply defined and are separated by such a profound abyss. When you see one of those omnibus-drivers sitting with so much solemnity on his coach-box, you appear to see in the gravity of his air, in the majesty of his countenance, the first of senators seated on his wool-sack, presiding over that high chamber which only had equal or resemblance in ancient Rome. And, notwithstanding, if physiology, if nature has not made differences between aristocrats and plebeians, how much, how vast are the differences made by the laws! On the other hand, the Neapolitan plebeian is a plebeian in the broadest signification of the word—a plebeian by his origin, a plebeian by his nature, a plebeian by his habits; and, notwithstanding, he imposes his will, his opinion, upon the aristocracy, with which he is mingled, by a happy mixture of lightness, of grace, and of personal dignity, born of the innate consciousness that whatever may be the nature or position of a man, whatever be his calling, he is sufficient for himself.

Is there any modern people who keep up a drama for itself alone? That intuition of the people in the fifteenth and sixteenth centuries which erected for themselves a theatre, and infused into it their ideas and sentiments, no longer exists in Europe. The Spanish drama was born, like that of Greece, in a cart which went from fair to fair, from festival to festival, followed by the people—a cart sacred as that of Thespis, over which floated the genius of the people. Little by little, after the death of Lopes, as soon as the supernatural lightnings of the minds of Shakespeare and Calderon were extinguished, the theatre ceased to be used for religious performances, the popular pieces were abandoned, and the drama became the vehicle for academical laws, the pleasant pastime of the lettered aristocracy. Till the war of the classical and the romantic, in which they pretended to represent the spirit of the people, that spirit which engendered the Homeric poems and romances, they did not touch the lower classes, who never even appeared in pamphlets or reviews. But Naples has her own stage—a stage whereon she has employed herself in all times, even those most stormy, in bitterly censuring the customs and at times the politics of the day.

It is true that this theatre can not hold any literary character, the pieces being written and performed in the local dialect, made up of a mixture of Latin and of the language of the country. A labor of six centuries carried on by men of the highest talent, without giving to dialects the absolute perfection of Latin, has shown that they possess much literary interest, and converted some into classic languages. This poor Neapolitan dialect, alas! can never aspire to so much! The chief personage of the Naples stage is always Polichinello, brother of the Pasquina of Rome. But still in its modest humility it shows that there is love of literature, a love of life and dramatic action in the people who support it, and who enjoy its pointed and sarcastic allusions, sometimes truly like those of Aristophanes. When I went to see a performance at this theatre, they bitterly criticised those patriots who lounge from seat to seat in the Roman cafés, lazily sipping lemonade, but do nothing for Rome or Italy, either in the electoral councils or in the field of battle. Politics only supported by illusions are worth little; but the drama throws light on the popular manners, and the relation of those manners, and the passion of passions—love. At all events it was curious and interesting to follow the ecstatic anxiety with which the people beheld their own imaginations reflected in the drama.

Both in the little theatre of the people and in the great theatre of San Carlo, one of the largest and most beautiful in the world, I observed the profound interest taken by the public in theatrical representations. Their nervous temperaments burst forth at every moment in tumultuous manifestations, either of censure or applause. The public becomes at the theatre a real actor. Its voice, and if not its voice, its accent, its murmur, accompanies the performers as the blue waves of the Piræus accompanied the choir of Grecian tragedy. When they are pleased, the applause reaches delirium, and the expression of disapprobation is absolutely pitiless. An actress would think herself despised and neglected if her ears were not saluted with a tempest of approval, or if she was not nearly buried under showers of bouquets. During the entire performance the excitement and curiosity of the people are extreme. They are never indifferent. They are a people who love or hate. The dawn of criticism rather spoils their frank, artistic nature. They feel acutely, and sing with taste and expression—putting their whole hearts into a romance of Bellini, a melody of Cimarosa, an air of Passiello. There is in their accent some echo of the Greek songs which the mariners chant in the Isle of Capri, at the Cape of Sorrento, at the foot of Vesuvius. As in the serenades of Schubert and of Mozart there is something of the music of Andalusia, so in the Andalusian song there is something of the sublime accent of the Moorish cadence, accompanied by the breeze of the desert.

But notwithstanding this, in my observations of the city which the Greeks call Siren, there is something which disgusts me—the excess of noisy gayety in conversation, the excess of movement in their gestures, the excess of giddiness in their dances, the excess of accompaniments of the most discordant instruments in their songs and their tarantelles. And often, wearied of so much commotion, I ascended the hill of the Carthusians to look upon the heavens and the Mediterranean, and to reflect that the varieties of peoples and of races are lost in the immensity of the infinite.

Chapter XI.

PARTHENOPE.

A SOUTHERN town can not have for us Spaniards, and particularly for Spaniards of the South, the novelty it possesses for the French, the Germans—especially for the French and Germans of the North. We have towns which for the clearness of their skies, the brilliancy of their light, the loveliness of their fields and suburbs, the beauty of their women, the ingenuity of their citizens, the art of their monuments, and the purity of their atmosphere, bear comparison with the richest and finest Italian cities. Who can forget Valencia, begirt with its Moorish and Gothic towers, reclining gently on the banks of the limpid river, which in its course fertilizes the adjacent plains, encircled by the fertile orchards which interlace with the bright branches of the mulberry the dark boughs of the pomegranate; while at the foot of the palms, softly waved by the sea-breeze, innumerable orange-trees delight the eyes with the golden harvest of their fruit, and the air is fragrant with the scent of their white blossoms? Who could weary of admiring the oriental Cordova, with its Mesquita, unique in Europe, where are heard the echoes of Moorish poetry, at the foot of that Sierra Morena, enameled with groves of roses? There is not in the world another Seville, when her luxuriant plains are caressed by the spring zephyrs. See the city in April, rising above the sea of tender green, her spires, her buttresses, her arched windows, her towers, under a sky of resplendent light, the air laden with the echoes of oriental melody and the intoxicating essences of flowers! The eyes never tire of looking at and admiring Cadiz—her white buildings, adorned with green balconies; her fine windows and crystalline inclosures, where float curtains of gay colors; flat roofs with turrets of florid hues, some erected among the rocks where the waves dash and break in foamy cataracts, surrounded by vessels which leave clouds of vapor in the pure air, and ride gracefully with their swelling sails and picturesque banners; the dark and massive wall on one side of the bay, with its white houses, its aqueducts and pyramids of salt, sparkling in the glorious light; its distant chain of mountains surmounted by rolling clouds, now violet, now crimson, according to the hour and the rosy shades of the ambient air; while on the other side the azure sea expands, retracing in its bright waters all the tints of the heavens; all together composing, with its winds, its waves, its breezes, its currents, its tempests, and its terrors, a continual canticle to the Infinite.

In the midst of the most smiling towns of Italy I always remembered our own beautiful Granada: the mountains with their snowy peaks, the extinct volcanoes with their pyramids of lava; the extensive plain all covered with a green carpet of rich vegetation, and bounded in the distance by the hills of Loja; the hoary Albaicin in the background, girded with aloes and Indian fig-trees, as if still awaiting the sons of Africa and of Asia, and still repeating the melancholy song inspired by the desert; the sacred mount crowned with pines; the confluence of the rivers Darro and Genil, which divide the gardens and refresh the groves of almond-trees, filberts, and cacti; in the centre the Alhambra, its towers bronzed by the sun of ages; above the eminence with its woods of tender green, at whose base sleeps Granada, and on the summit of which stands—outlined against the sky with all the beauty of oriental poetry—the minarets and the arched windows and the red towers of the Generalife, half hidden among grottoes and murmuring cascades, fragrant jasmine, melancholy cypresses, and flowering shrubs, whose whispers and odors invite to the joys of Moorish life, consecrated, after war and religion, to sleep, to love and poetry.

We have laurels to crown poets; we have myrtle-groves worthy to be habitations for the gods of antiquity; palm-trees under whose broad leaves the genius of Asia seems to wander; coasts of golden sand and of celestial waters; bays and promontories which the setting sun gilds and variegates like the classic shores of Greece; the air perfumed with orange-flowers and jasmine; figs luscious as those of Athens in our orchards; grapes as sweet as those of Corinth in our vineyards; warm days when is heard the chirp of the grasshopper, which delighted the ancient poets like the harmony of soft music; nights clear and tranquil, like those of the East; serenades in whose plaintive cadence is heard again the immortal accents of Moorish poetry, with all their intensity of love and all their profound melancholy.

But though I have seen all this, I was much struck with the wondrous beauty of the Campagna of Naples. There may be something wilder, more sublime, or grander on the earth; there can be nothing more classic, more worthy of the antique eclogue, more suitable for the refreshment of the soul which takes its tints and inspirations from nature. Thus, as sculpture is pre-eminently the Pagan art, the art which harmonizes and forms conceptions in dignified repose, the Campagna is the land of the eclogues and the Georgics, the pastoral country in which the monks repeat the undying echo of the soft flute of Virgil, and plants and animals are transformed in the vision of our thoughts with the metamorphosis sung by Ovid.

Good heavens! What richness of shades, of tones, of colors! What gradations from the clear azure of the bay to the violet and deep amethyst of Vesuvius! How the mountain-chains toward the east, adorned here and there with glaciers which sparkle like diamonds between emeralds and turquoises, contrast with the rosy tints assumed at sunset by the hills of the west, by the headland of Miseno and around the island of Nisida, like promontories of burnished jasper! Behold that pure horizon and those columns of white smoke escaping from the volcano; that sea varying with the clouds, their repetition and their mirror; that soil with its black and shining lava, between whose jetty blocks shoots up the luxuriant vegetation! I have never any where seen the light break into such varied refractions, or present such rapid changes of color. I have never beheld in any other country contrasts more remarkable than these abrupt descents to smooth sands; the wildest groves beside the most cultivated gardens; towns thickly populated and solitary ruins; a land now threatened with death by the volcanic streams and the caves of burning sulphur, by sudden earthquakes, by violent eruptions; nor life more gay and joyous, which delights itself in the song, in the dance, in games and pleasures; refinements of civilization, mingled with the repose of the country, old memories wandering over the indolent modern forgetfulness; the column of fire which the volcano shoots forth like a gigantic torch lighting up the summits of the snow-topped mountains.

Here I saw beech-trees and the oaks of Virgil; goats wandering on the heights and browsing among the shrubs; sheep with their rich fleeces of wool and their udders filled with milk, followed by their tender bleating lambs; brambles on the steeps, with whose berries shepherds tinge their cheeks and eyebrows when chanting their bucolic verses; on the banks of the stream the reeds with which the god Pan formed his flageolets; festoons of vines between the stately elm-trees, whose foliage shelters the wood-pigeon, and whence is heard the coo of the turtle-dove, beneath the flowering lavender; upon the hills there are the sweet-scented thyme and the hyacinth; at the entrance of the cavern, in the trunk of the evergreen oak which stretches across, is the honeycomb, with the wild bees buzzing around and extracting the luscious essence from the flowers. Within the cavern reposes Silenus, intoxicated with life and wine, in his hand his amphora, and his garland on his brow; by the flowing streams the white naiads weave their crowns; by the sheepcot on the height the young shepherd twines the wild rose and the narcissus, the white lily and the honeysuckle, to offer them to his beloved; in the broad sea, rippled by the breeze and variegated by the changing light, there is the antique siren among the waves, singing eternally her seducing chant of love and melancholy, the undying poem of nature.

Besides these eclogues, what terrible tragedies are presented by this tormented country! The ancients did well in calling her the siren who attracts and the siren who destroys. Frequent and awful volcanic eruptions have burned and buried entire towns and villages. Shocks of earthquake spread terror and desolation over the whole region. The buildings balance themselves like ships upon the waves in a tempest, and then come clouds of hot and stifling vapors, rains, showers of ashes, fearful hail-storms, floods of lava. The sea boils and foams, the heavens shoot forth their dreadful fires, as if the beneficent rain-clouds had turned to burning ovens. The volcano gasps like a Cyclopean forge, or lightens and thunders its eruptions like a legion of tempests. On all sides volumes of red-hot lava, rain of black ashes, whirlwinds flinging upward stones and pieces of rocks, the horrible roaring of the mountain, the terror and despair of the valley, sulphurous smoke, exhalations of poisonous gas, dark and angry clouds crossed by reflections of the flames and filled with little aerolites, a border of scoriæ below the crater, and streams of boiling water; the infernal regions blended with the earthly paradise, as pain and pleasure in the soul of man, as error and truth in his mind—a faithful copy of the great drama of our existence, of the strange contrasts of our being.

The burning mountain is a gigantic laboratory, from which issues with equal power death and life, as nature is a combination of forces which compose, decompose, and recompose. Of its extremes, its convulsive tragedies, the ancient dwellers in Pompeii and Stabia might complain; the modern peasant of Resina and Torre del Greco, who in our sad days sees his vines, laden with the celebrated sweet juice of Lacryma Christi, disappear under the burning bituminous flood. But the chemist, the physiologist, discover something fruitful in these exhalations—soda, potash, and divers kinds of mineral salts, a testimony of communication with the Mediterranean; deposits of iron, with all the colors of precious gems and of wild flowers; streams of chloric acid and of sulphuric acid; ammoniacal substances and pieces of sulphur on the dark scoriæ; deposits of thermal waters which cure many diseases; and continual exhalations of the gas azote and of carbonic acid, so fatal to life and so precious to science.

Without having seen the wonderful contrast between the smiling serenity of the fields and the sinister aspect of the volcano, it is impossible to form an adequate idea of its effect. When imagination wanders over those sylvan scenes, and the eye looks with delight upon those classic shores, passing from the hill to the vale, and from the vale to the grove, from the grove where interlace the olive and lemon trees to the celestial sea, where, like flocks of white birds, curl those beautiful lateen sails used in the Mediterranean, you almost believe you behold the shepherds of Virgil, the mariners of Theocritus, singing—the former among their sheepfolds and meadows, the latter among their nets and vessels—verses which are repeated by the waves and the breezes. But afterward look at the volcano; behold its awful flames and its torrent of fiery lava, hear it roar and thunder, believe that its heights outline among clouds of smoke the legions which now tread those high summits, the legions of the eternal victim, of the immortal outcast, of Spartacus, the noble defender of slaves, whose blood-stained and tragic shade overhangs those scenes as did the infamy of slavery all the beauty and harmony of the ancient world.

What excess of cultivation in life and of originality in nature! Here there were placed four or five distinct civilizations one above the other, from the Pelasgic to the Christian; and the volcanic soil, in its peculiarities, in its convulsions, in its vapors, seems to belong to the time in which the planet was still incandescent matter, filled with intense heat and thundering electricity. I can fancy myself in the caverns where the archetypical ideas—the mother ideas, as Goethe calls them—wove the web of life, or where the fabulous giants formed in colossal forges the immovable granite bases of the earth. This spot has always been Pagan. The holy water falling for fifteen centuries upon the fields has not yet baptized them. The gods of antiquity refuse to depart. In vain the aged sibyl of Cumæ, her vision dimmed with gazing into futurity, her tunic rent in sorrow, from the elevated point where she lingers, says to the children of Naples when they cast stones at her and ask, "What do you desire?" "I want to die." In vain the sirens have gathered round the Cape Miseno to lament the death of the god Pan. Here are still all the divinities—the same Ceres crowned with wheat-ears, and Bacchus girded with vine-leaves; Minerva with her olive-branch, and Silenus leaning on his cypress; Neptune with his sharp trident urging his foaming horses to the earth; and Vulcan reddening the iron in the profound abyss of his eternal forge. They have not *been* here—no, they *are* here, on the very ground, in the sculptured rock-bound headlands, in the fastnesses of the mountains, in the shadows of the coasts, in the living light which admits not of mystery and shows the meeting of the golden angles, to celebrate the nuptials of the spirit with nature, as in the times of ancient Paganism.

These lands, pre-eminently graceful and beautiful, attract the natives of all climes and races; they are the channel of perpetual communication among all men. They remain for the rustics of the soil, to preserve behind the defiles of their mountain chains, in the bosoms of the caverns, veiled by impenetrable forests, on heights only accessible to eagles, their safeguard being the danger of the marble rocks suspended over the valley; they remain for the wars of independence, the savage worship of ancient laws and ancient institutions. Here among those transparent waves, where the reflections of glorious light represent lakes and rivers, each of whose drops is a star; where phosphoric splendor, white as the soft rays of moonlight, leaves shining tracts in the calm nights of summer, like the path of the Milky Way in the heavens; here where the lovely shores are seducing as maiden beauty; where every tree exhales a delicious aroma, and every movement of the air is like a low sigh of love; upon the grass or over the waves, among the flowers of the field and the sea-shells on the strand, in the shade of the myrtle and the olive and the swelling sail —come the gods of all the temples, the pilots of all races, the conquerors of all towns, to live even for a moment, intoxicated with pride and pleasure in the arms of enchanting and voluptuous nature.

The same happens among ourselves. The Catalonian sees over again the Roman invasion a hundred times in his leathern buckler; the Asturian, without having the culture of Brutus or Cato, without hoping that Plutarch will relate and Lucian sing his achievements, prefers death to serfdom; the Navarrine from the high mountains will think over the old conquests of his people, and again make the soldiers of Charlemagne bite the dust; the Biscayan preserves, through so many revolutions and so many ages, laws and usages which have patriarchal characters, and ancient and purely primitive language, like the smooth and smiling beach of the Mediterranean, accessible to all vessels and nations, with its azure waves and its silvery foam, its golden sands and its graceful slopes, its olives, its myrtles, and its laurels; tinted by that dazzling light whose reflections give to the mountain chains their metallic touches, and to the East and the West those rosy clouds of indescribable beauty, to the stars and the wake of vessels their scintillation; while the air is fragrant with the intoxicating breath of flowers and balmy with the soft breeze of summer;

and people from all ends of the earth, vessels from all parts, come to her shores, which open and give themselves up of free will, or force, now to the sword, now to persuasion.

Thus it is in the history of the Spanish peninsula, as in the Italian peninsula, the northern cities form a nationality, and those of the south make it illustrious. The mountains of the north will be historic regions, the Conservative regions—if it is permitted so to speak; the southern shores will be the Liberal regions—the regions, so to speak, humanitarian. The one will give the people its proper and peculiar character, the second will succeed in bringing the people into communication with the other nations of the earth. The rude and vigorous Italians of the north, realizing the dream of fifteen centuries, sustain the independence of united Italy, as the inhabitants of the mountains of Covadonga, of San Juan de la Peña, of the steep and rocky Sobrarbe, descend to the plains with the impetuosity of their rivers to form the Iberian nationality. And as by Rosas, by Sagunto, by Denia, by Tarragona, by Calpe, by Algeciras, by Cadiz, came the Greeks, the Phœnicians, the Carthaginians, the Romans, the Moors, by the southern shores of Italy came almost all the invaders, from those who founded Magna Grecia in the Strait of Messina and in the Gulf of Tarento, to those who founded the Spanish monarchy in the plains of Etna and Vesuvius.

And in Naples all that exists of modern life recalls Spain —our Spain; so that we almost believe we are in Barcelona, in Valencia, or even in Madrid, when we see lattices and balconies, and the houses painted of different colors, and the monuments of the age of Alphonso V., or of Carlos III., so much of all that antique life which is to us more familiar —much more than the Italy civilized by the arms of Rome, the Italy civilized by the word of Greece.

Parthenope is Grecian — completely, absolutely Grecian. There the eternal harmony between the soul of man and the universe which surrounds him will never be broken or dissolved—true secret of the excellence of the Hellenic life not told in history. Naples appears to float in the ether of which Euripides sung, and to be filled with the choirs of the Muses and the melodies of Apollo; the waters have raised above their shining surface the golden ships in which went the processions or Greek theories celebrated in the Banquet of Plato; the isles seem to retain on their marble brows, like the antique Cytherea, the kiss of the goddess new-born in the snowy foam of the waves; those coasts, outlined as if by a compass, and those mountains, in harmonious proportions with all their surroundings, preserve the rhythm and the geometry of Euclid and Pythagoras; the Mediterranean is calmly sleeping there, not only to repeat all the shades of the luminous heavens, but to sport with the nymphs, with the sirens, with the divinities, whose temples, crowned with seaweed, with pearls and corals, are seen at each moment in the rays of sunlight on the variegated sands, within the transparent sea borders. And man is upon that earth, under that heaven, like the antique god on the sacred stone of his altar and under the roof of his temple; there nature is clear, transparent in relief, like that ancient classic conscience—

like that Hellenic language, the most distinct and precise, the richest and most harmonious of all human languages; there all these are invited to give themselves up to universal life—all to join the chorus of songs, the dances for the multitude, the Delphic courses, the Pythian games, the athletic and gymnastic exercises, the Grecian life—serene as its art—ruled by music and geometry, devoted to make of each body a perfect sculpture, of each soul a transparent heaven — a life in complete and eternal peace with nature, that chisels, carves, and paints itself, and submits itself to the spirit and to the conceptions and forces of man.

I have not beheld the beauties of the tropics, but I have heard them glowingly described by those who have seen and admired them. I have a friend who is an insatiable and untiring traveler, who frequently speaks to me of Cuba, of Hayti, of Brazil, and, above all, of the island of Java—that assemblage of volcanoes. All these must be beautiful—terribly beautiful. Our trees would appear like ladies' bouquets by the side of those gigantic trees, which are there in harmony with the landscape. Our rivers are but bubbling brooks in comparison with the great waters of India and Peru. Our flora dwarfed and miserable compared with that of the tropics, overflowing with sap and perfume. I have figured to myself a thousand times, on reading the narratives of great travelers, that island of Java, with its granite foundations—with its basaltic mountains—with its chain of volcanoes—its shore, covered with madrepores and polypi—sylvan groves, and woods overgrown with jungle — boiling rivers, drained from the mountains of fire, and flowing into the immensity of the ocean — tempestuous days, whose lightnings are fires, whose thunders let loose from the heavens their electric floods—nights illuminated, not only by the stars and constellations, but by the great fire-flies which dart about in all directions like clouds of animated aerolites; the cocoa-trees rising from the waters, sometimes from the waves, and rearing their lofty heads, crowned with fruit — the waving palm-trees—the bamboos at the foot of the gigantic plane-trees, through whose trunks flow the liquid amber—the leaves and the branches of this luxuriant vegetation interlacing so thickly as to form a perpetual shade, inhabited by green-eyed tigers, and monstrous bats with immense wings; the open country, covered with plantations of tobacco, tea, coffee, and of spices, which intoxicate us with their sap, their essences, and their exhalations, and perfume the atmosphere—the entire earth producing and devouring beings in continual and reckless extravagance, as if that extraordinary development of nature were the madness, the delirium, the frenzy of existence.

Beautiful it must be, most beautiful; but, with all its fascinations, man has reduced and conquered it. How different from the tranquil seas whose waves wash rocky islands; from the harmonious coasts which are ever hospitably open to the winds and waters; from the elm-trees, between whose graceful columns are festooned the flexible shoots of the vine, twining around them their soft green tendrils; from the artistic flora of the Mediterranean coasts, a flora of surpassing richness of color—the jasmine interlaced with the passion-flower; the verbena at the foot of the myrtle; in the hollow of the valley the olive, the pomegranate, the fig, the orange, and lemon trees; beside the torrent the rose-bay; on the mountains the sage, the thyme, the rosemary, the dwarf apple-tree, the arnica—all with healing or restorative powers; over the flowers the butterflies in their gay idleness, the bee, with his industry, and the sweet and gentle air, tempered by the sun in winter, by the breeze in summer; with the unceasing warbling of birds, with their gorgeous plumage. Humanity will always delight in this lovely and luxuriant nature, which invigorates with its warmth, nourishes with juicy fruits, regales with its odors, refreshes with its zephyrs; which bronzes and heals with its sunshine; which enchants with the changing beauty of its seas, and that rosy light over its hills, and the view of its horizon, and the architectural perfection of its mountain-chains—nature in which man lives as the faun in his ivy-covered grotto, and bathes as Silenus in the crystal of his fountains!

We all feel ourselves an integral part of the universe. We understand the near relationship which exists between nature and the soul. The minerals furnish the basis of our skeleton. Iron enters into our veins, colors and warms our blood. Even on beholding the human body we observe its relations and harmonies with the planets. This connection is still greater in the superior spheres of life. All animated creatures have affinities, physical, chemical, and physiological, with this human body, which includes them, crowns and perfects them. On all sides we feel ourselves united to the universe, and in relation also with the far-distant star, lost in the immensity of the heavens, as well as with the humble flower trampled beneath our feet. We are one with all beings, and shall we not acknowledge the closeness of the tie which binds us to our own species? Shall it be more easy and agreeable to us to feel ourselves one with the mineral, the vegetable, with the inferior animals, than with the rest of humanity, on whose brows is the light of the Spirit? And if we acknowledge ourselves united to other men by the fundamental identity of nature, how can we explain war and slavery? How the desire of corrupting, of enslaving, of conquering, of exterminating, which causes suffering to so many human beings, is so detrimental and so hateful to those who are in all things our equals? In this smiling land of Naples we remember its history. The pride of some, the tyranny engendered by that pride; and of others the serfdom, the degradation, the moral and material misery. Do I not see before me the Gulf of Baiæ, where Nero in his impious cruelty assassinated his mother? where Caligula in his madness and folly called upon the moon to share his couch? and do I not also behold the cone of Vesuvius, where Spartacus summoned the gladiators, telling them that instead of turning their swords against each other they should bury them in the hearts of their tyrants?

Let us give ourselves up to the contemplation of this beautiful panorama of the Campagna and of the city. I seem to have it now before my eyes. We are in the last days of April. The green and tender leaves cover the branches. The sea and the heavens smile joyfully. Toward the east, the snow-crowned crests outlined against the clear azure of the sky, are the Apennines, sometimes vanishing in clouds and again appearing in the ether; before us, toward the shore, at the northeast, is the truncated pyramid of Vesuvius, on whose sides, composed of lava and metallic rocks of dark crystals, the light shows shades of violet, blue, and lilac, which are almost magical; near the volcano, a mass of beautiful and verdant hills, is Cape Campanella; on the borders of the sea, among groves of olives and lemon-trees, of oak-trees and figs, of laurels and myrtles, are Castellamare and Sorrento, white as doves; toward the central curve of this vast amphitheatre, first the solitary ruins of Pompeii, then those thickly peopled villages of Portici and Torre del Greco, surrounded with lovely country-seats and blooming gardens extending for many leagues; toward the west, Naples, among her wharves of commerce, where vessels are grouped in hundreds, and boats in thousands; and then the Riviera di Chiaja, with beautiful and shady promenades, wonderful statues, and marble temples, bordered by a line of palaces, grandly picturesque with their flat roofs and balconies; behind these are villas, gardens, towns, a row of little volcanic cones forming graceful undulations; and beyond, green hills, on whose summits are churches, monasteries, castles, and all kinds of monuments, at whose foot are extended woods and forests on graceful slopes; further to the west is the grotto of Posilippo, celebrated for the tomb of Virgil—a genius which reposes there as in its proper home; still more westward the Cape Mesino, sung by the poets, eternally beloved by artists; the whole bathed in that rosy light which gives an unearthly aspect to the snows of the Apennines and to the smoke of Vesuvius; and toned by that sea of an almost indescribable azure, studded and made more beautiful by those towering islands which raise their lovely heads to watch, to woo, to adorn the goddess of sirens, the divine Parthenope.

THE END.

VALUABLE AND INTERESTING WORKS
FOR
PUBLIC & PRIVATE LIBRARIES,

PUBLISHED BY HARPER & BROTHERS, NEW YORK.

☞ *For a full List of Books suitable for Libraries, see* HARPER & BROTHERS' TRADE-LIST *and* CATALOGUE, *which may be had gratuitously on application to the Publishers personally, or by letter enclosing Six Cents in Postage Stamps.*

☞ HARPER & BROTHERS *will send any of the following works by mail, postage prepaid, to any part of the United States, on receipt of the price.*

FLAMMARION'S ATMOSPHERE. The Atmosphere. Translated from the French of CAMILLE FLAMMARION. Edited by JAMES GLAISHER, F.R.S., Superintendent of the Magnetical and Meteorological Department of the Royal Observatory at Greenwich. With 10 Chromo-Lithographs and 86 Woodcuts. 8vo, Cloth, $6 00.

HUDSON'S HISTORY OF JOURNALISM. Journalism in the United States, from 1690 to 1872. By FREDERICK HUDSON. Crown 8vo, Cloth, $5 00.

PIKE'S SUB-TROPICAL RAMBLES. Sub-Tropical Rambles in the Land of the Aphanapteryx. By NICOLAS PIKE, U. S. Consul, Port Louis, Mauritius. Profusely Illustrated from the Author's own Sketches; containing also Maps and Valuable Meteorological Charts. Crown 8vo, Cloth, $3 50.

TRISTRAM'S THE LAND OF MOAB. The Result of Travels and Discoveries on the East Side of the Dead Sea and the Jordan. By H. B. TRISTRAM, M.A., LL.D., F.R.S., Master of the Greatham Hospital, and Hon. Canon of Durham. With a Chapter on the Persian Palace of Mashita, by JAS. FERGUSON, F.R.S. With Map and Illustrations. Crown 8vo, Cloth, $2 50.

SANTO DOMINGO, Past and Present; with a Glance at Hayti. By SAMUEL HAZARD. Maps and Illustrations. Crown 8vo, Cloth, $3 50.

LIFE OF ALFRED COOKMAN. The Life of the Rev. Alfred Cookman; with some Account of his Father, the Rev. George Grimston Cookman. By HENRY B. RIDGAWAY, D.D. With an Introduction by Bishop FOSTER, LL.D. Portrait on Steel. 12mo, Cloth, $2 00.

HERVEY'S CHRISTIAN RHETORIC. A System of Christian Rhetoric, for the Use of Preachers and Other Speakers. By GEORGE WINFRED HERVEY, M.A., Author of "Rhetoric of Conversation," &c. 8vo, Cloth, $3 50.

CASTELAR'S OLD ROME AND NEW ITALY. Old Rome and New Italy. By EMILIO CASTELAR. Translated by Mrs. ARTHUR ARNOLD. 12mo, Cloth, $1 75.

THE TREATY OF WASHINGTON: Its Negotiation, Execution, and the Discussions Relating Thereto. By CALEB CUSHING. Crown 8vo, Cloth, $2 00.

PRIME'S I GO A-FISHING. I Go a-Fishing. By W. C. PRIME. Crown 8vo, Cloth, $2 50.

HALLOCK'S FISHING TOURIST. The Fishing Tourist: Angler's Guide and Reference Book. By CHARLES HALLOCK. Illustrations. Crown 8vo, Cloth, $2 00.

SCOTT'S AMERICAN FISHING. Fishing in American Waters. By GENIO C. SCOTT. With 170 Illustrations. Crown 8vo, Cloth, $3 50.

Harper & Brothers' Valuable and Interesting Works.

ANNUAL RECORD OF SCIENCE AND INDUSTRY FOR 1872. Edited by Prof. SPENCER F. BAIRD, of the Smithsonian Institution, with the Assistance of Eminent Men of Science. 12mo, over 700 pp., Cloth, $2 00. (Uniform with the *Annual Record of Science and Industry for* 1871. 12mo, Cloth, $2 00.)

COL. FORNEY'S ANECDOTES OF PUBLIC MEN. Anecdotes of Public Men. By JOHN W. FORNEY. 12mo, Cloth, $2 00.

MISS BEECHER'S HOUSEKEEPER AND HEALTHKEEPER: Containing Five Hundred Recipes for Economical and Healthful Cooking; also, many Directions for securing Health and Happiness. Approved by Physicians of all Classes. Illustrations. 12mo, Cloth, $1 50.

FARM BALLADS. By WILL CARLETON. Handsomely Illustrated. Square 8vo, Ornamental Cloth, $2 00; Gilt Edges, $2 50.

POETS OF THE NINETEENTH CENTURY. The Poets of the Nineteenth Century. Selected and Edited by the Rev. ROBERT ARIS WILLMOTT. With English and American Additions, arranged by EVERT A. DUYCKINCK, Editor of "Cyclopædia of American Literature." Comprising Selections from the Greatest Authors of the Age. Superbly Illustrated with 141 Engravings from Designs by the most Eminent Artists. In elegant small 4to form, printed on Superfine Tinted Paper, richly bound in extra Cloth, Beveled, Gilt Edges, $5 00; Half Calf, $5 50; Full Turkey Morocco, $9 00.

THE REVISION OF THE ENGLISH VERSION OF THE NEW TESTAMENT. With an Introduction by the Rev. P. SCHAFF, D.D. 618 pp., Crown 8vo, Cloth, $3 00.

This work embraces in one volume:

  I. ON A FRESH REVISION OF THE ENGLISH NEW TESTAMENT. By J. B. LIGHTFOOT, D.D., Canon of St. Paul's, and Hulsean Professor of Divinity, Cambridge. Second Edition, Revised. 196 pp.

  II. ON THE AUTHORIZED VERSION OF THE NEW TESTAMENT in Connection with some Recent Proposals for its Revision. By RICHARD CHENEVIX TRENCH, D.D., Archbishop of Dublin. 194 pp.

  III. CONSIDERATIONS ON THE REVISION OF THE ENGLISH VERSION OF THE NEW TESTAMENT. By C. J. ELLICOTT, D.D., Bishop of Gloucester and Bristol. 178 pp.

NORDHOFF'S CALIFORNIA. California: For Health, Pleasure, and Residence. A Book for Travelers and Settlers. Illustrated. 8vo, Paper, $2 00; Cloth, $2 50.

MOTLEY'S DUTCH REPUBLIC. The Rise of the Dutch Republic. By JOHN LOTHROP MOTLEY, LL.D., D.C.L. With a Portrait of William of Orange. 3 vols., 8vo, Cloth, $10 50.

MOTLEY'S UNITED NETHERLANDS. History of the United Netherlands: from the Death of William the Silent to the Twelve Years' Truce —1609. With a full View of the English-Dutch Struggle against Spain, and of the Origin and Destruction of the Spanish Armada. By JOHN LOTHROP MOTLEY, LL.D., D.C.L. Portraits. 4 vols., 8vo, Cloth, $14 00.

NAPOLEON'S LIFE OF CÆSAR. The History of Julius Cæsar. By His late Imperial Majesty NAPOLEON III. Two Volumes ready. Library Edition, 8vo, Cloth, $3 50 per vol.

HAYDN'S DICTIONARY OF DATES, relating to all Ages and Nations. For Universal Reference. Edited by BENJAMIN VINCENT, Assistant Secretary and Keeper of the Library of the Royal Institution of Great Britain; and Revised for the Use of American Readers. 8vo, Cloth, $5 00; Sheep, $6 00.

MACGREGOR'S ROB ROY ON THE JORDAN. The Rob Roy on the Jordan, Nile, Red Sea, and Gennesareth, &c. A Canoe Cruise in Palestine and Egypt, and the Waters of Damascus. By J. MACGREGOR, M.A. With Maps and Illustrations. Crown 8vo, Cloth, $2 50.

WALLACE'S MALAY ARCHIPELAGO. The Malay Archipelago: the Land of the Orang-Utan and the Bird of Paradise. A Narrative of Travel, 1854–1862. With Studies of Man and Nature. By ALFRED RUSSEL WALLACE. With Ten Maps and Fifty-one Elegant Illustrations. Crown 8vo, Cloth, $2 50.

WHYMPER'S ALASKA. Travel and Adventure in the Territory of Alaska, formerly Russian America—now Ceded to the United States—and in various other parts of the North Pacific. By FREDERICK WHYMPER. With Map and Illustrations. Crown 8vo, Cloth, $2 50.

ORTON'S ANDES AND THE AMAZON. The Andes and the Amazon; or, Across the Continent of South America. By JAMES ORTON, M.A., Professor of Natural History in Vassar College, Poughkeepsie, N.Y., and Corresponding Member of the Academy of Natural Sciences, Philadelphia. With a New Map of Equatorial America and numerous Illustrations. Crown 8vo, Cloth, $2 00.

WINCHELL'S SKETCHES OF CREATION. Sketches of Creation: a Popular View of some of the Grand Conclusions of the Sciences in reference to the History of Matter and of Life. Together with a Statement of the Intimations of Science respecting the Primordial Condition and the Ultimate Destiny of the Earth and the Solar System. By ALEXANDER WINCHELL, LL.D., Chancellor of the Syracuse University. With Illustrations. 12mo, Cloth, $2 00.

WHITE'S MASSACRE OF ST. BARTHOLOMEW. The Massacre of St. Bartholomew: Preceded by a History of the Religious Wars in the Reign of Charles IX. By HENRY WHITE, M.A. With Illustrations. 8vo, Cloth, $1 75.

LOSSING'S FIELD-BOOK OF THE REVOLUTION. Pictorial Field-Book of the Revolution; or, Illustrations, by Pen and Pencil, of the History, Biography, Scenery, Relics, and Traditions of the War for Independence. By BENSON J. LOSSING. 2 vols., 8vo, Cloth, $14 00; Sheep, $15 00; Half Calf, $18 00; Full Turkey Morocco, $22 00.

LOSSING'S FIELD-BOOK OF THE WAR OF 1812. Pictorial Field-Book of the War of 1812; or, Illustrations, by Pen and Pencil, of the History, Biography, Scenery, Relics, and Traditions of the Last War for American Independence. By BENSON J. LOSSING. With several hundred Engravings on Wood, by Lossing and Barritt, chiefly from Original Sketches by the Author. 1088 pages, 8vo, Cloth, $7 00; Sheep, $8 50; Half Calf, $10 00.

ALFORD'S GREEK TESTAMENT. The Greek Testament: with a critically revised Text; a Digest of Various Readings; Marginal References to Verbal and Idiomatic Usage; Prolegomena; and a Critical and Exegetical Commentary. For the Use of Theological Students and Ministers. By HENRY ALFORD, D.D., Dean of Canterbury. Vol. I., containing the Four Gospels. 944 pages, 8vo, Cloth, $6 00; Sheep, $6 50.

ABBOTT'S FREDERICK THE GREAT. The History of Frederick the Second, called Frederick the Great. By JOHN S. C. ABBOTT. Elegantly Illustrated. 8vo, Cloth, $5 00.

ABBOTT'S HISTORY OF THE FRENCH REVOLUTION. The French Revolution of 1789, as viewed in the Light of Republican Institutions. By JOHN S. C. ABBOTT. With 100 Engravings. 8vo, Cloth, $5 00.

ABBOTT'S NAPOLEON BONAPARTE. The History of Napoleon Bonaparte. By JOHN S. C. ABBOTT. With Maps, Woodcuts, and Portraits on Steel. 2 vols., 8vo, Cloth, $10 00.

ABBOTT'S NAPOLEON AT ST. HELENA; or, Interesting Anecdotes and Remarkable Conversations of the Emperor during the Five and a Half Years of his Captivity. Collected from the Memorials of Las Casas, O'Meara, Montholon, Antommarchi, and others. By JOHN S. C. ABBOTT. With Illustrations. 8vo, Cloth, $5 00.

ADDISON'S COMPLETE WORKS. The Works of Joseph Addison, embracing the whole of the "Spectator." Complete in 3 vols., 8vo, Cloth, $6 00.

ALCOCK'S JAPAN. The Capital of the Tycoon: a Narrative of a Three Years' Residence in Japan. By Sir RUTHERFORD ALCOCK, K.C.B., Her Majesty's Envoy Extraordinary and Minister Plenipotentiary in Japan. With Maps and Engravings. 2 vols., 12mo, Cloth, $3 50.

ALISON'S HISTORY OF EUROPE. FIRST SERIES: From the Commencement of the French Revolution, in 1789, to the Restoration of the Bourbons, in 1815. [In addition to the Notes on Chapter LXXVI., which correct the errors of the original work concerning the United States, a copious Analytical Index has been appended to this American Edition.] SECOND SERIES: From the Fall of Napoleon, in 1815, to the Accession of Louis Napoleon, in 1852. 8 vols., 8vo, Cloth, $16 00.

BARTH'S NORTH AND CENTRAL AFRICA. Travels and Discoveries in North and Central Africa: being a Journal of an Expedition undertaken under the Auspices of H.B.M.'s Government, in the Years 1849-1855. By HENRY BARTH, Ph.D., D.C.L. Illustrated. 3 vols., 8vo, Cloth, $12 00.

HENRY WARD BEECHER'S SERMONS. Sermons by HENRY WARD BEECHER, Plymouth Church, Brooklyn. Selected from Published and Unpublished Discourses, and Revised by their Author. With Steel Portrait. Complete in 2 vols., 8vo, Cloth, $5 00.

LYMAN BEECHER'S AUTOBIOGRAPHY, &c. Autobiography, Correspondence, &c., of Lyman Beecher, D.D. Edited by his Son, CHARLES BEECHER. With Three Steel Portraits, and Engravings on Wood. In 2 vols., 12mo, Cloth, $5 00.

BOSWELL'S JOHNSON. The Life of Samuel Johnson, LL.D. Including a Journey to the Hebrides. By JAMES BOSWELL, Esq. A New Edition, with numerous Additions and Notes. By JOHN WILSON CROKER, LL.D., F.R.S. Portrait of Boswell. 2 vols., 8vo, Cloth, $4 00.

DRAPER'S CIVIL WAR. History of the American Civil War. By JOHN W. DRAPER, M.D., LL.D., Professor of Chemistry and Physiology in the University of New York. In Three Vols. 8vo, Cloth, $3 50 per vol.

DRAPER'S INTELLECTUAL DEVELOPMENT OF EUROPE. A History of the Intellectual Development of Europe. By JOHN W. DRAPER, M.D., LL.D., Professor of Chemistry and Physiology in the University of New York. 8vo, Cloth, $5 00.

DRAPER'S AMERICAN CIVIL POLICY. Thoughts on the Future Civil Policy of America. By JOHN W. DRAPER, M.D., LL.D., Professor of Chemistry and Physiology in the University of New York. Crown 8vo, Cloth, $2 50.

DU CHAILLU'S AFRICA. Explorations and Adventures in Equatorial Africa, with Accounts of the Manners and Customs of the People, and of the Chase of the Gorilla, the Crocodile, Leopard, Elephant, Hippopotamus, and other Animals. By PAUL B. DU CHAILLU. Numerous Illustrations. 8vo, Cloth, $5 00.

DU CHAILLU'S ASHANGO LAND. A Journey to Ashango Land: and Further Penetration into Equatorial Africa. By PAUL B. DU CHAILLU. New Edition. Handsomely Illustrated. 8vo, Cloth, $5 00.

BELLOWS'S OLD WORLD. The Old World in its New Face: Impressions of Europe in 1867-1868. By HENRY W. BELLOWS. 2 vols., 12mo, Cloth, $3 50.

BRODHEAD'S HISTORY OF NEW YORK. History of the State of New York. By JOHN ROMEYN BRODHEAD. 1609-1691. 2 vols. 8vo, Cloth, $3 00 per vol.

BROUGHAM'S AUTOBIOGRAPHY. Life and Times of HENRY, LORD BROUGHAM. Written by Himself. In Three Volumes. 12mo, Cloth, $2 00 per vol.

BULWER'S PROSE WORKS. Miscellaneous Prose Works of Edward Bulwer, Lord Lytton. 2 vols., 12mo, Cloth, $3 50.

BULWER'S HORACE. The Odes and Epodes of Horace. A Metrical Translation into English. With Introduction and Commentaries. By LORD LYTTON. With Latin Text from the Editions of Orelli, Macleane, and Yonge. 12mo, Cloth, $1 75.

BULWER'S KING ARTHUR, A Poem. By LORD LYTTON. New Edition. 12mo, Cloth, $1 75.

BURNS'S LIFE AND WORKS. The Life and Works of Robert Burns. Edited by ROBERT CHAMBERS. 4 vols., 12mo, Cloth, $6 00.

REINDEER, DOGS, AND SNOW-SHOES. A Journal of Siberian Travel and Explorations made in the Years 1865–'67. By RICHARD J. BUSH, late of the Russo-American Telegraph Expedition. Illustrated. Crown 8vo, Cloth, $3 00.

CARLYLE'S FREDERICK THE GREAT. History of Friedrich II., called Frederick the Great. By THOMAS CARLYLE. Portraits, Maps, Plans, &c. 6 vols., 12mo, Cloth, $12 00.

CARLYLE'S FRENCH REVOLUTION. History of the French Revolution. 2 vols., 12mo, Cloth, $3 50.

CARLYLE'S OLIVER CROMWELL. Letters and Speeches of Oliver Cromwell. With Elucidations and Connecting Narrative. 2 vols., 12mo, Cloth, $3 50.

CHALMERS'S POSTHUMOUS WORKS. The Posthumous Works of Dr. Chalmers. Edited by his Son-in-Law, Rev. WILLIAM HANNA, LL.D. Complete in 9 vols., 12mo, Cloth, $13 50.

COLERIDGE'S COMPLETE WORKS. The Complete Works of Samuel Taylor Coleridge. With an Introductory Essay upon his Philosophical and Theological Opinions. Edited by Professor SHEDD. Complete in Seven Vols. With a Portrait. Small 8vo, Cloth, $10 50.

DOOLITTLE'S CHINA. Social Life of the Chinese: with some Account of their Religious, Governmental, Educational, and Business Customs and Opinions. With special but not exclusive Reference to Fuhchau. By Rev. JUSTUS DOOLITTLE, Fourteen Years Member of the Fuhchau Mission of the American Board. Illustrated with more that 150 characteristic Engravings on Wood. 2 vols., 12mo, Cloth, $5 00.

GIBBON'S ROME. History of the Decline and Fall of the Roman Empire. By EDWARD GIBBON. With Notes by Rev. H. H. MILMAN and M. GUIZOT. A new cheap Edition. To which is added a complete Index of the whole Work, and a Portrait of the Author. 6 vols., 12mo, Cloth, $9 00.

HAZEN'S SCHOOL AND ARMY IN GERMANY AND FRANCE. The School and the Army in Germany and France, with a Diary of Siege Life at Versailles. By Brevet Major-General W. B. HAZEN, U.S.A., Colonel Sixth Infantry. Crown 8vo, Cloth, $2 50.

HARPER'S NEW CLASSICAL LIBRARY. Literal Translations.

The following Vols. are now ready. 12mo, Cloth, $1 50 each.

CÆSAR.—VIRGIL.—SALLUST.—HORACE.—CICERO'S ORATIONS.—CICERO'S OFFICES, &c.—CICERO ON ORATORY AND ORATORS.—TACITUS (2 vols.).—TERENCE.—SOPHOCLES.—JUVENAL.—XENOPHON.—HOMER'S ILIAD.—HOMER'S ODYSSEY. — HERODOTUS. — DEMOSTHENES. — THUCYDIDES. — ÆSCHYLUS.—EURIPIDES (2 vols.).—LIVY (2 vols.).

DAVIS'S CARTHAGE. Carthage and her Remains: being an Account of the Excavations and Researches on the Site of the Phœnician Metropolis in Africa and other adjacent Places. Conducted under the Auspices of Her Majesty's Government. By Dr. DAVIS, F.R.G.S. Profusely Illustrated with Maps, Woodcuts, Chromo-Lithographs, &c. 8vo, Cloth, $4 00.

EDGEWORTH'S (MISS) NOVELS. With Engravings. 10 vols., 12mo, Cloth, $15 00.

GROTE'S HISTORY OF GREECE. 12 vols., 12mo, Cloth, $18 00.

HELPS'S SPANISH CONQUEST. The Spanish Conquest in America, and its Relation to the History of Slavery and to the Government of Colonies. By ARTHUR HELPS. 4 vols., 12mo, Cloth, $6 00.

HALE'S (MRS.) WOMAN'S RECORD. Woman's Record; or, Biographical Sketches of all Distinguished Women, from the Creation to the Present Time. Arranged in Four Eras, with Selections from Female Writers of Each Era. By Mrs. SARAH JOSEPHA HALE. Illustrated with more than 200 Portraits. 8vo, Cloth, $5 00.

HALL'S ARCTIC RESEARCHES. Arctic Researches and Life among the Esquimaux: being the Narrative of an Expedition in Search of Sir John Franklin, in the Years 1860, 1861, and 1862. By CHARLES FRANCIS HALL. With Maps and 100 Illustrations. The Illustrations are from the Original Drawings by Charles Parsons, Henry L. Stephens, Solomon Eytinge, W. S. L. Jewett, and Granville Perkins, after Sketches by Captain Hall. 8vo, Cloth, $5 00.

HALLAM'S CONSTITUTIONAL HISTORY OF ENGLAND, from the Accession of Henry VII. to the Death of George II. 8vo, Cloth, $2 00.

HALLAM'S LITERATURE. Introduction to the Literature of Europe during the Fifteenth, Sixteenth, and Seventeenth Centuries. By HENRY HALLAM. 2 vols., 8vo, Cloth, $4 00.

HALLAM'S MIDDLE AGES. State of Europe during the Middle Ages. By HENRY HALLAM. 8vo, Cloth, $2 00.

HILDRETH'S HISTORY OF THE UNITED STATES. FIRST SERIES: From the First Settlement of the Country to the Adoption of the Federal Constitution. SECOND SERIES: From the Adoption of the Federal Constitution to the End of the Sixteenth Congress. 6 vols., 8vo, Cloth, $18 00.

HUME'S HISTORY OF ENGLAND. History of England, from the Invasion of Julius Cæsar to the Abdication of James II., 1688. By DAVID HUME. A new Edition, with the Author's last Corrections and Improvements. To which is Prefixed a short Account of his Life, written by Himself. With a Portrait of the Author. 6 vols., 12mo, Cloth, $9 00.

JAY'S WORKS. Complete Works of Rev. William Jay: comprising his Sermons, Family Discourses, Morning and Evening Exercises for every Day in the Year, Family Prayers, &c. Author's enlarged Edition, revised. 3 vols., 8vo, Cloth, $6 00.

JEFFERSON'S DOMESTIC LIFE. The Domestic Life of Thomas Jefferson: compiled from Family Letters and Reminiscences, by his Great-Granddaughter, SARAH N. RANDOLPH. With Illustrations. Crown 8vo, Illuminated Cloth, Beveled Edges, $2 50.

JOHNSON'S COMPLETE WORKS. The Works of Samuel Johnson, LL.D. With an Essay on his Life and Genius, by ARTHUR MURPHY, Esq. Portrait of Johnson. 2 vols., 8vo, Cloth, $4 00.

KINGLAKE'S CRIMEAN WAR. The Invasion of the Crimea, and an Account of its Progress down to the Death of Lord Raglan. By ALEXANDER WILLIAM KINGLAKE. With Maps and Plans. Two Vols. ready. 12mo, Cloth, $2 00 per vol.

KINGSLEY'S WEST INDIES. At Last: A Christmas in the West Indies. By CHARLES KINGSLEY. Illustrated. 12mo, Cloth, $1 50.

KRUMMACHER'S DAVID, KING OF ISRAEL. David, the King of Israel: a Portrait drawn from Bible History and the Book of Psalms. By FREDERICK WILLIAM KRUMMACHER, D.D., Author of "Elijah the Tishbite," &c. Translated under the express Sanction of the Author by the Rev. M. G. EASTON, M.A. With a Letter from Dr. Krummacher to his American Readers, and a Portrait. 12mo, Cloth, $1 75.

LAMB'S COMPLETE WORKS. The Works of Charles Lamb. Comprising his Letters, Poems, Essays of Elia, Essays upon Shakspeare, Hogarth, &c., and a Sketch of his Life, with the Final Memorials, by T. NOON TALFOURD. Portrait. 2 vols., 12mo, Cloth, $3 00.

LIVINGSTONE'S SOUTH AFRICA. Missionary Travels and Researches in South Africa; including a Sketch of Sixteen Years' Residence in the Interior of Africa, and a Journey from the Cape of Good Hope to Loando on the West Coast; thence across the Continent, down the River Zambesi, to the Eastern Ocean. By DAVID LIVINGSTONE, LL.D., D.C.L. With Portrait, Maps by Arrowsmith, and numerous Illustrations. 8vo, Cloth, $4 50.

LIVINGSTONES' ZAMBESI. Narrative of an Expedition to the Zambesi and its Tributaries, and of the Discovery of the Lakes Shirwa and Nyassa. 1858-1864. By DAVID and CHARLES LIVINGSTONE. With Map and Illustrations. 8vo, Cloth, $5 00.

M'CLINTOCK & STRONG'S CYCLOPÆDIA. Cyclopædia of Biblical, Theological, and Ecclesiastical Literature. Prepared by the Rev. JOHN M'CLINTOCK, D.D., and JAMES STRONG, S.T.D. 5 vols. now ready. Royal 8vo, Price per vol., Cloth, $5 00; Sheep, $6 00; Half Morocco, $8 00.

MARCY'S ARMY LIFE ON THE BORDER. Thirty Years of Army Life on the Border. Comprising descriptions of the Indian Nomads of the Plains; Explorations of New Territory; a Trip across the Rocky Mountains in the Winter; Descriptions of the Habits of Different Animals found in the West, and the Methods of Hunting them; with Incidents in the Life of Different Frontier Men, &c., &c. By Brevet Brigadier-General R. B. MARCY, U.S.A., Author of "The Prairie Traveller." With numerous Illustrations. 8vo, Cloth, Beveled Edges, $3 00.

MACAULAY'S HISTORY OF ENGLAND. The History of England from the Accession of James II. By THOMAS BABINGTON MACAULAY. With an Original Portrait of the Author. 5 vols., 8vo, Cloth, $10 00; 12mo, Cloth, $7 50.

MOSHEIM'S ECCLESIASTICAL HISTORY, Ancient and Modern; in which the Rise, Progress, and Variation of Church Power are considered in their Connection with the State of Learning and Philosophy, and the Political History of Europe during that Period. Translated, with Notes, &c., by A. MACLAINE, D.D. A new Edition, continued to 1826, by C. COOTE, LL.D. 2 vols., 8vo, Cloth, $4 00.

THE DESERT OF THE EXODUS. Journeys on Foot in the Wilderness of the Forty Years' Wanderings; undertaken in connection with the Ordnance Survey of Sinai and the Palestine Exploration Fund. By E. H. PALMER, M.A., Lord Almoner's Professor of Arabic, and Fellow of St. John's College, Cambridge. With Maps and numerous Illustrations from Photographs and Drawings taken on the spot by the Sinai Survey Expedition and C. F. Tyrwhitt Drake. Crown 8vo, Cloth, $3 00.

OLIPHANT'S CHINA AND JAPAN. Narrative of the Earl of Elgin's Mission to China and Japan, in the Years 1857, '58, '59. By LAURENCE OLIPHANT, Private Secretary to Lord Elgin. Illustrations. 8vo, Cloth, $3 50.

OLIPHANT'S (MRS.) LIFE OF EDWARD IRVING. The Life of Edward Irving, Minister of the National Scotch Church, London. Illustrated by his Journals and Correspondence. By Mrs. OLIPHANT. Portrait. 8vo, Cloth, $3 50.

RAWLINSON'S MANUAL OF ANCIENT HISTORY. A Manual of Ancient History, from the Earliest Times to the Fall of the Western Empire. Comprising the History of Chaldæa, Assyria, Media, Babylonia, Lydia, Phœnicia, Syria, Judæa, Egypt, Carthage, Persia, Greece, Macedonia, Parthia, and Rome. By GEORGE RAWLINSON, M.A., Camden Professor of Ancient History in the University of Oxford. 12mo, Cloth, $2 50.

RECLUS'S THE EARTH. The Earth: A Descriptive History of the Phenomena and Life of the Globe. By ELISÉE RECLUS. Translated by the late B. B. Woodward, and Edited by Henry Woodward. With 234 Maps and Illustrations and 23 Page Maps printed in Colors. 8vo, Cloth, $5 00.

RECLUS'S OCEAN. The Ocean, Atmosphere, and Life. Being the Second Series of a Descriptive History of the Life of the Globe. By ELISÉE RECLUS. Profusely Illustrated with 250 Maps or Figures, and 27 Maps printed in Colors. 8vo, Cloth, $6 00.

SHAKSPEARE. The Dramatic Works of William Shakspeare, with the Corrections and Illustrations of Dr. JOHNSON, G. STEVENS, and others. Revised by ISAAC REED. Engravings. 6 vols, Royal 12mo, Cloth, $9 00. 2 vols., 8vo, Cloth, $4 00.

SMILES'S LIFE OF THE STEPHENSONS. The Life of George Stephenson, and of his Son, Robert Stephenson; comprising, also, a History of the Invention and Introduction of the Railway Locomotive. By SAMUEL SMILES, Author of "Self-Help," &c. With Steel Portraits and numerous Illustrations. 8vo, Cloth, $3 00.

SMILES'S HISTORY OF THE HUGUENOTS. The Huguenots: their Settlements, Churches, and Industries in England and Ireland. By SAMUEL SMILES. With an Appendix relating to the Huguenots in America. Crown 8vo, Cloth, $1 75.

SPEKE'S AFRICA. Journal of the Discovery of the Source of the Nile. By Captain JOHN HANNING SPEKE, Captain H.M. Indian Army, Fellow and Gold Medalist of the Royal Geographical Society, Hon. Corresponding Member and Gold Medalist of the French Geographical Society, &c. With Maps and Portraits and numerous Illustrations, chiefly from Drawings by Captain GRANT. 8vo, Cloth, uniform with Livingstone, Barth, Burton, &c., $4 00.

STRICKLAND'S (MISS) QUEENS OF SCOTLAND. Lives of the Queens of Scotland and English Princesses connected with the Regal Succession of Great Britain. By AGNES STRICKLAND. 8 vols., 12mo, Cloth, $12 00.

THE STUDENT'S SERIES.
    France. Engravings. 12mo, Cloth, $2 00.
    Gibbon. Engravings. 12mo, Cloth, $2 00.
    Greece. Engravings. 12mo, Cloth, $2 00.
    Hume. Engravings. 12mo, Cloth, $2 00.
    Rome. By Liddell. Engravings. 12mo, Cloth, $2 00.
    Old Testament History. Engravings. 12mo, Cloth, $2 00.
    New Testament History. Engravings, 12mo, Cloth, $2 00.
    Strickland's Queens of England. Abridged. Eng's. 12mo, Cloth, $2 00.
    Ancient History of the East. 12mo, Cloth, $2 00.
    Hallam's Middle Ages. 12mo, Cloth, $2 00.
    Hallam's Constitutional History of England. 12mo, Cloth, $2 00.
    Lyell's Elements of Geology. 12mo, Cloth, $2 00.

TENNYSON'S COMPLETE POEMS. The Complete Poems of Alfred Tennyson, Poet Laureate. With numerous Illustrations by Eminent Artists, and Three Characteristic Portraits. 8vo, Paper, 75 cents; Cloth, $1 25.

THOMSON'S LAND AND THE BOOK. The Land and the Book; or, Biblical Illustrations drawn from the Manners and Customs, the Scenes and the Scenery of the Holy Land. By W. M. THOMSON, D.D., Twenty-five Years a Missionary of the A.B.C.F.M. in Syria and Palestine. With two elaborate Maps of Palestine, an accurate Plan of Jerusalem, and several hundred Engravings, representing the Scenery, Topography, and Productions of the Holy Land, and the Costumes, Manners, and Habits of the People. 2 large 12mo vols., Cloth, $5 00.

TYERMAN'S WESLEY. The Life and Times of the Rev. John Wesley, M.A., Founder of the Methodists. By the Rev. LUKE TYERMAN. Portraits. 3 vols., Crown 8vo, Cloth, $7 50.

TYERMAN'S OXFORD METHODISTS. The Oxford Methodists: Memoirs of the Rev. Messrs. Clayton, Ingham, Gambold, Hervey, and Broughton, with Biographical Notices of others. By the Rev. L. TYERMAN. With Portraits. Crown 8vo, Cloth, $2 50.

VÁMBÉRY'S CENTRAL ASIA. Travels in Central Asia. Being the Account of a Journey from Teheren across the Turkoman Desert, on the Eastern Shore of the Caspian, to Khiva, Bokhara, and Samarcand, performed in the Year 1863. By ARMINIUS VÁMBÉRY, Member of the Hungarian Academy of Pesth, by whom he was sent on this Scientific Mission. With Map and Woodcuts. 8vo, Cloth, $4 50.

WOOD'S HOMES WITHOUT HANDS. Homes Without Hands: being a Description of the Habitations of Animals, classed according to their Principle of Construction. By J. G. WOOD, M.A., F.L.S. With about 140 Illustrations. 8vo, Cloth, Beveled Edges, $4 50.

www.ingramcontent.com/pod-product-compliance
Lightning Source LLC
Chambersburg PA
CBHW031904220426
43663CB00006B/756